the DRAGON MASTER CREATRIX

Conversations with a Female Spiritual Teacher for These New Times

ALISON J. KAY, PHD

DocUmeant *Publishing*
244 5th Avenue
Suite G-200
NY, NY 10001
646-233-4366
www.DocUmeantPublishing.com

THE DRAGON MASTER CREATRIX: *Conversations with a Female Spiritual Teacher for These New Times*

Published by
DocUmeant Publishing
244 5th Avenue, Suite G-200
NY, NY 10001

646-233-4366

Editor: Philip S. Marks

Cover, Layout, and Design by: DocUmeant Designs
www.DocUmeantDesings.com

Library of Congress Control Number: 2021930899

ISBN: 9781950075256

DEDICATION

FOR ALL OF you who are seeing how we are being asked to change, lighten up and evolve. Thank you for your desire to contribute to bettering our world by bettering—lightening—yourself, your consciousness, your body, your carbon footprint. May your path be easier, enriched and more playful from reading this book.

CONTENTS

PREFACE
The Master

THIS BOOK SEEKS to give a window into working with a female spiritual teacher, with access to the intimate teachings, and connections to women—and men!—seeking that experience. This is a sharing of key concepts, tips, techniques, to give such women—and men!—tools to step into their power at entirely new levels, both personally and collectively.

Success in the world is important. And yet to have it requires spirit. For the spiritual woman, seeking to accomplish everything she can in both spiritual evolution and material terms, this book is a must-have inspirational companion to the journey.

Reading this book will empower women—trigger their own Knowing of the ancient power mysteries, show them to a community, normalize spirituality and the understanding of subtle energies, consciousness, and evolution, and give them clues and bread crumbs to follow their own paths.

Individual women make up the collective and as such, are the ones who individually create the collective experience. As the individual evolves so too does the society and world in which they dwell. It is said that one evolved person raises up 100,000.

And I am looking for heroes. Heroes are defined by running into the thick of things, to be "part of the solution" and they get up, stand up, and choose joy—no matter what. Let's end the sole reliance on science and logic only as we rebalance it with empathy and intuition, and get started magically creating the evolutionary leaders, who will do the work to raise up oneself and the collective.

Is that you? Consider this book your invitation to come and play.

ACKNOWLEDGMENTS

THANK YOU TO the Divine for this life force that pulses through me. Thank you for this gift of life, this precious, exquisite life of mine to live. Thank you for all the clear Guidance, Love and Support that is constantly there, all around me.

Thank you to my family and friends for your love and support and cheerleading. It is oxygen, of sorts. And for the laughter, adventure, and fun! To all of my team, thank you for your strong commitment to this beloved Vibrational UPgrade™ System, to me and my mission.

Claire, you are all of this; thank you for your generosity of spirit and genuine seeing of me, for all your love and support, while busy wifing, momming, and daughtering. And thank you, to each of you beloved VUP Dragon Masters, Grand Dragon Masters and VUP Practitioners. We're up to such GOOD stuff here. May the laughter, light, joy, ease, love, abundance, and Service continue!

Thank you to all of my students, clients, AYM, 3M and MM program participants, and subscribers for your loyalty, trust, and respect. It is an honor to Serve you.

Let's PLAY!

No unicorns were harmed in the production of this book. In fact, they were supported and nurtured, with contributions made to their continued growing existence on planet Earth at this time. Fairy and fey folk were also consulted. As were the crows ibis, while the dragons breathed their fires behind and around the words.

INTRODUCTION
The Student

MY PREVIOUS EXPERIENCE . . . Enlightened woman from a male teacher's viewpoint.

We were 22 in number, women aged between 22 and 55 years of age. We were meeting in the living room of a female student to learn about enlightened women. It was mid-1980s in Los Angeles—Arnold Schwarzenegger was The Terminator rather than The Governator. Sylvester Stallone's Rambo was another image of power. Along with CEO's and Generals and Presidents—all males.

Into this my then Zen Master decided to bring a public meditation evening, an event just for women, called, "Why Don't More Women Attain Enlightenment?" and the atmosphere in the almost full house was thick. These women were angry.

He came at it from a sexism-free, everyone-can-get-there possibility. He let us know that the historical divide-and-conquer that men used to separate women from their power and each other was in large part to blame, yes.

But he said, everyone there could change it. Change for ourselves the backbiting and competition. Change for ourselves the focus on external standards of appearance that were given to women to keep them distracted from the essence of their true worth. And the system of cultural conditioning that has caused women to feel they needed to get what they want by manipulating other people. All this is to the detriment of claiming their own power.

They were furious. At him.

A few nights later these women students, myself included, were invited to a beautiful home, high in the hills above Laguna Beach, to have some direct experience of meditation—and to ask questions about the material he had presented those few nights before.

I don't remember much of what was said that night. Rarely a drinker, I remember having wine to try and assuage the skin-crawling tension and anxiety I was still feeling from a few nights before. In between these nights, during a dream, I had woken suddenly, gasping in fear as I fell down a cliff.

The part I do remember was the following. I wrote it in my journal because I knew it was a significant moment in my life. I still remember it quite clearly today.

Questions ranged from clarification of the points of the evening, to whether or not there were any examples of women we could take as role models for a different way to live. At a certain point, after several women asked the same question in a variety of different ways, seeming to avoid the subject of power altogether, my master sat up a little straighter and moved his legs into full-lotus position and said,

"I am going to meditate now. If I meditate and you watch me do it, you will be able to see what I mean. The truth is that I can't give you any examples. We haven't seen a fully enlightened women in historical memory. In caves no doubt they existed. Sure. But there isn't anyone I can point to. So, I am going to channel one for you who has agreed to come here for you to see."

And as he sat, while we dutifully watched, a corona of light began to surround him. Then light seemed to start coming through his pores—at first gold then white, then gold with red tones. And suddenly I realized that his face had changed. The features had a feminine cast to them. He held up his hands, as if to bless the room. Two sharp exhales and the room went white, and I was looking into a furnace.

My mouth was fully open at the sight of this. I could almost hear a woman's voice in my head. I couldn't understand what she was saying. Then one more exhale and I was looking at something I now know is the birth of a star. Fully embodied, quantum, generative potential, and power. My spine was stick straight and I couldn't have moved even if I'd thought about it. It was as if I could hardly breathe, so strong was the heat. My mind laughingly joked that I would probably have no skin left after this.

And then it was over. I don't know how long it went on because it turns out that I had fallen backwards. I woke up when my teacher asked me if I had enjoyed myself. There were still quicksilver colored light tones in the air—which had nothing to do with the many regular incandescent bulbs in the lamps throughout the room.

And that was my first experience of what it might be like to work with a female spiritual teacher. My then master spent the remainder of his life working with women, and men, to help them step into their power. The fully luminous, free, and choice based life of energy and fun and service. He told us that the true nature of a human being is joy—unalloyed, perfect joy.

After he passed away, I studied with other teachers, learned more about the feminine principal, and meditated. I learned from men and women. And there were some things that I noticed in the styles of the women that were different from that of the men.

So, when in 2016 I encountered the work of Dr. Alison J. Kay, PhD, and deepened with it in 2017 to the present, I was pleased, yet somehow unsurprised to find that she too had these hallmark differences.

I saw right away the opportunity to help people to recognize what she is doing and how they can gain so much benefit for themselves and how they can further their missions and callings by connecting with her and her work.

This book is set during one of the epic Mastermind retreats that Dr. Alison offers to her students twice per year. She told us she offers these retreats intentionally timed at the two most pivotal turning points of the Celtic Wheel of the year, Beltane, and Samhain. This timing is also known as the beginning of Spring and near the end of Autumn, where Beltane's Celtic roots in essence is thriving and Samhain's is about releasing. These retreats are held in ancient Celtic sacred land, known as a nexus point of Ley lines across the planet, that culminate as the heart chakra for the planet, Glastonbury, UK.

Yet beyond the retreats being held within this sacred land and all that Dr. Alison encompasses within the retreats due to this, she gets to so many other layers, all at once, to deliver a life-changing event. During these epic retreats we experience an expert and fluid combination of connections with sacred land including ancient historical power spots, megaliths, stone circles and elementals, blessings and initiations, land clearings, all culminating in deep energetic transformation. The transmutation and transformation are so resplendent that we all typically spend the following four to six weeks having to integrate how high we got, into our daily lives. And integrate it does; she makes sure it does, with the follow up work afterwards.

These retreats really are beyond easy description. And yet I am going to offer here my own story for you to enjoy . . . until you have the chance to experience your own magical journey with her.

All student names are changed to protect confidentiality.

CHAPTER 1
Bird Signs and Synchronicities

WEDNESDAY NIGHT TO FRIDAY DAY

I DIDN'T KNOW I was beginning a journey that would change my life forever. *I didn't know* that my "before" and "after" pictures would be so different. *I didn't know* I would make friends to last a lifetime and be shown a sacred vision of the planet and my own body. When I started on my epic journey across the sea, I just knew that I wanted more. I had to gain access to more of myself and these emerging possibilities I had begun to see.

Five days earlier . . .

From the window of the train, speeding through the English countryside, the hedges fly past. Then there are fields. So, much green. We hurtle through a crossing and a crow flies up from the side of the tracks. A few seconds later I see several large crows rising together. Since working with Dr. Alison I increasingly see crows. Everywhere.

I've seen this consistently occur with every engaged student of hers. She says these crows show up via her connection with them and our connection with her and her teachings. It's really a wild phenomenon as newer students start to post pics and videos of how often crows have begun to be around them. There's a sense of benevolent stalking, as if a calling to initiation.

Also, there are cardinals, woodpeckers, and hawks. So, OK, perhaps I could have seen them before working with her. But I never did. New York City does have them if you're looking. Some would say, though, it isn't really known for the avian wildlife as much as, say, Belize or England.

As I watch another huge flock of crows fly up from a field, my mind takes me back to my flight from The City to the taxi enroute to JFK Airport. To the problems I feel like I am fleeing in my personal life.

My husband and I met and married early. We had a dream of having a family, a home, a second home. And when no children came, we poured ourselves into our respective careers. But the impulse for building a nest egg, the urge for expansion had died for us. We each spent increasing time in our offices, with our colleagues. With our male and female friends. And we grew apart.

As I reached my forties, I began to feel like I wanted to try something new. I began to read expansive literature and take online classes. Then I ran into Dr. Alison's free monthly call. The Vibrational Upgrade™ system appealed to me because it emphasized choosing. It emphasized life force. It emphasized joy. Joy was something a bit thin on the ground in my house.

Don't get me wrong, I wasn't lacking anything necessary. I had a roof over my head when others were homeless. I had a spouse when so many friends were unhappily single. I had my freedom of bedtimes when some of my friends, those with infants, were sleep deprived and miserable because of it. My sex life was regular and adequate. My health was fine. I was "fine."

And yet, with everything at this "fine" level, I enrolled in the Magic, Manifestation and Money Flow course that is Dr. Alison's signature program. Her first book's title is, *What if There's Nothing Wrong?* And it was like this for me when I signed up for the Magic, Manifestation and Money Flow program. I wasn't there to fix anything, really. But I knew there was something within it that was calling to me.

Suddenly, I found myself asking for more. It was super helpful and healing, despite having the sense that I didn't have the kinda stuff to heal that so many other folks seem to in other programs. Well, people in Magic, Manifestation and Money Flow *did* have traumas to heal, and they most clearly did so.

But this was different. While there was healing, deep healing, I've become tracked to have all that I'm learning and we're doing in this program to be applied to my daily life. Like I'm going for living out my greatest human potential. Literally. And learning to live in the possibilities, rather than problem solving, figuring stuff out and my intellectual constructs. And let's face it, I'd made a success of my life from my intellect.

But Dr. Alison's work is different. I understand now why it was calling to me. Because I was completely unaware prior to working with her that I even had this opaque, heavy film—that the majority of us in the world seem to live with—coating my life. And that I could not only take off this coating but turn the Technicolor ON!

This is her work with the vital life force energy, where she says that while we've learned to build up our brains and intellects, (she has a PhD, so I take her word on this) there is *so* much more available and possible, when we learn to work with all levels of our consciousness. Not like this is something that's out there, it's just that when we do this, we're more capable of accessing subtle energy. This then has us capable of wielding energy and our consciousness to our advantage, while we actually exert less effort. It's massively logical. And it is so relevant to all that's going on.

Another way she says this is through her yoga teacher framing. She is speeding up the results of a regular meditation practice, exponentially. Here, she activates us and coaches more mindfulness out of us after she's cleared enough of the old out of the different layers of consciousness where we carry the old around, unknowingly. A regular meditation practice does this too, but that takes at least a decade to see results like we do in the first year. It's like I'm being super connected beyond my every day, conditioned mind to my Higher Self and then even, to the Divine. Like I'm being unplugged from one level and plugged into a much higher, faster, lighter one and stuff is just easier. And how I've become? Clearly, somehow, this was missing before. As it is for most in society.

And increasingly, over time, I realized that she was helping me peel back that opaque layer and reconnect to my own truth, so it wasn't only taking her word for it. I am now seeing much more aliveness to not just me, but much of life outside of me, all around me. Like stuff is pulsating and alive. And I began to really feel what my own truth feels like. I don't mean just listening to my intuition. I mean I just cannot get away with fooling myself or living "off" in any area of my life the way I once could. I don't rationalize decisions anymore.

As I sit here traveling towards my fellow Masterminders and my first-time meeting Dr. Alison in person, I am realizing massive shifts have occurred with how I now look at life from the inside out. I've actually begun to realize why she quotes Traditional Chinese Medicine, saying "blood follows chi." The physical follows energy, in other words. When she first said it, I thought it sounded cool and murmured as much. But I had no idea what she really meant, until I had begun to see just how interactive my consciousness can be with all of life.

Yet within my marriage, that has become the remaining challenge; Dr. Alison referred to it as part of an initiation I am undergoing. It's like how I deal with it and myself within this challenge *is* the initiation, not the result, is how she put it. Which is totally opposite to how I think about it. My mind still demanded to know the end result! Is it ever going to change? Stay in or leave?

As I found myself in the yellow cab to the airport, with the evening light slanting into the window, I squinted my eyes to let the golden rays shine on my face and picked up my mental musing. I found myself returning to that omnipresent energy and topic again, and began to turn over in my mind, again, the subject preoccupying me for weeks now—should I leave my marriage?

Ugh, I still loved my husband but other than regular arguments and problematic communication about household tasks and chores, we didn't even see each other anymore. Is there more for me?

Checking my suitcase went smoothly and finding a place to sit was easy. When the time came to go through security, the agent stopped the line one person in front of me and let us start a new queue, so my time through the checkpoint was very short.

I went to the news agent to buy some water and found they were having a one-day buy one get one free due to a double shipment which they did not have room to back stock. Smooth. Just like most of the process of arranging to travel for this retreat.

My boss gave me an extra week because I hadn't taken a break in a while and they had decided to redecorate my department's entire floor during my trip. My team thanked me for the extra time off as well. I mean *really* smooth.

My husband said he thought it would be good for me to get away so he would take care of the dog, the cleaning, and everything else that I usually did—even though we both worked the same number of hours and brought home nearly identical pay checks.

I slept well on the plane, waking quite refreshed when the PA system announced that coffee and a boxed breakfast would be served. Welcome to London! I had never travelled by myself before. Friends had done it of course. Dr. Alison lived this life! So, I wanted to do it myself. This time I decided to expand my horizons and stay overnight in the city where Royalty lives, before traveling on to Glastonbury the next day.

I saw the sights, had afternoon tea, and went back to my room early as I felt a bit off although not really tired. I continued reading, *Reasonable Dragons* that evening, again. I felt like re-reading Dr. Alison's last book would help me be more prepared and able to get even more out of this retreat.

I wanted to have myself geared up to best experience this place— Glastonbury not London—that is known to be so mystical. Dr. Alison had shown us that, when she was there herself and we were on the calls with her from there. My god, her energy and intuition were even higher and stronger.

Then, while being in such a place, I'm also going to have to be able to handle these high attunements and blessings I'm about to get, along with the training in Vibrational UPgrade System™. I didn't know if I was actually going to become a VIbrational UPgrade Practitioner with a full-on business, like others in the program. I just knew I wanted the huge leap forward in my progress all this was going to give me. I know whatever I do on this retreat will be assisting me to upgrade my life back at home. I know that's her goal—that we change from these retreats, not just *on* them. She told us that.

So, being practical, and knowing how quickly Dr. Alison moves, I am going to read myself to sleep.

The next morning I set off to the GWR train in Paddington Station. Taking the subway—tube or underground here—was interesting. Some of the cars seemed very small after the New York transit models. Paddington station was charming, and I kept thinking of the literary bear by the same name. That made me smile. What a historical place.

. . . And so now I am back to the final train ride, the one I began this telling with, and the hedgerows whizzing past. Getting off at Bristol Temple Meads was another feast of history. The old stone station gave onto a kind of plaza where buses and taxis, pedestrians, flower and food vendors and many well-behaved dogs on leashes all moved around in a kind of dance. It smells different here.

Walking down to the right I found out I was walking on the road, which I had thought was a sidewalk. I was walking on the wrong side for safety. But nobody ran me over. And the States drive on the different side of the road than here. Whew. Many differences. I am being forced to be more present. OK.

And a man in a uniform came up to me and asked where I needed to go. He directed me to the bus stop. I remember Dr. Alison talking about traveling in Asia, and how she spoke conversational Mandarin but didn't read it, and how she'd match the characters from her guide books in English to signs as she traveled. Glad it's English here. Geez!

I caught my correct one and walked upstairs to the upper deck. Watching Bristol disappear to be replaced by greener and fields, I wondered about my time ahead. What would it be like to be on the land with Dr Alison? What would she be like in person? How would it be to connect with the women I had only met online, but who'd come to know me so well?

The energy had been building in intensity for a few weeks. I already knew, from being around Dr. Alison's programs for a while, that she always created this kind of energetic container. So, for the retreats, she added Energy Medicine and special blessings into all our lives leading up to the retreat and we each could see it at work. She said it was to help us get the most out of the retreat.

And I know now how to recognize that increased "smooth sailing" where stuff like finding seats easily, and extra specials like that

BOGO on the water—there's this signature flow of ease that I've come to learn is Dr. Alison at work. This makes me smile. Plus, she told us she was enclosing us in these extra special "safe and easy and timely travel" bubbles. Well yes, she clearly had!

"Wells next," said the driver. Once we stopped at the bus depot in Wells—England's smallest city—I came down to the lower level, went up and asked him if he could please let me know when we got to Glasto (as I had heard someone else call it earlier in the journey).

"Do you need the center of town in Glastonbury, or are you staying in the outskirts?"

"In town," I said.

"OK."

I sat down in a seat just behind the driver so I could hear him. Butterflies in my stomach now. What would it be like?

Then we were there. I grabbed my bags from the overhead rack while the bus driver got the bigger bag out from the luggage bin underneath.

Once I got my bearings and looked in all directions around me to understand which direction Dr. Alison had told me to go from this exact point I was standing at and in the direction I was facing now off from where the bus had dropped me, I noticed that one of the ladies, Heather, from the group was sitting at a cafe across the street from the bus stop.

So, I was pulled into the flow of the retreat right away, as she recognized me from her little table on the sidewalk and beckoned me over.

Heather offered me tea, telling me how much earlier she'd arrived via train from where she lived in another part of the UK, then showed me where we were staying. Did I want her to walk me there and then show me where to meet at 5PM? Yes please. Easy.

Walking towards the building our housing was in, we passed the town hall. This was where Dr. Alison told us she would give her evening talk the following evening. Good. Check!

We saw another one of the people in the retreat basically standing right in front of the town hall. She had shopping bags in her hands. She looked the exact same from her photo in the private Facebook group where we spent time together chatting almost daily, as fellow members in this Mastermind level program with Dr. Alison. We'd all gone through Dr. Alison's signature program, the Magic, Manifestation and Money Flow program too, at different times, but we'd each been especially invited into the Vibrational UPgrade Mastermind. And we'd all been looking forward to meeting each other in person on the much-anticipated retreat.

Looking around at Glastonbury I was surprised at how small it seemed. And how it *was* so much like a New Age Disney World. Like a historical *and* New Age theme park with ancient myths, apparent medieval ruins, and the 15th century George & Pilgrim Inn, (that I'd later learn from Dr. Alison is haunted, as she'd learned due to the manager showing her a binder of pics and articles, from when it had been in the national press. The pics actually caught ghost figures in the images! Dr. Alison later taught us how to feel out where it's haunted.) And the 16th century tribunal Hall . . . And then loads of crystal and Celtic and book and herb shops, along with loads of cafes and gathering spaces and meditation spaces and treatment clinics. And yet also where people actually lived. Wow.

There was something about the atmosphere that is special. Something like a sound or a smell, some kind of silence. Later, I would find out how a very special Abbey was a stone's throw from this place where I stood, yet it was all so new and different. When I started to cross the street and a car rushed by from the wrong side, I felt disoriented. OK, I said to myself, I am not in Kansas—but I don't know where

I am instead. Maybe I'll learn how to click my magic red shoes . . . ooh, look at me, making jokes!

I thought about how I'd been increasingly wondering what it might be like to walk around in a magical world. In fact, this is one of the first things I see people readjust to, when they enter into one of Dr. Alison's programs as they notice that they're engaging with something quite different. Granted, the many actual physical changes in the body are probably what *actually* happen first. It's as if it's planned; feel the magic, but GET in your body, before we proceed. But there's just this different scent in the air there too.

So, being around her programs for a while now, and seeing new people come in, it's quite consistent, their changes as they first start to work with her. I'm able to see newer folks go through their shifts within Magic, Manifestation and Money Flow because part of our Mastermind program has us continuing to access and participate in the Magic, Manifestation and Money Flow program, to enrich both our and the newer folks' experience.

So, I've seen these newer folks come in and as soon as they begin their first level of shifting within the first week or two, they consistently report better sleep, being less triggered, having more energy, better moods; these are the most repeated. Also, people begin to experience many more synchronicities which seem to further their understanding that there really is something magical here.

Part of these increasing synchronicities is that people begin to see animal synchronicities. Dr. Alison teaches this animal medicine, as well as how to interpret it, as a way of increasing *our* fields' communication with the greater field of all of life and the means with which the Universe communicates *back* to us.

Woodpeckers, Magpies & Crows, oh my. She had years of training in bird and animal signs' interpretation, including time with Native Americans in study and medicine wheel ceremonies, along with training for her second tour guide position as an intern during her Masters with the Audubon society.

They trained her in local—Florida's Gulf Coast—bird life and how to identify, speak about, and become a naturalist interpreter to lead boat tours out to, I think, it was a migratory bird island in a bay, for the Audubon Society.

And then upon graduation, Dr. Alison set up her own kayak and canoe trek business. She apparently would do both the naturalist and symbolic bird and animal life interpretation. This was as a side business while she waited to place in a job using her masters. She tells these wild stories about getting super close to alligators and teaching people how to bang on their canoes or kayaks with their paddles so the alligators will just slip away. Honestly, as cool as that sounds, I am glad we're not doing that on this retreat.

So, Dr. Alison is able to share the significance of the appearance of the many animal sightings. And it seems like animals tend to flock to her. I know cats and dogs consistently react to her over the computer and phone lines. I see it within our calls and events.

I get this Disney like image of Dr. Alison in the woods with animals just flocking to her outstretched arms, landing there and on her head, gathering around her. I think that's from Dr. Alison making fun of herself; yes, she actually mentioned that first.

Yet after a certain level of work with her, people *really do begin to see crows!* It's as if, well it seems like there's this "ON" switch that activates the crows to show up. Seriously, it's *that* reliable. And mystical, frankly.

Crows are symbolic of the magic that is contained within every moment that we may not visually or physically be able to see because it's "behind or beyond the physical" or metaphysical. As Dr. Alison says, this magic that is contained within every moment that we cannot necessarily see, we can become a certain vibration, with our mind, body, heart, and spirit "arranged" in such a way that it is more able *to see and perceive this magic*. And then by our choices, weave it into our physical existence to affect our day to day "mundane" lives.

She speaks so much about these times being about re-balancing the invisible with the visible, the material with the spiritual, the mundane with the sacred. The crows seem to in one way really be aiding her work with us all so that we have a sort of "proof" of this magic and are thus able to believe even more in its actual existence. Yet it's also so that we too are able to—and meant to—be accessing it.

It's funny. Dr. Alison presents it in such a mundane, matter-of-fact daily life way, that it's like the Universe is getting her back by bringing in the mysticism and magical connotations by the crow being a part of this. I've never heard Dr. Alison say anything at all about intending to work with the crow, or any special ceremonies invoking the crow.

And it's not just the magic outside of us, but also the magic within us, that the crow symbolizes. Dr. Alison continually emphasizes this, that the magic is woven in through our choices, and learning to live in the possibilities within every moment. But that these choices, where we access more magic, and live in more possibilities, is meant to change our everyday life. That's the bottom line with her.

There is something joyful about sharing the stories of sightings. So, many of us post videos and pics when we do. Dr. Alison will provide an interpretation of it to aid our perception of the possibly symbolism messaged from the Universe. It's such a real, tangible, and FUN part of working within her programs. Our whole worlds get so opened up.

So, let me share some with you so you too can experience this. Here are some of the interactions I and fellow VUP (Vibrational UPgrade

System) Masterminders and Magic, Manifestation and Money Flow program participants have had with these animal synchronicities and then some with Dr. Alison's interpretation. You'll see how we're becoming trained to opening up to the invisible field of all of life all around us, and how this life force permeates all of life and *connects us all*. And we can communicate with it, and it with us.

"I am sitting outside with two cardinals and a crow for half an hour as they communicated continuously."

"This is what it sounds like when I walk outside into the backyard. My crow—yes, we have claimed each other—follows me. Around the block he would fly ahead and stop on a light. And then yesterday afternoon when I got out of the car, there he was again on the light and carrying on with whatever he was trying to communicate to me."

AJK: "OK, so it seems your Crow is saying to you: 'Please recognize the magic within and all around you at all times that Dr. Alison has been helping to remind you and further attune and activate within you and all around you. You have in each and every moment, my most beloved 'student,'—she used the person's name here—the opportunity to choose to create from this magic, *more* magic.

'You're doing a great job learning to live within the possibilities, within the flow of true Power and light, and to increasingly create from there, *no matter what you see in the outside world.* For this is in great part, the crow's message; that your power is *within* first, and what shows up in the outside world *is the result of* what's going on—or not- *within you* and your consciousness and vibrational field. Keep tuning in, we're here supporting you, reminding you of this power you have in each and every moment. You are loved. You are SO magical. We totally endorse what You're up to on behalf of your own path, karma and life, beloved.' How's that, student's actual name?

"Now tha's a message! I think I will print it out and hang it by my desk."

And she did. She referred to it other times, as it sat right next to her computer.

"Thought I'd share with you some magical wildlife that showed up for me yesterday. The crow was really close and when I turned my head a butterfly flew right past my face. A cardinal was actually in a tree about 6 feet from me. I also saw my first dragonflies for the year. Oh, and there was also a red pileated woodpecker. Sigh."

"On my way to take my child to her sporting event, a crow flew in front of my car with a big piece of food in its mouth."

AJK: "The crow catching its prey flying right out in front of you is ALWAYS a good sign, the prey in mouth symbolizing a win, or a capturing of something you've been desiring."

Student: "Two mornings in a row I have been woken by the calling of the crow. Thank you for this, Dr. Alison, as I can sense your hand involved here!"

AJK: "PERFECT! I've been doing more remote work with you all, from Saturday onward especially, with and for you, due to what You're currently shifting through. So, grateful and happy to hear this. No surprise the crow had been letting you know. So, grateful You're noticing it and getting what's happening. You are welcome!"

Student: "I can feel the work. Crows keep coming in to my present and it always brings a smile. And I allow my whole being to receive their beauty and magic."

AJK: "Well your response right here led to a smile on my face. I can perceive it in the daily energy sends, that the magic is WAY more present in your life and you've totally up-leveled your capacity to allow it.

"Welcome to your new life, my dear!"

AJK: "Hi there. As you began your Facebook Live, a woodpecker trilled out. Then a crow flew up, landed close by, then—not kidding—a red tailed hawk landed right next to me and grabbed a worm out of the ground—catching your intention there and manifesting as symbolism. So, the messages I received while you did your FB live, is that level of subtle messaging from the Universe that we have to look for and to really be open to when working at this level."

During the initial three months of COVID-19 hitting the West, Dr. Alison and her trained and certified VUP Practitioners, all volunteered to do daily FB lives to send healing and light focused on whichever areas of the world were the hardest hit. The work was done for support, to help grief, pain, loneliness, worries about money, feelings of instability about the future and supporting the front-line workers. This is the FB Live Dr. Alison is referring to. These have become a special playlist, by the way, on Dr. Alison's YouTube channel, if you need.

"A friend of mine was gifted with this picture of a crow, and she posted it. Now the crow is showing up on Facebook."

AJK: "Yes that is how this stuff works. Once it begins, it lets you know, increasingly, of its Presence."

As the energies of Dr. Alison's programs are very much about abundance and abundance for all, we see the animals showing up with these signs as well.

And people start both having unexpected money show up in many different forms (i.e., people who'd owed Dr. Alison's student money for years suddenly pays them back, clients with long overdue invoices of Dr. Alison's students suddenly pay them, raises, grants suddenly come through in the millions, divorce proceedings turning out way better than ever thought even possible . . . I could go on and on and on. And yes, this list is direct from Dr. Alison, lol.)

As people start working with Dr. Alison in the Magic, Manifestation and Money Flow program this also consistently happens; they begin to find unexpected money in the street, around the house, hidden in cushions, in the mail. . . . Such magic is very inspiring. These synchronicities can give an immediate lift to the mind and heart when they show up.

Student: "When I was sitting on a bench in an important conversation, I noticed a large toad not far from my feet."

AJK: "Toads and frogs are symbols of abundance in the Chinese culture. Nearly every traditional Chinese home—and even modern, due to it being part superstition, part Feng Shui—has Chinese Toad wooden carvings with a Chinese coin in its mouth—Fabulous that you got this sign show up right next to you!"

Student: "Today I was experiencing a bit of a joy—rather new for me—this high feeling open to limitless possibilities, which was great!"

AJK: "You're experiencing your own version of living in that awe as it all magically and synchronistically falls into place. The post I did today was very much for you. . . from the post you did the other day and the great work You're doing on your ego-mind managing down its fears and worries about money.

"You've SO got this. I have your back and the Universe is showing you that it does, as does your Higher Self–that's what all these synchronicities are helping you to see. So, step out now with more courage than ever before, and confidence. Yes?

"Being grateful when desired things show up, and watching for them, primes the mind to look for what IS working in our lives.

Later, when we have more experience, we can be grateful for whatever shows up. As we begin to see changes as happening FOR us instead of TO us, we begin to work with the dual energies of surrender, and command.

"So, it's something along the lines of stand, command, let go, and surrender. They are steps. One doesn't work without the other, and they need each other. When we stand command and command it HAS to be done with a balance between holding the vision and then letting go and surrendering to the Universe and our Higher Selves to be able to create something greater than what our minds are able to envision. That means: attachment to the bigger dream with detachment as to how it shows up, and trust in that it will show up in the most helpful version. This is what the increasing animal messages are helping you to uplift to and live from."

Student: "While I was cleaning yesterday, I found loose change in the sofa cushions and a twenty-dollar bill in pants in the dryer!"

AJK: "It's started!!! Keep your eyes and awareness peeled, whether cleaning at home, or walking outside markets in the parking lot. Woohoo!"

Student: "I've walked on an evening down a summer path and seen 22 adult toads up to their fertility rites in the Spring. By now, I have long taken in the toads' symbolism of abundance, because frequently of what they're up to during our group calls (Note to reader: in the rainy season for her in Florida, you can hear the singing toads in the cypress swamp in her backyard, both on the live calls and then when we re-listen to the clearings and activations.) And the number 22! Mastery number it is.

"Dr. Alison you know how we've been working with me to no longer separate the spiritual and material in the crippling way I had been, making it harder for my spiritual business to take off because I had to clear those old, erroneous, unconscious beliefs I held about what money is and isn't, and what spirituality "should be" when it comes to money."

AJK: And then activate, right, what is current to the new paradigm, these new times? Abundance for all, yes?

Student: "Apparently! Because I've just gotten a new, big client who wants me to also come into his business and work with his employees!"

AJK: "HA! Look at you, rock star! Living in the possibilities!"

Same student, later on in Summer:

Student: "After the first big rain, I walked through a mill-pond field near the path as at least 1000 baby toads, all emerged into their world. It was incredible to see, and gave me a feeling, an awareness of magic primed by the energies of fertility in this program! I have also seen dozens of crows, rooks, and magpies. I almost stepped on a toad in the street, only to see what looked like the same one sitting in the back garden."

AJK: "GREAT receiving and perceiving, my dear!"

I have found 20 and 50$ bills, hundreds of coins, heart-shaped stones, winning lottery tickets. And then there are the lucky meetings, emails, introductions, or random conversations which have answered a question or solved an issue or allowed some sort of expansion. And then the natural, organic, exponential building of my business.

In the time in these programs, I have come to expect all this stuff. The magic and signs are part of a larger energetic backdrop, where I am learning to collaborate with life, to co-create and experience the joy of seeing things turn out well. I am expanding my business, sorting out old relationship patterns, and receiving deep clearings which lead to healing in the body that have moved me out of and beyond old medical diagnoses.

Female Teacher—Collaborating

Student: One of the qualities often seen in female spiritual teachers is a focus on co-creation, and a collaborative spirit in their dealings. Can you talk more about that, please? And how competition does or doesn't fit into that, including for business?

AJK: Sure. Thanks for asking such a great question! As many of the women we find as teachers or leaders in traditionally male-dominated sects have had to follow practices and techniques created for men (i.e., spiritual teachers, think—dare I say?—"gurus" and Chi Gong and Tai Chi "Masters" or documentary show hosts, entrepreneurs, politicians, sharks in "Shark Tank" . . .) they more typically find themselves seeking or even creating less competition and instead, more win-win situations with their colleagues and fellow students from the very beginning. As they follow the dictates and rule for advancement, frequently there needs to occur tweaks and changes to allow room for the women to advance.

And that's just at the very start, where women have approached a male dominated sector and had to play the games by their rules, first. This happened in business for many years as women advanced through the management ranks. And it happened in politics, where the first women in congress did not wear dresses, but business suits. I used to love monitoring the fashion of those earlier female leaders in congress.

Collaboration here is defined as working with someone to produce something. The sense of hierarchy and top-down "commands" delivered from bosses dictating certain outcomes and projects is not.

This model of collaboration has served women well in times of contention or conflict (whether creative or destructive).

When faced with conflict people tend to respond in one of five ways:
1. Compete
2. Avoid
3. Accommodate
4. Compromise
5. Collaborate

Each produces social consequences and outcomes. Female spiritual teachers seek the best outcome for the development of their students, and fellow residents on the planet. So, there are some up and down sides of each response.

If we look to compete, there will always be the possibility of at least one party losing. The word competition is from Greek word, "competere" which means, "*to seek together*" namely each becoming better due to having someone else to spur you on.

Problems occur when motivation to win or improve is not equal or high in everyone working on the project. While men have often used competition to improve themselves and often approach it in that spirit, the situation for women has not been that.

Through history, due to socio-economic systems, women needed to compete for the support of men to ensure survival of themselves and their children. Recent decades have produced more "girl power" attitudes in several cultures, whereby girls and women are choosing to stand together for mutual support. The world of sports in a growing number of cultures is introducing healthy competition, and economic self-determination is shifting the negative competition bias from female culture as well. Are you with me so far?

Student: Yes, absolutely.

AJK: OK, great. Both avoidance and accommodation as conflict resolution styles have been found in female culture for a long time. When faced with having to deal with a person of greater physical or economic strength, many women have circumnavigated around this or avoided conflict outright.

Or they have practiced accommodation.

The thing with both of these methods is, the person practicing them does not have the option of getting "their way" or their preferred choice out of the conflict. Both of these are ways to manage either perceived risks or outcomes that are *all* undesirable.

Compromise gives a chance of getting some of what you want, through "give and take." This doesn't work well in the case of spiritual teaching, where integrity, skills training and blessings are often involved. Paying attention to quality, and doing right by the students, the material, the outcome, and oneself, it is clear the only model that really works is collaboration.

In collaboration, if done correctly and sincerely, then everyone can get what they desire. Hence the "win-win." In collaboration people come together, each bringing their best to the process. In spiritual teaching this is the only model that really works because both teacher and student need to give 100 percent in order for the process to work. And each needs to play their part.

In collaboration it can be arranged that each one does what they are either very good at, or what they really need to learn; i.e., the teacher teaches and the student applies themselves.

Part innate and in part, due to having been a classroom teacher and administrator for twelve years, my supporting everyone to live up to their potential is well-practiced. Competition was not a part of this, except when it was taught as competition within one's self, and how far one can take themselves. Otherwise, collaboration was the name of the game. Remember all those group projects in school? Yes. That!

I remember when standing up in front of a classroom full of diverse students at the high school level and I was talking with them to boost their confidence. I gave my vision of the world as optimally functioning when it resembles a quilt.

Student: Yes, I remember you having used this example before.

AJK: OK, great. So, within this metaphorical quilt, each person has their own unique talents and genius zones which they love to do and rock at. It does not matter how "big" or "meaningful" society deems it, but that we need every person to shine in their own right, to produce the best "quilt" possible of—and for—humanity.

In this discussion of collaboration, when in this context of rebalancing between the masculine and feminine and my own career as a female spiritual teacher when historically it has been males in this role nearly all of the time, it becomes relevant to talk about how I have worked with each and every student on their fifth chakra.

This always, consistently comes up, whether the student is in Activate Your Magic membership, a customer who purchased the Chakra Attunement Audio Series signature product, or a Magic,

Manifestation and Money Flow signature program member or even you all, in the Mastermind. It does not matter. Each and every time this has always needed to get addressed. People and their blocks around communication. You likely remember when we first focused on this within you, yes?

Student: Oh yeah . . . still a work in progress with this one, too.

AJK: (Laughing) I know . . . and it's one of the more gradual learning curves and changes,

It is typically earlier on that I work with clearing out the blocks within the fifth chakra in regard to speaking up for one's self rather than the unleashing of the capacity to choose to co-create from the field of unlimited possibilities. The latter is the more advanced work within the fifth chakra that we explore more in depth, afterwards, once this communication aspect of speaking of for one's self is a bit healthier. Because it helps to feed our work at that higher level of the throat chakra—where You're recognizing your power to choose where you once did not even see the implied choice.

So, there comes a time, when I consistently, with each and every student at the level of wherever each of them are within their own growth of speaking up more for themselves, that I have to engage in addressing the expectations of conflict.

As one is learning to more easily and fluidly speak up truthfully about their feelings or thoughts or desires, this typically includes the expectation of confrontation if/when the do speak up for themselves. In fact, I'd go so far as to say it's contained within the collective unconscious—that *if someone is speaking up for themselves, that is naturally signaling conflict.* And it's very nuanced.

So, as one learns how to speak up for one's self and gets more used to it, the unconscious expectation of speaking into conflict consistently needs to get cleared, along with the other clearings I tend to be shown I need to do all around and during this huge learning curve.

But this unconscious false belief in the collective unconscious that if someone is stating how they feel about something that is not a "Yes" to what the other speaker is saying, this perceived disharmony-to-conflict spectrum that is automatically triggered makes collaboration more difficult and has helped to keep the collaborative model further out of reach.

This massive rebalancing between the masculine and the feminine, and the healing that needs to occur to bring back into the proper positioning the divine feminine, is a major part of this new paradigm. This is for the health and thriving of us all. And the collaborative model is where competition has died down in its confrontational or out of balance mode. So, the outdated form of competition is able to die off and be replaced by something healthier, more functional, and desired by all. Now the real stuff can actually get done, rather than power plays and dips into ego land, that block progress.

CHAPTER 2
Walking It . . . Every Day

FRIDAY AFTERNOON

WE ROLLED OUR suitcases to the B & B, which was really a converted apartment block. We each had our own spacious room with kitchenette. We put away our baggage and met out front to go exploring.

Walking through the old and charming streets gave us a lot of time to chat. What would it be like to receive these trainings? How would we end up being, then, when we returned home? Dr. Alison had said so many times that this retreat, being sandwiched within our Mastermind program, was meant to catapult us forward. Yet while integrated within us afterwards, so the gains are applied to our daily lives and not just a one-off event that's great while we're there and then we lose the momentum after being back in our daily lives three days later.

We spoke about the recent Mastermind call. Sometimes we do this integration from the work on our calls on our own, while other times we seem to desire support, especially when it involves really profound stuff. I found myself really enjoying doing this sharing experience in person with the other Masterminders.

And then, "Ooooh, a crystal store".

"Wow a goddess temple!"

"Look at this wall. It has a crystal Celtic Green Man!"

"Look at that dragon!"

"Check out that copper pyramid in that meditation center! Wild!"

At the end of our walk, we each decided to make our way separately to the restaurant for dinner. That is where we'd meet the other members of our group, and Dr. Alison herself, for the first time in person.

"And so here we are. Woo-hoo! What else is possible?" Dr. Alison says, smiling as she greets each of us with a hug.

During dinner, after we've ordered various ciders and ginger beers, Dr. Alison makes a toast.

"Here's to your first retreat together. May blessings shower down upon and all around us for this time together, sanctifying our sacred, sweet group."

We have a lively, whacky conversation, full of laughter, non-segues from one topic to the next and tons of jokes about the New Age and how it shows up as an industry, while noting which shops we wanted to return to later.

Dr. Alison tells us when the weekly farmer's market is, the arts and crafts market, and then gives us a sense of the flow of our days coming up, so we can plan accordingly our free time. She also tells us where the closest co-op and then health food store each are on High Street close to our lodgings, to stock our kitchenettes if we wanted, while also letting us know the main restaurants in town that'll be open for our dinners, once we're done with our trainings each night.

The mind is often saying exactly the opposite of what is actually going on. This is one of Dr. Alison's most repeated teachings. That our ego-minds interpret the exact opposite of what the Universe and the Soul actually mean by something.

I think of this as I look around at my fellow Masterminders and Dr. Alison, seeing how different this first night of our retreat is than I'd expected. It was a lot lighter, a whole lot more human, than what I seem to have expected—serious discussion about energy medicine and how to apply it for the benefit of ourselves and eventually, who'd we be serving as our clients. And the bigness of what we're each, and all, up to together.

After dinner, Dr. Alison asks us if we're still awake and alert enough after our travels to want to hang together for a light intro session that night.

We all happily say yes, no matter how little sleep we've each gotten, following what excites us. Despite that we'd all traveled for the past twelve hours or so across the planet and had gotten little to no sleep, we were excited to get more time with her in person and get down to whatever business this training and retreat hold in store for us. We'd been living in so much anticipation, increasingly as the time drew nearer, in these past two months after first paying for the retreat and then after, booking our flights.

As we walk up the stairs from the family pub atmosphere, we'd eaten dinner in, to a small ballroom above it in this apparently 15th century building, I reflect on this aspect of choice that Dr. Alison works on with us so much. I suppose it was because I was so proud of myself and pleased that I'd made the choice to even take on Dr. Alison as my spiritual teacher/mentor/coach and enter into first her Magic, Manifestation and Money Flow signature program, then accept her invitation into the Mastermind—feeling privileged to have been invited, because I know only like a third of folks in 3M ever receive this precious invite into the 2M. And happy with myself that I'd chosen to do whatever it takes to make this retreat.

Some programs I've seen and have been in focus on affirmations or analytical coaching and intellectual guidance to better choosing.

That is so not the case here! The Vibrational UPgrade System that Dr. Alison created focuses on how subtle energy flows work both in our bodies and the Universe, and then how to align within and engage that flow of energy. It feels like a whole load of energy and magic are going in the direction of increasing my joy—in all areas of my life.

So, while that may seem complicated—it's actually the exact opposite of that, because Dr. Alison has truly taken boatloads of such complex ancient wisdom and Universal Laws and has broken it down for us into more digestible pieces that then fit together in a comprehensive, yet succinct package. Seriously—it's one of the things we all comment on that we appreciate a lot about having her as our teacher. There's so much she can address. One time when I told her as much, Dr. Alison laughed and said that yes, her first assistant thanked her for her first book, saying that it saved her from having to read like eighteen others.

I could feel this joy bubbling within and between all of us as our cheerful, bubbling group made our way up the iron spiral staircase. Ooh this felt good!

As we get into our sacred space for this time together on this first night and we all settle into our little areas, Dr. Alison seems to be clearing the space and adjusting the lighting. I think about how grateful I am for who I have become today due to this work, as I watch others really in their own heads, quietly arranging themselves in their bit of space, as we take our seats. How much more alive I've felt since really having my first major shift out of who I'd been when I'd started the program. And wow, had this been noticed by so many of my friends, colleagues, family and yes, my spouse.

I looked around at my fellow retreat goers as we all got ready to begin, waiting for Dr. Alison to get the water with lemon pitcher filled up from the server. I remember them as well, having had much the same experience of their loved ones around them commenting to them about how different they'd been increasingly seeming; somehow lighter and more spirited and alive.

And then it hit me—one of Dr. Alison's tagline for Vibrational UPgrade is, "Awake, Alive and Ready to Thrive." As I looked around at my compadres and Dr. Alison herself, we each had this kind of glow about us that totally translated that into reality.

I decide to do yet something else out of character. After we are all settled in and Dr. Alison opens the session with a playful invocation, she then asks us what we each want to ask or say, at the start of this retreat.

So, I raised my hand first.

"Wow, OK! Check you out, Maggie! What's up?"

I said, "I want to speak about the deep healing—and I know you don't even like to refer to yourself as a 'healer' and wow, now that's another example of what you talk about with how so much of the time the ego-mind makes the exact opposite interpretation or label of what is actually going on. Because you don't like to refer to yourself as a healer, yet that's at the core of what you do!"

Dr. Alison looked at me with a quizzical smile on her face. "Thank you, Maggie, for seeing that."

"So, I was thinking, you know, working with remembrance, because there's this remembrance, you know, this Isis goddess remembrance kind of a thing, it just keeps coming back to me. Like, you know, my personal experience with you is that I have been remembered. I can be put back together, you know?"

Dr. Alison switched her leg positions as she sat in lotus position and then leaned forward, her hand on her chin.

"Maggie, that's quite interesting—that you bring in goddess Isis. I don't speak about her directly, but she's one of the core teachings I work with and share the learning from. When I go into super strong clearings on behalf of the feminine, and when I'm transmitting or activating with that sense of fierceness—do you know what I'm talking about?"

"Yes." I looked around and a few others were nodding, but only half-heartedly. I'm not sure they were following what I meant. But I didn't care in this moment, it was so important, what I've been wanting to say to her. In person.

"Well Maggie, it's like, I feel the Isis energy is a part of why I have the nickname, 'lightning bolt.'"

"Yeah. That's the energy it is, Dr. Alison. And so, well then that allows me to remember who I am, because you're healing pieces, you know, there's a lot of dissonance, so that—as you help collapse that dissonance, I see that I'm well remembered. Yeah. And that remembrance is like, uh, you know, it's one of these secret women tools because the woman, the woman's body, obviously, you know, in terms of gonads, the, the male gonads are hollow and it produces, its 'seeds' as the man grows, right? But a woman is born with all the actual eggs she'll ever have in her body at the time she's born, they're all just stored inside the woman's body. You taught me that."

"Yes, I remember, Maggie. Keep going."

"So, we literally carry forward that unbroken body memory. So, one of the, sort of, to me, one of the forefronts that, that I feel you're working on and people are talking a lot about, you know, DNA redoing this and that, and that's great, but that reliance on science that you are talking about, people are picking it apart. Instead of what I see you doing is it's the massive cohere, cohere, cohere until the coherence resonates."

I was nearly breathless with excitement to finally be able to say this to her in person, and have the words come together in the way I had so wanted them to, so she'd see what I've been increasingly seeing about what she's up to with me—well, with all of us.

"And then, once you've aided our consciousness to get to a coherent state, that coherence then resonates. So, the Universe then gets our signaling more. It's just so much less complicated and so much more elegant!"

"Maggie, on this first night of the retreat, from all the great listening and perceiving you've been doing in your nearly nine months, first in Magic, Manifestation, and Money Flow then in the VUP Mastermind, you've really truly seen what I'm up to. I mean you've really pieced together where I've alluded to and implied some of the more advanced and hidden stuff that was too much to go into at that time, yet I left it there for breadcrumbs should any of you follow. And you have. WOOHOO!! Check you out, Sistah!

"So, Maggie, what you've just said, well it's another way to say what I'm up to, what You're getting ready to be able to do more of yourself—first, with yourself increasingly, and then on behalf of and with others. So, this is a really good timing for you to have had this all come together, as you step out of receiver-only-mode and into practitioner mode of the Vibrational UPgrade System of energy medicine and mindfulness, *applying it*. Now, not only applying it to yourself and your life and seeing the overall upgrade that has and is resulting, but then when working with your own clients, helping them upgrade and apply it to their lives.

"So, much of what I do, while I will explain what is necessary to you all in the formal training sessions in the coming days, is actually implied and rather hidden. But before you get to that point, what I've done that you've experienced thus far, I set it up *in conjunction with the Universe*, by following my Guidance and allowing it to be infused by the Universal flow of vital life force energy for it all to piece together in that natural, organic way. And it has turned out way better than anything my own myopic intelligence could've conceived of. That's what I mean in part about it all fitting together. And why I sense You're using the word remembrance and also have that sense of piecing back together and cohere, cohere, cohere until coherence results.

"But we're talking about what the Native Americans called 'Great Mystery' and the Chinese have referred to as 'Ancient Chinese Secrets' and the Alchemists kept in mystery schools. I enjoy it most when the explanation just emerges in the results you get. And then you get it. While being lighter!"

The room was really silent. No one was moving. The ice machine outside the small banquet room we were in, that was supposedly one of the haunted rooms in this hotel that Dr. Alison told us about, dropped a bunch of ice.

Then Dr. Alison began again, "But it's not meant to be kept secret anymore, in that same way. We're in new times. So, I'm glad, so grateful, that you've pieced together when I speak about coherence and particularly coherence in the heart's field, how that combines with alignment, and having the chakras perennially opened and flowing the chi, combined with the overall Universe's flow of chi, the law of magnetics and manifestation. And while I'd love to just sit in awe and watch us work the Universe's laws to help humanity, it's no longer those times anymore.

"I have chosen to be who I am, be guided to move across the planet multiple times, learn what I've learned, and become a teacher of these ancient power mysteries and wisdom as methods to help all of us uplift, as we move into this new golden era. But for me, believe it or not with as much talking and speaking and teaching that I do—I'd rather imply it, and have you all infer it indirectly. And to use less words and more affects and results seen in the energy and your lives for you all to learn from. So, thank you!"

"Dr. Alison I feel like what You're talking about is another possibility for people outside your programs, in a different kind of configuration, say if they didn't want to be in the Mastermind, but they did want to get to this level of coherence you so naturally help folks evolve into. Like there's some sort of advanced level of almost like a priestess initiation for people—maybe you could offer retreats for just that—who are already doing a lot of work with other mentors and or even piecing it together themselves, but they're not having access to that coherence energy, that deep cohering energy, you know, they're working their butts off, out there."

"Oh my God, Maggie, I KNOW they are!"

"I know, right? And some of them are getting more and more fractured, even though they're doing, they're throwing themselves at evolution, you know, so that I feel you really have a part to play in that because you do have all the background and technical skill and knowledge and your integrity around all of it. So, that you know what needs to happen."

I got down from the banquet chair I'd been sitting in, took the pillow from the side of the room and sat on the floor now, with one leg bent behind me and one bent at the knee in front of me.

"Hey, just so you all know, where we will be for the formal trainings is going to be a whole lot more comfortable," Dr. Alison said, as if reading my mind. "This was just an impromptu session tonight."

"Will we need our yoga mats?" Arabella asked.

"No, but you can bring them if you want, sure. But make sure to bring those notebooks and pens. The formal trainings are when you'll most want to take notes."

Looking around, everyone was either holding theirs up in the air or already writing in them.

"Maggie, what I'm up to in the biggest way possible, including with you all after months of working with me and then coming specifically *here*, with what we will be doing specifically on *this* retreat out at the *very selective sites* that we'll be going to and then during your *formal training* hours, all of this will combine together in an entirely new way. That will begin to bring a whole lot more clarity about what you've been experiencing these past months as the receiver of all that I'm up to within the Vibrational UPGrade System and work that I do. Because your role you've stepped into, even with what you brought up tonight, is changing from receiver of this fantastic stuff to now also being able to do it for others. Your positioning and axis are in the process of shifting."

"I can't wait! I'm so happy to finally be here!" Molly blurted out.

"Yeah, me too! My god, I thought it'd never get here!" Jan squealed.

"I bought my tickets the minute Dr. Alison announced the dates, remember? What was that like . . . two months ago?" Sheila looked at us all.

"Yah, I remember you got a great deal on your flights, Sheila," Heather replied. Those two always commented on each other's posts within our private Facebook group. I could see that continues in real life. Hmm. More translation from on screen to real life. Good!

Sue then burst out with, "I waited too long, but I still did score a sweet deal. I was kinda surprised!"

"Yeah, I gotta admit, I was kinda counting down the days. I was driving my girlfriend mad." Sam had a sly grin on his face.

Dr. Alison sat there quietly taking us all in. "Maggie, what's up? You don't feel complete yet."

"Yeah, thanks. See . . . well . . . but how to say this?"

"Just take your time, Maggie. You know it'll come and just flow out."

"Well, like, what you do, what you are going to teach us to do our own versions of—if that's even possible 'cuz I recognize none of us are ever going to be you and you've warned us to not try to, and that, well, nor should we want to—"

"Right. Be your own best version of yourself. We need *you*. We already have me. But remember to be careful of using that word 'should' . . . I know, I used it in that regard, and it was in a light sense in that context—but overall, living in the 'should' world is just so heavy."

"Yes, for sure. I get it. And 'should' is not really the focus here, 'cuz I've done really good at working that out of my vocab."

"Yeah, I hardly ever use it anymore, and I've told my daughter why I've stopped using it. She loves not being told what she 'should be doing' as a teen!" Sue had this smile on her face as if holding in a secret. She had that look on her face a lot on our video calls and events, come to think of it.

I smiled at Sue then continued, "So, what I'm saying is, well, Dr. Alison, there's also this sense of what You're doing is wielding and, and, and, and making this crucible where people can 'cook' up their best combinations within themselves, while letting go of the proverbial ingredients they no longer want in their recipes for their best selves, right? And then they come out having been unleashed and become more than what their wildest dreams could've imagined were going to be the results. And you've explained much of how that works, you know?"

"Well, Maggie, as I said, I hinted at it throughout your time of working with me, enough so that you all could get why we were doing what we were doing, and with that understanding, make better use of the clearings and activations and teachings. Yet You're really going to see under the hood, the mechanics of much of it, again during the formal training sessions later on this week. But you got it! You've been seeing with clear perception. And that'll make this training so much easier for you." Dr. Alison smiled at me in a way that made me kind of go all warm and fuzzy. But I wasn't doing this to be a good student.

She just had done so much for me. I couldn't believe where I'd gotten to, how much freer and more alive I felt and how much this had been changing my day-to-day life. It just isn't like what those other spiritual "gurus" or teachers or mentors are doing out there. I actually got *better* results than what Dr. Alison had said we'd be working towards. I mean, seriously!

So, I was and am just so grateful to her. And this system she's developed that has set me so free and helped me to unleash my authentic power is just SO strong. I wanted to help her see from outside herself what she'd created. I wanted to reflect her power back to her. God knows she does it all the time for everyone else. So, I wondered, who did it for her? Well, I wanted to!

"So, so that, I think that the subtle energy maneuvering skills you have, Dr. Alison, allow for massive shifts in the body, and I've seen this, you know that. Yet this is also while we're able to reach such joy levels, that we end up being given new criteria for decision making. Really and truly, we end up being able to function from an entirely new, elevated set of criteria. And this is SO different from how I'd learned to be out in the corporate world and on Wall Street. For this, I am just so grateful!

Dr. Alison nodding, responded, "Maggie, I'm so super stoked to hear this be your first offering on this here retreat. Because I can relate to how steeped in relying on the intellect you once were. And to even refer to choices as "decision making" is reminiscent of that.

Remember, I have a PhD, right? And was a classroom teacher and administrator for twelve years? So, the honoring of the intellect, and how it can help us make informed decisions towards our goals—or tests, as it was in the classroom when I was teaching in the public school system before the international one—hell, the glorification of the intellect, well yes, that's the majority of our conditioning. And during our years of deepest conditioning, to boot."

Murmurs of "yes" and head nodding were happening from everyone around me.

I then added, "But Dr. Alison, it's more than just that. You seem to have taken us from there to where we learn we're not even engaging in decision making as much as we're learning how to allow for the best choices possible. It's like an entirely different Universe! To go from logic and analysis, to—following our hearts' exaltation and then our intuition—and even learning how our bodies feel as the wisdom within them say yes to something, and all of this without having to have our minds agree—while calling it all a 'higher order of logic.' It's just a really functional packaging of a whole bunch of divergent wisdom applied in this really unique way. I'm just so grateful. It's beyond words how grateful I am for the massive transforming I've been able to do. This work is just priceless!"

More murmurs of agreement and heads nodding.

"Maggie, remember what you just said about this work being priceless when you are telling your first clients your pricing—and when you are creating your first price list for packages of sessions. Second, I'm so happy to hear that freedom You're expressing right now. It's what I've been working towards getting you all to each see in your own ways and lives. Woo-hoo! And yes, the mission here is to allow ourselves to choose the highest possible versions of ourselves and our lives. And to do this, to reach this, we have to go beyond analysis from the mind only. We have to go to higher wisdom both from our own Higher Self via our intuition and then from the Divine, and create from this elevated, aligned place where all possibilities reside.

"The ego-mind knows what it knows and prefers the known so it doesn't have to work as hard, and thus constricts us when we go to create something new or choose something different. It's the wrong tool there. You all are each able to appreciate the meaning of that by now. Rather than just words only.

"In this new paradigm, the task is to learn how to allow ourselves to co-create our lives using our inherent free-will, or power to choose, coupled with our reason, balanced with our intuition and informed by our heart's wisdom and spirit's joy *to get to* the most elevated choice that creates the most desirable buffet of further choices that our Higher Selves and the Divine would love to see us making. It's constant evolution, really. Remember how I've told you all stories about how I get uncomfortable with getting comfortable?"

"Yeah, it was one of my most eye-opening moments in the first weeks of working with you, Dr. Alison, after how I'd been living my life, these past seven years or so," says Laura, who came from Toronto to join us, and was one of my favorite fellow Masterminders.

"Wow. That's cool, Laura. Thanks for that feedback. I just take it for granted, because, well, it's how I am. You know? So, whenever I hear someone express surprise over something I've said or done, it actually helps provide more of a window into myself. I remember my fellow ex-pat teachers in Taiwan doing so when I'd be telling then my weekend travel plans or Chinese New Year travel plans. And for me, much of the time this further clarifies why I'm doing this work as *my* mission. For me, inside my own head, I'm just me following my intuition and living my life," Dr. Alison chuckles.

And then she continues, "It really is about learning how to unleash our seemingly hidden human potential. But even then, it's still beyond the intellectual 'Human Potential' movement in the States in the 70s. Why?"

Dr. Alison continues, answering her own question, "Because it's going beyond what seems to us to be the mind and its thoughts, or intellect, as the primary tool, even when the heart is involved with the mind.

"Rather, we are involving the subtle energy body and our many levels and layers of consciousness to engage on our behaviors as well, and rather than working against ourselves, say with self-sabotage. Meaning because you get cleared first of so many blocks at the identity and intellectual level (i.e., "ego-mind") and unconscious and subconscious levels, while also simultaneously getting activated for your highest possibilities and highest potential, as your subtle energy body is actually innately wired for, well that's only one, albeit huge, aspect of what we're up to. You're then cleared and activated in all the ways you show me you need, so you can *actually* choose what it is your heart and Higher Self really want you to be choosing.

"You're then attuned to the greater field of unlimited possibilities while your own fields are 'arranged' for you via the chakras to naturally call out to and *hook up with* this greater field of unlimited possibilities. Yet even after that, you're then taught how to engage that field with your own fields. And it's from here, that we further exponentialize your capacities to do this. And ultimately you can then help others get to this, as You're about to learn on this retreat!"

Sam cleared his throat then said, "Yeah, it really is a unique and results driven system and brings together just *so* much—and I've been around this spiritual path stuff for a long time . . . you know, coming from California and all." Sam smiles a sideways grin.

Dr. Alison nodding her head and smiling, responds, "Yah, I know what you mean there, Sam. I lived in San Francisco for three years after my bachelors at a university in another liberal hub on the east coast, where I'd first learned of the Human Potential movement and mindfulness. In fact, the first book written about mindfulness in The States was done by a prof at my undergrad school. I remember when I was working in politics down in L.A. and living there for months at a time, I went to used bookstores in the Santa Monica area and saw tons of books about it. But in the Bay Area, man, that was one of my favorite past times—going to the used book stores! I scored **so** many classics for and about this path."

Heather asks, "Dr. Alison, isn't that story about the purple book about meditation that fell off the shelf and stopped you in your tracks, in a bookstore in San Francisco?"

"Wow, Heather. Great listening and memory. Yep. And that author became my first meditation teacher. I seriously could not take another step without stepping on the book, which is not in my DNA." Dr. Alison giggled, then paused for a moment while some of us reshuffled in our chairs.

"You all, if you want, get out of the chairs and onto the floor if it's more comfy. We'll be done what feels like soon. I'm following your energy levels for this discussion, to see how long to go on for."

Two people climb down off the chairs and stretch out on the floor, lying on their stomachs, with their notebooks open.

She continues, "So, the criteria that I consider now outdated that the majority of the world is used to using and being limited by when making—rather it is more like evaluating choices, well, these change from matters of intellectual-evidence-only decisions that serve to limit us and what we can create, into choices that lead to outcomes that contain more joy, uplift, fertility, and abundance because we're working from our connection to the Divine, to our Higher Self through our intuition, and to the field of unlimited possibilities. So, it's able to be as big as possible—and as easy as possible! And because it's not like it's one choice and then we're done—it's that buffet of choices we live from, making one, then observing its outcome and either making more of the same if we like the outcome, or not making it again because we did not. But this requires that neutral mind I speak about, which results from the increased mindfulness you each now have."

Dr. Alison paused for a moment, her eyes looking up to the sky as I've seen her do frequently when we've been on video calls and events as if she's listening for what seems like packets of intuitive information. That's her word, not mine. But I get why she says it that way, like it's bigger than just when responding to a simple question one of us will ask her when seeking her intuitive Guidance with whatever situation we want her to get our backs on.

"But this increased neutrality and mindfulness is even able to become so accessible without requiring years or decades of meditation because your mind-body-spirit systems have been cleared, activated, and attuned towards your highest possibilities and your highest potential, over and over and over again. Right?"

Dr. Alison pauses as she waits while some of us take notes.

Then she continues, "The combination of the energy medicine with the mindfulness component speeds up your progress by decades, literally.

"I don't know if you remember hearing me say this to somebody, like Jan, as an example at one point: 'Wow that took me five years of meditation to get to the point you are at now and you have only been working with me for like a year and a half.' Haven't you all heard me say that or something along that line?"

Many: "Yes!"

Dr. Alison says, "Well, that's how it is. It speeds up the effect you can get through meditation. I don't know the measure in years, but it's just exponential. It's a major part of the design of the Vibrational UPgrade System."

Tiya then asks, "So, could you say not only that it speeds it up, but that it is more direct?"

"Yes! And faster!" Dr. Alison responds.

Tiya presses for further clarification, "Faster and more direct, to the point, kind of thing?" Tiya is an Indian born, American citizen who lives in DC.

"Yes!" Dr. Alison responds, nodding her head, while taking a sip of her green tea. Well, I'm assuming it's green tea, she's always drinking it. I think she said it's jasmine green tea at some point. I love the visual I got when she described her daily habit of driving up on her scooter to green tea stands in Taiwan and being able to get clean, organic, unsweetened green tea freshly shaken at any time she wanted it—for like .25 US dollars.

"You all, I've said this so many times, you likely already know it. But yes, during this retreat, some aspects that have gone by unregistered by you, because you were in the midst of clearing out some unconsciousness, or of applying it and experiencing it for yourselves but weren't yet ready to conceptually understand it—or not fully—that this is what was happening at the time, well now You're more ready and in the proper space to take it in, and have it make crystal clear sense. So, yes, in fact, you are going to want to have those notebooks with you most of the time."

The amount of daily work, personal practice, mindfulness, and attention that Dr. Alison puts into what she delivers to us, and all her students and clients, but especially us Masterminders, is extensive. Those who get to work with her over time are introduced to "Beast Mode" where she ends up accomplishing five or six times more in a given amount of time than most people. Expecting things to work, and commanding that they do, means that even things like tech issues that might take considerable time and effort, often result in rapid upgrades of capacity, rather than delays and difficulties.

So, it is typical that she repeats for us, because we are, as she just said, typically going through either clearings and activations or the application of one—or a few at a time! of the tools and experiences she's describing. So, our conscious minds can be a bit knocked out, as if either we're just not fully consciously for a moment or we get spacey, in order for the clearings and activations to go where they need to—where we're unconscious or to our subconscious.

She expects nonetheless that we get multiple layers of meaning at a time, due to her capacities, and yet, at the same time, allows for whatever repetition is required, for us to get it. I would be realizing this at entirely new levels throughout the training days during this retreat.

Dedication to vision, mission, and service mean that all the investments she makes into her life and business are turned around and offered to us—her own students. Empowerments, blessings, courses, coaching, continuing education, ceremonies, and even holiday trips to powerful land spots are shared. I know she makes special equinox and solstice trips to sacred sites so she can get the special energy at these times and then share with us—as well as her cool videos of these places, from where she'll do energy transmissions for us. She did that equinox one for her birthday trip to Mexico City, where she sent us healing energy from the top of the Mayan Pyramid of the Sun for like five minutes. Wow, did it zap me! And now we're here in person with her and we're going to sacred sites with her. Man, I was buzzing with excitement and gratitude. Really, this woman models the new paradigm's "Abundance for All" that she talks about.

In fact, I've seen her invest in the collective "out there." Her free monthly call is one of these. And then I've seen her post stuff on her

Facebook business page and then boost it, paying money to send the support out to not just her following, but in general, people on Facebook when she senses something is up in the collective and that they could use the support from knowing of this certain aspect going on at that time.

Consistently, over-and-over-and-over again, Dr. Alison always brings it back to the reality I'm in, or any of us are in, as if she's looking out from my eyes, because she's so able to accurately tune in intuitively to what's lurking within my consciousness as a block that's limiting me. I don't mean all the time. I do have to ask her to tune in! But still, so much of the time I don't have to ask. I don't mean she can read my mind—but at times she can—when it seems helpful. I just mean she has this uncanny ability to sense what's up for me while she seems to be tracking with me. And she repeatedly retrains us that our power is within what's behind these eyes of ours looking out, not the other way around. This power is what she spends so very much time attuning us to.

So, I snap out of my reverie I'm sitting in, interacting with Dr. Alison in person for this first time, and blurt out, "Dr. Alison, I'm just so happy to be here with you, finally!"

I guess she had been in the midst of saying something because she stopped. And she turned her head to look at me dead in the eyes, smiled, and said, "Me too, Maggie! Me too."

Someone else—I'm so lost in my own review and glee over finally being here that I don't even know who it is, so I shake my head and blink my eyes—it's Molly, from Germany, "Dr. Alison I'm just so grateful how you have clarified in so many different ways at so many different times how around 90 percent of what we see show up outside of our bodies in the external world, is created by what's behind our eyes. It has helped restore this sense of power to me that I never knew I had yet always seemed to want to get to, while not knowing I was giving it away. I had been feeling powerless to change something. So, you flipped me right side up again or turned me from inside out to right side out again. Thank you!"

Sheila, who lives in Michigan with her husband and three boys, "Me too, Dr. Alison. Words can't express how grateful I am. Truly. My husband credits so much of all the new goings on in our lives, including his new business, to my working with you."

Wow, Molly had been talking about exactly what I was thinking. Does that happen a lot within this program? I wonder if it's going to happen even more now that we're in person together. I know Dr. Alison has talked about how carefully she selects and then invites the specific people she does into this advanced Mastermind. Well, come to think of it, she does it too, just in a different, seemingly less intensive way, for the Magic, Manifestation, and Money Flow group program. What I do know is that we have this kind of cohesion and supportive community that is nearly indescribable.

Dr. Alison responds to Molly, "Molly, thank you for that expression of gratitude. You know I always love to receive the feedback from you all. And that gratitude—always good to keep our hearts light. It's the quickest shifter, right? So, yes, you've taken in that reframing really, really well. Do you see now that the first meeting point to having the kind of influence over what shows up outside of us, is to relate to the medium that our consciousness behind our eyes is using to be here, in the physical?"

There's quiet for a few moments. Then Jan pipes up, "Our bodies?"

"Yep. You got it, Jan. Our bodies. You know how much I focus on the body within this program as the key, while so many 'spiritual' folks ignore it."

Jan responded, "Yah I know."

Arabella, a soft-spoken American from Oregon, then says, "Being joyful to be in the body, to enjoy, share and explore the mysteries and delights of life here on planet Earth, that's how we're able to focus on bringing more possibilities in, to all of us. Isn't that what You're saying, Dr. Alison?" Arabella looked up from her yoga mat, where she was sitting on her heels, kneeling.

"Arabella, yes, in part. Well done. I couldn't have said it better myself."

Jan exclaims, "Well you ARE the one who said it!"

There are a few giggles as Dr. Alison stands up. She's actually shorter than I somehow expected. I thought she'd be taller. She's only like 5' 5".

Dr. Alison says, as if in closing for this first night of retreat, "This quality of focusing on the body is a crucial quality of working with a female spiritual teacher. Why? Because it IS the body that is the way to get in touch with your feminine consciousness. And that leads to the consciousness of our Earth. All of which we'll be delving *way* more into in the coming days of this retreat of ours! So, with that, I suggest we all retire for the night and get as much rest as possible."

We all take a few moments, then suddenly realize what she's just said and wake up to the fact that we need to pack our carry bags and get ready to leave.

"Some of you I know are already taking the homeopathic jet lag pellets I suggested. The health food store up on High Street that I gave you directions to—again, go out this front door and go left, it's up at the top of the hill, on the left. It has them if any of you want to pick some up in the morning.

"While others of you I know will go for drinks. There's a great pub and restaurant directly across the road from the front of where You're staying. From where we are, if you walk out the door at the base of this spiral staircase, that'll bring you out to the car park and the entry door to your lodgings. So, walk to the front of your building and look diagonally across the street to your left and you'll see it. Pubs close here earlier than You're likely used to. Whatever you do, rest well and sweet dreams. I'll meet you out in front of where You're all staying, opposite the exit here, tomorrow am at 11 o'clock. Make sure you have your sheep and cow poop-friendly shoes for walking and moderate climbing. You all brought a pair like I told you, right?" Dr. Alison has the closest I've ever seen her get to looking concerned look on her face.

Everyone responds with a nod. Seems like we're all getting lost now in the ideas and images of sheep and cow poop and the reality that we're finally here and day one is tomorrow.

"Ok then! See you all in the morning. Last one out of here please just make sure the door is closed. Good night."

And with that Dr. Alison was gone.

FEMALE TEACHER—EMBODIED

Student: We are seeing more people starting to look at the body as a tool of consciousness and as an aid on the spiritual path.

AJK: "I don't see that. This path of consciousness, yes, particularly as yoga becomes even more practiced throughout Western culture. And Chi Gong and Tai Chi infiltrate Western society more. Yes, and jiujitsu. I know that in great part I have the specific training and certifications I do, including being a Chi Gong teacher, and why I'm a certified personal trainer and an India certified yoga teacher and why I jumped out of a plane, and why I've hiked mountains, and in part why I love to dance, and make love, and swim, and surf, and lay on the beach . . . because of my love for the body, and my love of discovering the body's potential.

But on the spiritual path, or the New Age culture, part of my fundamental—I don't know how to say this . . . disagreement? What I take issue with the most within those communities is how much they focus on angels, ascended masters, channeling, tarot readings etc. but it's done as a bunch of talking heads, filled with projection typically so it's not even clean, accurate perceiving—while leaving the body totally out of it.

I'll never forget one of the energy medicine modalities I'm trained in, my basic training before the advanced level. And then another energy medicine modality I have attended quite a few events for where the other folks way more into the modality, more advanced in the trainings than me, because it didn't make sense for me to continue further—how in both these, we were asked to be in practice sessions with various partners throughout the days and how in one of these trainings every single partner I had was *completely projecting!* There was *no clear perception. No* accuracy!

Then in that second modality, at those events, overall, the people were *so* in their heads, barely in their bodies, and the majority of them really incessantly talking without any self-filtration. Just not grounded nor present. While ironically, this is one of the more materialistically applied modalities.

Meaning it's as if they only work with their heads; what I would call their top chakras and go up and out of their bodies in order to "be spiritual" or do the readings or channeling or connecting to guides or angels. It's the same check-out that gets done with money. Bottom line is that it's the perpetuation of the old paradigm, where the material and spiritual have been seen as mutually exclusive. This is dysfunctional, moving forward into this new paradigm.

So, the disembodiment and disconnection to the body is a symptom of this greater lack of unity, where the spiritual and material are meant to be mutually complimenting each other. Not only that, but the recognition that the material is a result of the energy, or consciousness existing first.

Yet specific to women, this has been a conditioned disconnection to the body, in great part initiated back when the patriarchy gained in control.

Student: OK. Yet I see that it has been mentioned quite a lot that women live their spirituality as a function of their body. Culture often says that the fact we are tied to it is sometimes a miserable fact due to all the possible pains that culture tells us are likely for us to feel, especially as we age.

AJK: Yes, the model in the West is that pains, illness, and decay are likely for you to feel, especially as you age. While in the East, I saw loads of elders out having fun in their bodies doing chi gong and tai chi in the parks in the mornings, with great agility to their bones and muscles. And that it's considered a *good thing* to age there, because of the wisdom you gain, *and the ignorance you lose.*

For those of you in the United States, when you fly for meeting me on retreats, and You're in the US airports, notice the amount of older folks in wheelchairs, with special assistance at the gates. Then, once You're at the UK or EU airports, depending on how you come in and what you do before or after, notice how much less of a presence of that there is. And how folks in the West still, even compared just to the US, when aging outside the US, aren't decaying in that same way.

To your first point, about having seen it mentioned quite a lot that women live their spirituality as a function of their bodies—that's typically only if they've been taught to understand the connection between their bodies' power to create, give birth, mother, be empathic, and finally how that yields more connection to unconditional love and the Divine. Yet still, these result from patriarchal constructs. I just don't see more advancement than that, certainly not to the level You're speaking about. Sorry! I look forward to when I can say YES! To that. It's in great part what I'm up to . . .

Student: And yet also a great spiritual master of Tibet said that if all things are equal in terms of evolution and conditions then a woman's body is actually superior for attaining enlightenment.

How do we square all this? Who should women seek out as their teachers and demand from themselves on the path? Let's talk about Feminism.

AJK: OK, so now You're asking the best question—how do we square all of these various tendrils so it becomes a complete, or holistic, understanding, so we can then work with it in a functional way?

So, let's talk about how we see our bodies and how we are seen. And let's even relax the stigma that got catalyzed by that word, "Feminism." Is it not part of the game—to have us shy away from using that word, as I know I have, even though I took Women's Studies courses in college, and went to a liberal college in a liberal part of the States, marched in a women's march in D.C. for women's right to choose what they do with their bodies? And then moved to another massively liberal city within the States for my Masters, San Francisco, as a heterosexual woman. Feminism can be synonymous with "butch." Ironic, too, how close the word, "butch" is to "bitch."

Student: Yes. Because boomers were told we had the choice of what to do with our bodies but were also not allowed to actually *make* the choice. You could have free love, but it had to be under the terms that the man in the equation wanted it to be.

We were told not to want marriage, and that we didn't need to have children—even if we wanted them. It was like you:
- Can't want to win
- Can't want to play
- Can't want to stay home

AJK: Yes. As if you were trapped and whatever you chose wouldn't be "the right" choice—or that you just couldn't win. The theories in those empowering slogans were there, but the actualization of the possibilities were just barely seeds, unable to yet sprout above the concrete, so to speak. If you went into the workplace and wanted to succeed you had to do it as a man, dressed as a man. Hence that "pantsuits" culture. I mean during my Masters, I actually spent time watching congress at work, and found myself focusing a lot on how the women dressed, seeing how much they were parroting men.

Student: Then in came all the generation X-ers girl power with the millennials following close on their heels. This in many ways did help a lot and yet also a fallout from that is where we see so many girls and young women of that time dressing like pop idols and being in the same kinds of competition and jealousy/self judgement dynamics that all the previous generations were facing.

AJK: Social media has played a big role in adding *back* in that cat-fighting, back-stabbing dynamic that the earlier boomers as flower children with sisterhood power somewhat spearheaded by Gloria Steinem, had brought in. Generation Xers were sandwiched somewhere in between these two dynamics, with *all of it* their experience, rather than one end of the spectrum or the other.

Yet in having this cat-fighting, competitive, "mean girl" gig brought back in, on top of it they didn't even feel their bodies had any sacredness or intrinsic worth outside of a sexual experience. And that is not freedom.

So, in this great paradigm shift, considered humanity's greatest evolutionary leap ever!, from 2012–2032, one of the massive aspects really demanding to be brought into balance for us all to move forward in a more cohesive, functional and even, yes, beneficial way is the learning to honor the sacred divine feminine.

And in that honoring, also comes collaboration, co-operation, and community. So, the Gen-Xers and Millennials have this much more in place and ironically somewhat also due to social media. Yet these collaboration, cooperation, and community aspects that are listed in the column of divine feminine traits have helped to counteract social media's heavy influence to compare and compete the superficial aspects of the female body, without connection to the sacred sisterhood.

Instagram usage, by the way, is associated with a greater prevalence of orthorexia nervosa symptoms. Orthorexia nervosa, yes, a cousin to anorexia and bulimia, is an out-of-balance obsession with clean eating. Orthorexia is a term that was coined in 1998 and means an unhealthy obsession with "proper" or healthy eating.[1]

And did you know that according to the National Eating Disorder Association, a recent study of women between the ages of 18–25 (highest age bracket of users, by percentage, of both Instagram and Snapchat, but not as much of the total percentage on Twitter and Facebook) showed a link between Instagram use and increased self-objectification and body image concerns, especially among those who frequently viewed fitspiration pages.[2]

Furthermore, "Americans spend around two hours a day on social media potentially exposed to unrealistic ideals of beauty, diet talk, body shaming, thinspiration, weight loss posts, and more."[3]

There is a path and there is an experience to be had that is necessary to take one out of the hatred of the female body, the twisting and contorting to make the female body show up as a certain size and

1   "All Foods Fit: When Being a 'Healthy Eater' Becomes Disordered." Magnolia Creek Treatment Center for Eating Disorders, March 5, 2018, Leigh-Ann Bamberg, MS, RDN, LD, magnolia-creek.com

2   "Social Media's Impact on Eating Disorders" Awareness and Advocacy, Jessica Jarrett, Magnolia Creak Treatment Center for Eating Disorders, May 23, 2019, magnolia-creek-com

3   Ibid

shape that is diametrically opposed to this experience of the female body as a way to honor the sacred feminine, and a way to reach into your own sacredness, or spirit and hence spirituality.

That is of learning how to honor the feminine. *And that starts with the female body* and *learning how to honor that.* And when you take a moment to really consider that you can recognize just how entrenched into our collective unconscious and then our own individualized unconscious *not* doing that is.

So, this dismantling of the patriarchy is what, in great part, we're talking about here. And its influence on society, on marketing, on mass media and its ensuing images. On how women relate with each other, rather than in the typically competitive model of the non-divine masculine, but the divine feminine form of collaboration and cooperation. Not the non-divine feminine form of 'cat-fighting', back stabbing, and passive aggressive 'mean girls' attack and competition.

It's not just about rebalancing the masculine and the feminine. It is also about the rebalancing that brings about, "I'm now living as a healthy, empowered woman with all choices open to me. Where it isn't just me rebelling against what others told me to do or told me not to do, but it's me choosing for myself. Whatever is good for me."

While I was in the classroom teaching for 12 years, with the millennials, indigo children were much the buzz, and those girls showing up (beyond the normal self-esteem challenges for high school girls) with little to no self-esteem, I eventually realized much of this was from asking them because of social media.

I remember discovering this as a Gen X, and asking, "Did the feminist movement of the boomers never happen, or what?" Like there had been so many advancements made for the women of the Gen X by the boomers and then we advanced that further, and then it was like *splat*. Gone.

Much of this is the comparison made due to so much now being about a visual culture via social media. Suicide, anorexia, and bodily self-abuse are all on the increase since widespread usage of social media began, starting with Facebook. And with that came an increased pressure of wanting to look as good as possible and as frequently as possible, just in case someone was filming . . . skin cream advertisements geared towards preventing lines, crow's feet and wrinkles for 20-somethings! Botox for 30 somethings! And the increased pressure of feeling as if someone is always inspecting how one looks.

This is WAY beyond what I've experienced as a Gen-Xer within the gym-rat culture of forcing one's body to conform to what one desires through weight-training and cardiovascular workouts. While that had the sense of forcing one's body, it was done more through a sense of appreciation for the aesthetics of one's body and the ability to sculpt one's body. And the eating restrictions around carbs, the high-protein diets, sure as a personal trainer, I'd experienced seeing some of these extremes.

But what we're talking about is not even that. What we're talking about is devoid of appreciation or even connection with one's body, as a female. Instead, it feels more like the destruction of it.

Student 2: One of the things about women's traditional roles is that they tend to be comprehensive. To the point of *a wife* is actually from an old Germanic word meaning, *woman*.

As women in some parts of the world gain freedoms of self-determination their "privilege" as wives also breaks down in that they cannot "hide" in the home. They must go out and earn a living and also keep the home and also raise the kids, care for the elderly and so forth. And vote and participate in politics, pass along cultural treasure, and on and on.

How to focus on our spiritual path in all of this? It has to be there if we are going to evolve. So, much post-feminism seems to have given women the masculine path of empowerment—career, action, and power. Somehow, we need a way for all of this to come together. I am a woman 100 percent of my day. I am not spiritual only part of that time, I need and want to be spiritual as a being, as a whole.

One thing that shows up in your teachings is the idea of aligning one's self to the life of the soul's highest and best possibilities. When we look at systems of spirituality, they usually offer a recipe for gaining the benefits of the system. What is your suggested "recipe for success"?

AJK: We are not only talking about re-balancing the masculine and feminine. It is also about dismantling from the point of view of now being a fully developed and empowered woman who has all the choices available to her. While at times that choice still gets made that it's the woman who stays at home with the kids because the man will still be able to earn more money due to inequity in pay when the woman actually has more training, experience and a proven track record in that same career and positions, and while the USA is one of the only industrialized countries without paternity leave, let's function from the positioning of you have all choices available to you, consciously.

But when looking at unconscious sabotage and limitations where You're restricting yourself, if when rebelling against an old choice, one that say your mom, if You're busy unconsciously rebelling for rebelling's sake, then You're not making a conscious, expansive, progressive, *nor free* choice. You've made a choice that leaves you with no actual choice because you are busy rebelling against that choice of hers, in order to go in the opposite direction.

So, that even if you liked her choice—let's say it's as a part time paralegal who'd never completed college due to quitting so she could work two jobs to pay for her wedding and then later to be around for the kids after school because the father was viewed as the one with higher earning potential—you couldn't easily choose that because you are meant to rebel against what her generation of women chose.

Like You're *not* supposed to choose being a stay-at-home mom, due to the limitations restricting her choices so you, as a woman, have to rebel against how she did it due to those constrictions, and do it differently. *That you have to choose "more" than she was able to, for the sake of all womankind, your sisters.*

And so, this rebellion doesn't involve my authentic choosing either. It's still locked into a certain tract, that does not honor *your actual desires* towards reaching your highest potential and living out your greatest possibilities that are true for you—whether it's to be the best mom you can be to your kids with no career, or it's to be the best CEO you can be with a husband and two kids, or a CEO who is married to her best friend and they have great sex and travel a lot because they don't have kids, or any other version of "to marry or not marry", "to have kids or not have kids", or "to have a full time career or not" . . . If any of this is made out of rebellion and not genuinely listening to what will make *your* heart sing and that honors *your* own unique being and your path, then You're still not authentically choosing nor honoring your co-creative capacities to choose how you will live your life, with as many possible choices open to you.

And it's the same thing for men. Those who feel like they *do* just want to stay at home and due to the woman having more education (more women have been entering college than men, increasingly, over the past five years) she can earn more, but who pursue working anyways, due to it being uncomfortable to "just be a Stay-At-Home-Dad."

Just last week, do you all remember me issuing that contest testing your intuition on the Magic, Manifestation, and Money Flow group call, asking which one of you—without googling the answer, could tell me which diaper company now has a dad on its box?

I do know that we Gen-Xers have freed this up a bit so that the Millennials have more choices with fewer stigmas. Yet they're into rebelling, for good reasons, but there is still some lack of freedom in there.

Another aspect of rebellion where there's no authentic choice made from listening into yourself and what's real and true for your own unique being, is about how much of a "girly girl" to be. How much cleavage to show, how much pink to wear, how high of heels can be worn "while still being able to be taken seriously, or professionally."

We're talking about, instead, where you have all choices available to you now. All choices are possible. We are in co-creator time and all things come from choice.

And when you feel as if "You have no choice" or You're automatically, seemingly robotically, going along a path and feel kind of listless or like there's a grey cloud over you, that's kind of a good tell-tale sign, let's say symptom, that You're not really tuned in to yourself and your freedom. And when You're not, *others are making your choices for you,* like the unconscious desire to be accepted and fit in, so you choose what those around you are. But that doesn't light you up, so you end up feeling kind of bleh.

Yet in this co-creator mode it means realizing where *You're limiting* yourself from *within your own beliefs.* These beliefs are not the ones we typically hear. That's only possible if we're able to hear the thoughts our minds are always pumping out—especially the hidden, silent ones. So, a vast chunk of stepping into an even more empowered role where you are the most free to choose what is really going to make you come alive and live up to your own unique version of your greatest possibilities, is to come out of the most nuanced meaning of the phrase "victim mentality."

To do that requires the internal work on clearing limiting, *hidden* beliefs—those stored in the unconscious and subconscious. And then freeing yourself up to make the highest possible choice in the moment. By highest, I mean what is most self-honoring that'll lead to the most freedom that your inner voice of your Higher Self really wants to be choosing, in this time, in this lifetime.

Then there's this other irony you've brought up here. It's in regard to that "doing it all" version of super working mom and caring daughter and rocking spouse and excellent employee and responsible citizen . . . It's ironic in that within the divine feminine model, where we're honoring the divine feminine traits rather than the non-divine, we're looking at traits such as collaboration, cooperation, and community. Whereas in the non-divine feminine model we're looking at aspects such as no self-care, no self-nurturance, over-giving, frustration/blame/resentment/anger.

So, our own chakra system, when we have full health in mind, body, and spirit over what the aspects of life the heart chakra covers as its areas of "responsibility"—these essentially guide us to the divine feminine.

If you are *over-delivering* as a woman in the workplace *to prove that You're worth equal pay,* well you've just become aware of an unconscious belief. If You're not asking your spouse and kids to support you taking time to do what you love—whether You're a father or mother—then You're not working collaboratively, cooperatively, nor in a community of your nuclear family. And when You're not, you end up with that range of frustration, blame, resentment and eventually anger—all of which closes down the heart chakra.

So, to honor you as a woman who can do it all—stop being her. Just stop that. You're honoring the patriarchy in doing so and You're just throwing your divine given life-force away. Just be you. Take some time for yourself. Ask for more collaboration and cooperation. Seek out more community.

Engage in more self-care and self-nurturance. This will then build a new momentum towards increased opening towards them instead of the old paradigm of woman-who-does-it-all-and-holds-her-multigenerational-family-together to honoring the divine feminine, and honoring you as a female, in coming out of the old patriarchal, worn out model.

And if You're a man supporting women to do so, then You're moving into even more honoring and balance within the new paradigm and could be considered progressive—and desirable! Ha, ha, had to say it.

CHAPTER 3
Connection

BEING JUST AROUND the corner and past a wildly colorful wall mural, the place we were to meet up for drinks was easy to find. Door after door on the way out of where we had been and over to where we were going were smaller than the ones I was used to. Some of the doors were so short that a tall person would need to duck their head. How quaint!

The door to the restaurant and pub, that Dr. Alison had given us the directions to, was a standard size, but the ceilings inside were just a few inches above our heads. Dark paneled walls were covered with local sports memorabilia and antiques such as washboards, pumps, china plates, and photos. There were several rooms to choose from as well as a beer garden outside, and a room on the right of the main hallway that led to a bar area containing several low tables and an even lower ceiling. The whole affect was comfortable, lived in, and very English country tavern. Which it may have originally been.

We chose a table at the back on the left, next to a billiard table. There were big oak chairs on the right, and bench seating on the left. Everything was clean and comfy. All the cushions on chairs and bench matched the decor. Most everyone was already there—six of us in all. Four people had chosen to go straight back to their rooms, including Sam, who'd wanted to Face Time with his girlfriend.

So, many conversations were flying amongst us once we'd ordered our ciders and ales and Proseccos. Of course, one was me speaking about my big "man" decision. Didn't someone say once that any five, OK six, women in a room could solve all of the world's problems, unless one of them was having a problem with her relationship? Ugh!

So, over our drinks under these dim lights and low ceiling, we all got to know each other even more, now in person.

The soul sister on my right, Sheila, enjoyed sips of Prosecco as we talked. "Maggie, so what do you want to choose in this moment? You seem like a person willing to go through whatever is needed as far as loyalty to the relationship."

I responded, "Yes that's true. I have always been someone who's willing to go through whatever it takes." I waited, thinking, "Oh ugh, am I being a savior or a victim?" So, I said as much.

"Wait just a minute, Maggie." Jan piped in. "What did Dr. Alison say about relationships? If there's no karma, then there's no sort of requirement to go through or complete a process with the relationship. So, then, what if it's simply about what do you want to choose?"

"Yeah, I know, Jan. Thanks. I keep that kinda on my forehead it feels like nowadays."

Then Tiya, surprisingly, came out of listening mode, "And what sexiness might I/you be feeling from any drama or heroics?" That question has always stopped me. Whether it's me procrastinating or relationship drama. I love that one and have been asking it so much of the time since Dr. Alison asked it.

Molly, who was on EU Central time but wanted to hang with us, said, "You know, I didn't even really understand that the first time she said it. I had to hear it explained like two more times before that made sense to me. But when it made sense to me, oh my god, did I get it! I do that so much with my kids and husband. But not with work."

I had been deep in thought while still half-hearing my fellow Masterminders, Oh, my, is this another old ego construct from when I was a kid? What if some of the drama in the relationship is stuff I am manufacturing just so I can prove that I am loyal and want to show I can stick it out? Ugh is it that case again of, what if the conscious mind is making the opposite interpretation from what is really happening? Oh heck, that is freeing.

And with that I got up and asked, "Who wants another round to celebrate finally being on retreat?"

"I do!" Sheila hopped up to go to the bar with me.

"I do!" Heather.

"Me too!" Jan.

"Me too!" Molly.

"I'm OK, I'm still working on my first one," Tiya said.

As we walked up to the bar, Molly said, "Yes, that's a big one. It does all seem to come back to choice. But conscious choice, you know, with as much consciousness and as little—preferably no—unconscious or subconscious hidden motives." Molly appears to be deep in thought, staring straight ahead rather than at us.

"Yes choice, and how clear we are when we send out our desires into the universe. And how receptive we are to receiving them manifesting," Jan chirped.

Sheila said, "Ha, ha, not sure I have ever had a conversation like this in a pub before."

Laughing, Heather said, "Well Dr. Alison talks about how all of this is meant to be lightening up our daily lives, like at that level. So, why not in a pub? But I am getting distracted by the dessert that woman over there at the table by the end of the bar with her date is eating. I am going to get one of those."

Jan, Molly, Sheila, and I all look over at what the woman is eating. Heather jokes, "Make sure you state it clearly to the server."

Sheila continues it, "Yeah. Ha, ha. True. Otherwise, you could get something else instead."

A group of noisy rugby players, apparently post game, came in and came up to the bar and began yelling their orders.

So, I slide over to make room for them, and still didn't have enough room, so I returned to the table where Tiya had been waiting for us. Heather sat down to my right, as the other three seemed to linger around the bar, in close proximity to the rugby players.

So, we got into a conversation about where we walk in nature. Heather shared about walking on the picturesque rural country-side near her house, further north near England's east coast, that apparently has a lot of the trees and plants from the druid alphabet, and about witnessing the striking beauty of the male pheasants in the area.

Tiya talked about how her daily run in her neighborhood had changed so much after one Mastermind call when Dr. Alison did a load of clearings and activations focused on the body. She then gave a blessing for feeling more connected to all of life. And then another too, about enjoying being in the body more. And another for being the perfect body size and type. So, Tiya seemed to be saying she was forcing herself less to move more, but was actually moving more.

"I used to run on the concrete but I've, since that call, changed to running in nature, along paths through the parks closest to my house. I get *so* much more out of it, and come home quite charged, rather than wiped out. It's just lovely." Tiya had this really sweet, pleased smile on her face. "Plus, I've lost ten pounds without trying."

"I remember when Dr. Alison did those clearings and activations that You're talking about, Tiya." Heather said. "And the frogs in the background at Dr. Alison's house were saying, 'bless, bless, bless' like those famous frogs in the beer commercial."

"I so love learning about the cypress swamps where those frogs hang out behind her house, and about all these other animal sightings!" I found myself exclaiming. It was making us all laugh. I sounded like a little girl.

Giggling, Tiya asked, "I wonder how much nature we're going to see while with Dr. Alison out in nature here?"

I felt so comfortable and happy to be around these women who I have only just met, but with whom I have travelled far in the program over the past six months. Being around these two now is a little like being in a troop, like when we were kids and spent part of our time being organized into small groups by our interests.

I am not 100 percent sure what interests I share with all these people individually but as a group I fit in perfectly. And that is a rare experience for me.

Such a feeling of belonging with all these people. It was SO easy!

Part of me always judges, and I judge people by how they treat other people. These people all seem really nice. So, glad I decided to get on that plane. So, glad I came.

FEMALE TEACHER—RELATIONAL COMMUNICATIONS

Student: Women are relational. We're communicators. Supposedly we have more wiring for being empathic. What are the best ways for us as women to guard our energies?

Or is it a question of guarding? I mean how do you do it? How do we stay happy, or in joy, so we can be in a higher vibration and be more precise in our manifestations? And bloody well how can I have more fun with it?

AJK: Well from what I've seen if we don't proactively make a choice for ourselves, and are instead waiting around, then we're looking for a choice to be made by default. Meaning, we're deferring to the Universe to make the choice for us, or we're deferring to someone else to make it for us. And then that's the exact opposite of what we're up to here. Yet I see this so much of the time, particularly within relationships, and what to do, stay or go—progress into it more—or not.

I totally follow you. I understand. I'm biting my lip to hold back from running a clearing on you, in fact. Because I just—while I hear you—I'm hearing and feeling and perceiving the contrast to the teaching I've consistently, continually given about, um, in the knowing of these times and how different they are right now as the old paradigm collapses and the new one comes in, going from the old version of victim/no choice/something outside of me knows better/has power over me (and is likely to abuse that power so I have to be on guard) to the new version of us humans as empowered co-creator/always choice/you-have-guidance-there-all-the-time-within-you-and-around-and-above-you wanting to support you/ courage to actually choose what this guidance says version.

Yeah. And I don't mean COVID-19 only this past year. I mean, like this is from 2012 onward. So, for example—how people used to use pendulums and ask it their questions with the framing of, "Is this _____ in my highest and best?" Do you remember me teaching you all this? And how key the framing of the question is with divination?

Student: Yes, I do. Of course. Fun stuff!

AJK: Totally fun, yep. But do you remember me clarifying that? How, now, instead, it's about anchoring in the *co*-creation, *directing what happens from our choice?*

Not this total surrender as if to something outside of you who always knows better than you so that You're abandoning yourself, your authentic feeling body, and your genuine desires within your own unique spirit. Rather it's meant to be the *combination* now of both the Surrender to the Divine and the guidance coming in via your Higher Self, coupled then with your own active choice making. Again, so it's that "*co*" gig, *combined, together.* So, You're involved.

And this more advanced level of Surrender involves, obviously, the first step of you learning how to Surrender more to that higher guidance vs. the controlling from the ego-mind and intellect, along with the control the unconscious and subconscious blocks not yet cleared exert as power over you that take away your conscious choice.

Because at that beginner level (which used to be considered advanced, in the old paradigm) when you are not Surrendered to Higher Guidance, then the past gets repeated over and over again because when working from the intellect, or ego-mind only, this not only involves the unconscious and subconscious blocks, but it also perpetuates *only* what is already known; so, it perpetuates the past. That's its only function. It doesn't have the proper design to be used for going beyond the known. It's the wrong tool to use to access the new.

So, without that first level of self-mastery in the Surrender, it's the intellect and ego-mind, infused with your unconscious and subconscious beliefs and blocks, that do the choice making. So, nothing changes, in form or essence. It simply can't; it's not the right tool. So, that first level of mastery over the beginner Surrender level is recognizing the limits of working only from the intellectual, ego-mind and learning how to go beyond that, to the Higher Self and Guidance that's meant to be helping you create your best life ever!

So then, You're able and ready, once you've mastered this beginner level of Surrender, to step into even more mastery over your mind-body-spirit system and the manifestation process and work at this higher level of discernment as to *when* and *what kind of* Surrender to apply.

And what I hear you doing in your current situation with your question about your husband, whether to stay or go, is floating. Yes, I "hear" you asking that question without having said it out loud. Of course I do, that's, in part, what you pay me for. (Laughing.)

You're floating along, rather than anchoring a choice that *then directs the energy*. Like you've given up, or never really felt you had choice, on your ability to actually have and make a choice within this particular context of your marriage. So, yes, this is your sticking point, and this is precisely where choice needs to get demonstrated so that you can evolve beyond this.

So, it feels from what I've seen, it's less substantial, less effective to allow the old version: where you Trust the Universe to get your back for your Highest and Best and you live in surrender to that, like that old way of framing questions to the pendulum, without making any choice yourself, as if you had no choice, nor any ability to perceive "the best" choice. You get it now, yes?

Student: I am following you, yes.

AJK: As if there can be "the best" choice. That too is old paradigm, old thinking, hierarchical and unkind—and untrue. As if you couldn't just make another one after observing undesired effects, should they occur, from the first choice. Yes, of course, rationally, there are some choices that are bigger than others. But not *all* choices are, in fact, most aren't. As if You're locked into one choice, only, ever. People make choice-making so bloody significant; it's so hyped *up*! Remember, I call life a buffet of choices.

And so, you make no choice. Or you allow the circumstances to end up speaking—typically to crisis point—when the choice gets clearer, typically to the point where it gets made *for* you, rather than *by* you.

Or you wait until "the other" makes the choice. Rather than recognize your own power and responsibility within that power to choose something different or more of the same. It seems more effective with this new vibrational backdrop of the new paradigm, and that we're being asked/commanded to step into this level of self-mastery and responsibility—*to direct the energy where to go, by actively using our capacity to choose.*

Especially when you're a higher vibration, via a choice *you* make. Like, isn't that in part why you want to be a higher vibration? Isn't that what you asked—applied in such a way so that you can have an easier and more fun time with the manifestation process? That's what your life *is*, over and over again. Each day, a plethora of new choices. Rather than wait or defer to someone or something else— like crisis—having to force you to grow more and evolve and take more responsibility for you and the direction—and fulfillment—of your life.

Student: Wow. So, you took this in a direction I was not expecting. So, yes, continuing on with the way You're responding, this . . . well it feels like labor. It feels, it feels wrapped up in the birth of something. So, there's a lot of, um, shedding that's happening at the same time. And there's a lot of dismantling all that kind of stuff that's happening at the same time. So, a lot of traction that's coming in. Um, and I still, I'm choosing, I'm choosing what I want and at the moment I can't have everything I want. So, I'm choosing, um,

I'm choosing, I'm trying to allow the universe to have some input about what will be the, what will be the, um, the way to get the most of what I want.

AJK: OK—*there* it is! You're getting it. Except I perceive some stickiness around you limiting yourself when you said, "and at the moment I can't have everything I want." While there's reality to that, sure, because you can't choose for your husband, in this context it seems to me that while You're saying the words that sound good, You're still weak with *actually believing you can have what you want.* So, you barely ask for it. It's like a mouse's squeak, your desire as it emanates out to the Universe showing it where to flow the energy, rather than a lion's roar.

Student: So, I am, I am doing it. I'm doing, you know, daily stuff and I'm holding the line and I'm doing this and all that. And then at the same time, there's also like pieces of my privilege. You know, it's not just white privilege, racial privilege. It's also my wifely privilege and there's a lot of, um, internal patriarchal stuff I've got going on. It's all shutting off. So, there's a lot of stuff, getting a lot of mileage out of this, you know, as, as you do, um, as one can, if they choose to, as one can.

And so, this to me, this really feels like, um, the birth of, of a being, as opposed to, you know, I mean, I've just landed in my body and really began to live from here rather than way out there, floating above my head, like a couple of years ago, when I first came to you, right? I was fresh out of the hospital at that time, remember? I had just come back from near death. And you've helped me beyond that.

At the very most, if we go to the very outside of the outside leading edge of where we could possibly say that I was even remotely embodied, we're talking like I'm two years old in this body. And we both know it wasn't just that illness. I've been learning how to be spiritual as well as good within the material. Instead of that floating, spiritual person, or that stressed out, money focused person on Wall Street, right?

AJK: Right. It's integration now. And balance between the two.

Student: So, you know, yeah, I'm this great being in this moment. And so, I'm really trying to make it all authentic. Um, I don't want to keep doing this looping thing where I go forward and back and forth and back. So, I'm not, I'm not, um, acquiescing I'm, I'm holding and then kind of commanding that the universe can conform to what I'm, I'm wanting.

AJK: What are you wanting? I want to hear that. I want to hear that out loud. I want you to say it out loud and see if you can claim it without your voice quivering.

Student: Well, I want to be free, you know, I really want to be free. And of the relationship with him in its current form.

AJK: OK! There's a choice. Now to be clear, when you say free, you don't mean split up, you mean free within yourself?

Student: No, no, no. I don't want to be free from that. If it can, if there's any way for it to be adjusted, but it may not be. And so, in that case, that'll be, that'll become obvious.

AJK: Yeah. I get it.

Student: Yeah. Yeah. And it's more, I think it's more suffering. If anything, for others, it's not, it's not so much suffering for me because I'm, I'm sort of, I'm holding out for what I want, but it's like when I had an experience with a person a few years back and it provided one of the biggest breakthroughs up to that time where, um, I had this really strong, passionate attachment to somebody and it was, it was really almost obsessional. It was really strange.

It was very strange, but you know, given my history and whatnot, being basically a monk, um, and it just, at the time my heart was breaking up. I'd never felt my heart before. Be that as it may, um, the person was married and there's no way in hell that I was going to follow through on that. Um, and so there's this whole thing where my dad had left my mom for the secretary. In this case, I was a secretary, and the man was trying to have me on the side with his wife and this whole thing, right? And there was a part of me that was, I never would have gotten into this, but I was trying to, I was trying to be authentic to myself for a change instead of being authentic to what my head was telling me were the rules.

So, I let it run a bit, it was a big risk, but I let it run and I allowed my feelings to develop. And so, I remember at one point where I was literally on my knees in my office, praying about this feeling because I could not shake it. And part of me was like, there's no way I'm going to follow through on it. So, I'm literally torturing myself.

I finally asked, why do I love this person so much? Because this was an obsessive love, but it was, there was a love component there as well. But as I said earlier, I can love a box. You know what I mean? What I'm saying is I'm somebody who could love, who can love an inanimate object.

AJK: (Laughing.) Indeed!

Student: I am a source of love. So, for me to love something is not unusual, right? But for me to feel *this* is unusual. It wasn't usual. So, I was, I was there on my knees and I was praying to, to my, the protectors of my life saying, you know, why is it that I love this person so much? And all of a sudden everything broke. It, it crescendoed as a volcano. And then it broke through to complete silence. And the voice was, you know, not a voice, but the knowing was, it said, actually you're asking the wrong question. The question for you should be, why don't you love everybody that much?

And that was one of the key initiations that shifted my path. And so, this is, this feels, this has the same feeling to it. This is, this is the answer here. It's me having what I want. And yet there's still parts of me that wants things which are not healthy.

AJK: OK, now you've gotten to it! Up until that last sentence, which is an entirely different topic, right?

Student: Yeah. But so, it's like, well I'm staring all that stuff down at the same time, you know? Um, um, I refuse to, to abuse myself or judge myself or, you know, violently try to control myself, anything like that. I'm, I'm trying to love myself through this with the compassion of somebody who knows that, you know, daddy's little girl is, is in here in the mix, you know? And so, there's a whole thing going on with that. So, I think I'm doing pretty well with it and I'm remaining very grounded within it. Um, and I have a bottom line I'm thinking I pretty much know what's going to happen, but I'm also leaving it open.

I'm allowing for a magic to come home with it. That is what is going to be the best. Um, but you know, I want to be done with this. Otherwise, I, I know I will just choose another similar situation if I don't, because it's time, the problem here, you know what I'm saying? I know you do, Dr. Alison, that was just rhetorical, right?

This is like the second shoe dropping of the, of the reverse spiritual narcissism that you've been helping me move beyond. This is like the, um, the spiritual denial, right?

Why would I want to be in something where I wasn't getting what I wanted? You know what I'm saying? So, there's this whole unraveling that's happening. In the meantime, I'm just, you know, going through and doing what I'm doing, but it's coming close now it's winding down one way or the other.

AJK: OK. Yes. I hear you. So, when you were talking, you made this hand motion as you were talking about your solar plexus, in front of it. The energetic you were implying with that is the exact match of the energy I perceive of what You're actually needing and up to there so you can get beyond this pattern. It's the necessity, of you there, *grounding that empowerment.* And I mean that in all ways, yes. The solar plexus has our empathic equipment, and when we're closed down there from unconscious and subconscious patterns, our boundaries are not strong, and we take in other's stuff. Yet at the same time, our boundaries are emanated out from a strong, clear solar plexus.

Power struggles also occur within the third chakra, our solar plexus. It's also where our confidence and self-worth and self-esteem all sit. Interestingly, it's also of the fire element, and this fire we use for the manifestation process! To hold our power in order to manifest what we desire. Right? So, this chakra evolving beyond old patterns with these very aspects of you and how you live your life is what You're in the process of moving through.

All that stuff you mentioned that you feel You're fielding?

It's because your growth point now is to ground there, and that includes grounding in your body yes, but also *grounding in your own empowerment,* and then *root that down, via your choices,* within this seeming power struggle—and by that I don't necessarily mean power struggle with "other," I mean within you—and experience what that feels like.

So, it is as huge as you perceive this all to be, because after working with me for three years You're now in the process of successfully evolving beyond this foundational pattern of being ungrounded, and thus at the mercy of what others are doing around you, without much real choice. This is a *samskara* you're overcoming, a life, not lesson, but a pattern that your soul has incarnated as one of the main patterns to evolve beyond in this lifetime. In how to be in your body, stay and *hold your ground,* while you choose what it is you desire, and allow yourself to have that manifested. All of which are different steps of equal importance.

You are a sovereign Divine being with spiritual license and freedom. OK, I can tell I'm going into transmission mode now. You do not need permission from anyone to be who you are and live your life as you so choose. This is your Divine birthright. Be the proper custodian of this inestimable jewel that it is and remember that you are a child of this Universe.

Within we each hold great jurisdiction, spiritual authority, and free rein to be the sovereign ruler of our own self and life. We don't have to control life or others or even the milieu around us. Yet with this dominion and freedom, we have the corresponding responsibility of complete and blooming choice to become as spiritually awake, free, and self-determined as we wish to be. This naturally includes consummate and unqualified choice as to what our values and behaviors will be this lifetime.

There is no permission required from anyone, apart from yourself, to be and live out your mandate. There are many voices that will challenge you on the path from chimerical chains of fear, loss, or abandonment that may hold you back or tempt you into giving your power away to others, so they choose for you.

And there is more responsibility when having spiritual authority than just recognizing that it lies within you. There are times when you must *act* on it and be a sentry for it. This means recognizing when others seek to press leverage over you for their own reasons, or when you are being manipulated out of your own mastery, becoming blind to your own power of choice and instead believing that things just are the way that they are, and you cannot question nor challenge nor make a different choice because it's being presented as if there is no choice.

So, becoming aware of all the areas throughout your daily life where you do, in fact, have choice where you'd not clocked that You're actually making choices because they're so unconscious, or assumed it's the way it gets done, or You're used to someone with more authority making them, is key.

And during this learning curve of increasing empowerment, to exert your own spiritual dominion requires that you stand your ground and remain true to your knowing, your choices, and your desires. This is not as much about achieving a specified outcome, or attempting to control something or someone, or even forcing things to show up as you wish they would.

Standing your ground means always identifying when You're lying to yourself, and not violating something that has genuine meaning for you. It is *not* about making someone else see things the same way you do. It *is* about honoring your own clear perceptions and if You're evolved enough to include compassion, then honoring the other, even when the other is differing with you or seeks to impair you out of their own fear. If you feel that another has to agree with you in order for your sovereignty to be intact, then it isn't genuine inner authority at all. The fact that you don't need to have the agreement of others in order to live an empowered life is exemplary of an awakened, evolved human.

You have the divinely given power to create and occupy your reality and you don't need permission from anyone else to do this. Honor your spiritual sovereignty. Stake that lightning bolt into the earth!

And I understand the pull you spoke of. I remember you in the parking lot on the last night of the last retreat as we stayed talking, with your sweet tears as you spoke through the pain about how much you love him and don't want to lose him, and I know you're not quite there anymore. That You're stronger within your own feelings, recognizing and also learning how to honor them and yourself within the context of this relationship.

I understand the pull as the wife that You're describing within the dynamic between you two that you've mentioned at length before. And that wifey privilege as well as duty you feel within your relationship.

I understand both what you're saying and not saying, too. I hear you.

And I hear the old paradigm around relationships from the collective's influence and conditioning, as well as the masculine and feminine rebalancing at work within your relationship dynamic too. So, while I acknowledge the sheer pull of the old habits and the many sources and levels this influence is pulling on you from, I also see you are getting your head above the proverbial water and are becoming much more solid and grounded within your body, listening to your body's wisdom, learning how to honor your actual feelings, speaking of them at a new level of expression for yourself, and holding your own while not falling back into old patterns. Like feelings of guilt and shame and you should just be happy with how it is. I see and hear and want to acknowledge you asking for more and giving your spouse space to respond to it. And that's HUGE!

You are basically following the Taoist principle I've talked about so many times, *following nature's way*. Remember that TCM (Traditional Chinese Medicine) premise I frequently mention of *blood follows chi*? Well, you're applying that premise here: comfort can turn into complacency which can turn into stagnation. And to shake that complacency up so that stagnation does not result—hell even more maverick'esque, is to not *require* comfort—ensures the more awake, alive, and ready to thrive you are. And then the relationship can also, as a result, be that, depending on your spouse's capacity for awakened aliveness and tolerance for thriving—and his choices. Yes?

Student: Well, thank you. And yes. Hence some of that sense of waiting and seeing, to allow it to play out.

AJK: I get it. Well done, my dear. You're going through massive evolutionary growth here!

Student 2: Dr. Alison, I know that I seem to be afraid that the more I am actually changing, I hear in me this fear of "If I change too much, I'll lose my spouse or my friends." Can you help me clear this, please?

AJK: There was this recognition I had a couple of years into dealing with more of the masses from having more presence on social media with my mission how much this work, or path, requires a stable, healthy egoic structure, *because we are dismantling it.*

So, when winding down after exercising at night, I've been watching a show on YouTube from the UK about old barn conversions into cool, modern homes over in the UK. To relate to the egoic structure and change, I'm thinking of the roof's wooden beam that's shaped like the top of an "A." And then the four walls coming down from the roof of a barn, as the legs of the "A." So, I see this frequently, after they've stripped a barn of its old, worn-out roof, as they are getting ready to renovate. So, this is the A-frame, because it's shaped as an "A," right?

As somebody is thinking about changing, and wondering well who will I be then? With all the ensuing fears like the ones You're asking about, it is like this A frame structure. The term "ego-mind" has ego in it and connected to the word mind here because it's indicating all the stuff in the mind, that is wrapped up in one's identity. This is a type of framing. It creates this structure around one's identity.

So, it's like people then walk around with that frame, despite the fact that it's holding up the old, worn out parts of one's self and life.

Who would they be if they renovated the frame?

This which you ask, is in great part able to *even be* a fear due to the over identification with the external. The over identification with the yang. The over identification with the masculine, outward flows of "what have you manifested so I can gauge and judge and label you and get onto other topics, with this unknown of you, as I just meet you, satisfied away with a label?" laziness that everyone exists within, if they've not done the proper clearing and cleaning within, nor the recognition of balance.

It feels like this over-identification with the external has helped to not only to create, but to keep in place people's identification and attachment with their identity. This is their personality level self. And this is what others can point to and say, with the label, "Oh yeah, that's how he is." Or, "Oh yeah, that's typical of her." So, the mind has to do less of what it prefers—living in the unknown of the question, of curiosity—rather than the conclusions of the known. It works less with conclusions.

Which creates, then, more focus on the kind of fear that You're speaking about: that if I were to listen to my inside and feel and notice and observe when my heart gets uplifted, when I think about _____ and if I were to choose that, then change will result and I may lose someone or something if I go for that change.

YET it seems like by not listening to that inspiration and instead living in that, "Well, who will I be and how will I make my money and who will my friends be?" Well, this orientation to the external framing is so much of the time the cause of why people push down new inspirations and stay with the status quo.

It feels like for so many people, their common reaction is to go to that frame that's outside of them—which comes from others' projections. This is another level of living *based on what others are doing and projecting into you and your world* and seeing and thinking. It's another level of fitting in. Sure, everyone likes to fit in. But You're meant to have this fed from *within* you, not relying on outside forces for this. That's where the trouble starts.

It almost feels like a combination or one of the following: a fear of being alone, and a fear of having to face oneself and a fear of having to listen to oneself, and a fear of having to trust one's self. So, if I just go along with what everyone else is doing, that's easier.

And so, following along with that thinking, if I stay outwardly oriented then I'll get the "all is well" feeling of being safe—of not challenging anyone, including myself, or anything. I won't upset anyone.

One of the biggest stops I've seen for people in making changes they actually desire is by asking and being attached to the response, "What are my family and friends going to think about me if I do this or make this change? Will I be accepted in this new environment? Who will I lose?"

Here, that first place of deference isn't self-connected and co-creating with the divine. Rather, the orientation is outward. It seems to be coming from the "will you approve of me?"

It still comes down to a certain level of this: in order to be sovereign, you have to have that cohesion within you. Meaning, where you are able to have so much of the egoic needs of being approved of no longer acting as a leakage. Much of this occurs within the root, third, and fourth chakras' aspects. And instead, you have turned that around to a subconscious and conscious embodiment of you having confidence, self-approving, not worried about not fitting in, and feeling entirely safe doing so. It has to come from within. And that's some of the internal work of what we're up to.

So, that you replace this leakage of needing others to approve of you and needing to fit in with what it's really asking for—to feel safe, and to be confident there, in your body, because you inherently believe you have every right to be here. That's the root chakra's "right"—each chakra has one—yes? Or there, in that room of that party or board room of that meeting, that you inherently have the right to be there.

Meaning, you belong. And you embody that sense of having the right to be here, which is the core belief needing to be grounded in, in order for the root chakra to be healthy, functioning and feeding you and your mind-body-spirit system that vital life force energy.

So, having your root chakra and third chakra really re-wired out of the unconscious and subconscious blocks, and activated back to its native state without carrying the old density of the past around, you will at all levels of consciousness *stop* the dance with fearing rejection and seeking approval from outside of yourself beyond the healthy, natural levels. So, that leakage of your power is no longer running the show and affecting what choices you do and don't make. And you become more capable of owning your sovereignty.

So, we're talking about needing to clear blockages resulting from both your conditioning and imprints growing up, and then what you came in with and as.

It seems like without that solid foundation, what I end up seeing in people is a less stable egoic framing.

Student 3: How do I stop caring so much about what other people think about me? In particular, that I am in a program like this, and enjoy the spiritual path, which they dismiss as "woo-woo"?

AJK: Ultimately, this is a power leakage within your own system. What I'm getting at with where I got to via that A-frame reference is that it seems like there is an element of dysfunction there and *it's no longer relevant in this new paradigm.* IF we are using this outward cuing and we are holding the A-frame in place with our identity, we then have to scan our environment to see how we have to be in order to fit in—which is, "Don't talk about this stuff because you will be considered a quack." "It's quackery." "Don't talk about this stuff because it's considered woo-woo." I feel that label for understanding your internal world and working with it and understanding how your own mind-body-spirit system optimally functions to live your best life is ignorant. The tables have turned. The internal wants— and is in fact, demanding—to be balanced with the external, both getting equal focus and working collaboratively, as intended to reach optimal potential.

The easy, convenient labeling that the ego mind does in order to structure all of the sensory data that we are picking up through our perceptual equipment is lazy. It is an old way of operating. It feels like we're being upgraded to a higher level of actually seeing with accurate perception, so we don't walk around with this A-frame that we automatically throw and cage others with.

Being locked into an identity doesn't allow you to have that malleability you need in order to make new choices to honor *your own sovereignty* so that you *can be the co-creator of your life;* conscious, awakened, aware, and thriving. Even with the parts of you that love what people label you with; I'm talking about not letting them stick. All of that's separate from the inherent you.

It would be helpful to look back to see how you've been since childhood in your more innocent moments in your teen years and your more innocent moments in your twenties. Not at when you are living up to expectations when you have already conformed in order to receive confirmation and validation.

You can see hints and signs along the way. If you look at what you were most interested in as a kid or what were the hobbies you had as a kid. You can see whiffs of whoever you are beyond the divine spark. If we have the divine spark there is a part of us around that divine spark that isn't all the way out here. That part of you that is encircling the divine spark, closest to it but not it—that *is inherently you.* That brilliance is what you are here to bring forward and create a revenue stream from and choose where to live and choose where to move and choose who to marry and choose who to be friends with.

That is you hearing yourself while connected to the divine and thus the divine part of you, or your Higher Self, because you are listening to the heart get elevated from a choice you just made, or the heart getting uplifted or enthusiastic or excited about something new. That's you being tuned in to your spirit to where you connect to the divine spark.

Instead of living life from the A-frame of the ego-mind with all its conclusions and intellectual thoughts wanting to prove how smart it is, and caring what other people with their identity, claim and project onto you as your identity. Also, understand there is a part of you that seems like, from what I have been able to gather, when we leave our bodies (die) it's been seen by this global study, as a grey mist, repeatedly. So, we still have some elements of our essence that is beyond the divine spark that is actually me instead of Molly, for example. Meaning, each of us has our own unique beings.

This part of each of us beyond the divine spark that is inherently *us*—It's up to us to choose if we do evolve. Again, we live on a free-will planet. If we do choose to evolve, then we go into the yumminess of sovereignty. And we have successfully accomplished what we as a soul incarnated for and moved beyond identity-based existence.

If someone wants to make fun of your choice to do that, clearly, you can see, of the two viewpoints, where the ignorance lies. That's the biggest threat to enlightenment according to Buddhism—ignorance. So, then, we can have compassion for folks who are choosing to still exist there, but then not let that have any effect on what we choose . . . right?

If we can drop that A-frame structure or at least let it be *outside* of us, then that is optimal. There is a teaching I got when I worked with Native American medicine wheel communities and I love this imagery. When somebody is a thought and they say, "Sue, you are like this." Act as if you have a handmade basket made from willow in front of you and that person's projection is an arrow and it lands in the basket in front of you. It doesn't automatically go inside of you. It doesn't automatically become a part of your A-frame. You can choose: does that serve me; does that help me or not? There is that level of teaching where you have the opinions of others, based on how other people want to label you that's more due to their background and their unclean consciousness and all of their projection, than it has to do with you. And then they go to put that on to you. You could pull that proverbial arrow out of the basket and let it fall to the ground and take in others—when it's helpful.

Student 3: It's your choice, you mean? You first put the arrow in your basket out in front of you. And then you can use it, as you see fit.

AJK: Look how you labeled me as maverick—which I love. It's apt. It's beyond pioneer. It really captures the intentional rebellion that's been chosen with a higher purpose in my intuited action plan. It's hot for me. Let's say instead of that becoming part of my A-frame, I have the arrow out in front in my basket; I've not dropped it down to the ground. I've chosen to allow it to remain in my basket.

That "Dr. Alison You're a maverick" goes into my basket, not my A-frame. Then I can pull it out, to use "being a maverick" when it helps me, but I'm not *stuck* being a maverick. Because I love going with the flow; I have a surfer's and ex-pat's mentality of "no worries, mate." I also like to not be in control, not always the one driving; you know? I don't always want to be the leader. I like to sit in the passenger seat and let somebody else drive and I want to face out and look at the beauty of nature.

Student 3: I like that imagery of the basket and arrow and that I have a choice. It feels much kinder. The flowing river of malleability is good too. The phrase that anchors that for me is honoring myself. That feels like a sovereign thing—honoring oneself.

AJK: I see what you are saying but I'm even beyond that because you are still stuck at some level of focus on the external, in that me versus them. It's beyond honoring oneself. It's honoring the life force. The divine within you.

Student 4: Until I get to that point Dr. Alison, how to I deal with the fact that when I show up as different sometimes people in my life seem to bully me?

AJK: What if that bullying is actually not what your mind is interpreting it as? This proverbial "not fitting in"? Here's a story: I was wearing Toughskins jeans from Sears as a middle schooler. Some of you will remember them if you are American. Their primary tagline? Selling "durability." Blech from a middle school girl's point of view; fabulous from a busy mom of four young kids, managing the household budget from her husband's more generous salary than her part time one perspective.

Here is an aspect of me wanting to fit in. Yet, in neutrally observing my motives now knowing myself as an adult woman, I don't know how much of it was an aspect of me wanting to fit in and how much was I actually liked Levi cords better than the Toughskins, lol. They just had a slicker look to them. Toughskins—well I didn't like the X on the pocket nor how it made my little middle school girl butt look. It wasn't as hot as like a Levi cord. That cool inverted V on the back pocket seemed better.

So, I begged and pleaded, definitely went at my mom for quite a while to start letting me have a budget for my school clothing elevated beyond Sear's Toughskins, and into the world of the Gap's Levi cords. We clearly had the money; I knew we did. It wasn't that. I finally won. So, I'm entering sixth grade and I get my first pair of Levi cords and they were brown.

Student 4: I can picture them. I think I know the exact model.

AJK: Not bell bottoms though!

Student 4: No! No! I can totally see them.

AJK: So, it's recess and I'm on the school yard and there was this girl—let's just call her Debbie. As I'm sitting here, I'm considering how to describe our dynamic. I'm thinking about had she every bullied me before. No! What I perceive was she circled me kind of from a distance. She was more aware of me than I was aware of her kind of a thing. I remember playing four square, which I loved. (Laughter) Totally dug the feel of pounding on the jelly ball and being in the server's box. I was there a lot. (Laughter.)

So, this one day, I was in the server's box and I was winning. All of a sudden, I got pushed from behind. I fell down and my knees got scraped. My hands thankfully caught my fall, which got those painful scrapes when you stop a fall on asphalt with your palms. I got back up with my hand ready to go, turned towards and began to wail on whatever that force was, and so a fight ensued. Someone yelled, "Girl fight!" And so, you know—that kind of a school yard fight scene ensued. We went at it for a bit. We had that ring of people watching and making the noises one does when in a circle watching a school yard fight.

Once a teacher's whistle blew and we were broken up, we were escorted to the office and got disciplined accordingly. After school, as I was walking towards where we loaded into our buses to go home, she did it again. She pushed me from behind on my backpack as I was getting close to getting on my bus. Just a message as if to say, neh—because she didn't like not having kicked my ass.

After getting up off the ground, climbing back up and getting on my bus so I could catch it to get home (and not get in any more trouble) I ended up in tears with my mom because my brand-new brown Levi cords that I had fought so hard to have, now had a big hole in the knee.

As so my mom out of her God blessed love for me and her inherent sunflower like sweetness found a yellow patch that had sunflowers on it. Not only did she put that over the hole on the brown cords at the knee, but she cut it in the shape of a heart. I could never wear them out to school again. (Laughter). My brand-new Levi cords are ripped and who wears a yellow heart shaped sunflower patch on them!? (More laughter.) Now *that* was pressure to fit in!

Student 4: I give your mom big marks on not saying "You know if you were wearing Toughskins, you wouldn't have broken through them and scraped your knees." My bother used to wear Toughskins and you could drag some across the floor and nothing happened.

AJK: (Laughter.) Yeah, I was surprised that the Levi's ripped so instantaneously. I don't believe it was the Levi's that inspired Debbie to come at me. I believe that jumping on me from behind, as I just really leaned into for the first time ever today just now, I realize she had been watching me and observing me and wanted something I have in me.

Student 4: Your vibe was elevated. You shifted your vibration with that clothing. Clothing is enormous—that's why people spend so much time on it.

AJK: I love that you said that because I've always had a thing with fashion. As soon as a thing becomes trendy, I drop it. I don't want to be trendy. I want to honor what my body wants to be sensual in and wear. Fashion has been important to me increasingly as I've grown up and went out on my own and bought my own clothes.

Yeah, she didn't like the light that I had, or was jealous of it and wanted to capture it, so she jumped me from behind as if to smoother it. I never felt bullied by her. I never felt insulted by her. And, to top it all off, later on around one of our high school reunions, it came out that she was a lesbian. "Ohhhhhhh, so *that's* what it was!" when I found *that* out. So, it was the earliest example of . . . well you know how I said I became aware, after the fact, that she'd actually been "circling" around me? Where she'd been noticing me, hovering around in the shadows so to speak, and I'd not noticed her?

This may sound obnoxious but it's my light—she was the first example of a stalker, it seems. I've had a few. Here's another story. There was a boy on the school bus in elementary school, he used to make fun of me and tease me. I know both his first and last name; that kind of a deal. Never just the first name. You know what I mean, right? So, I came to find out years later back when Facebook opened up and the general masses all started to join, and he was like one of the first from high school to ask to friend me. This confirmed what I'd come to sense by high school—that he had had a crush on me.

So . . . what if it is the exact opposite of what your mind is interpreting as bullying? I just said this yesterday, bullies are the least confident people. That's not really revelatory. They're cowards. Hence their attempt at outer control even *more*, rather than inner self-management.

Like I say about the black sheep in the family, you became the black sheep in part because they could not handle the higher vibration you had or how much of their fears were challenged by your bolder choices and how that reflected on them. Who you were choosing to be and choosing not to be ruffled their feathers, possibly made them feel badly about themselves, and that made them afraid, and you became the one that didn't fit in because you were a higher vibration, likely thus more evolved, and so you triggered this resistance. So, rather than them taking their own responsibility over their own fear and managing themselves, they projected that onto you, and in pushing away mode. Attacking you, going at you, instead of what was bullying them, *within*. We've had great examples of that in recent American society . . .

It is the same thing about not fitting in out there with the masses. You should be cautious if you *are* fitting in.

At an initial stage when you have done little to no work on your consciousness and you are concerned about not fitting in, again, you are limiting yourself.

If you are being bullied by somebody or being targeted by somebody it's highly likely it's because you've done more work on yourself and you are a higher vibration. They don't know what to do with their negativity—this is all unconscious and subconscious suppression of their own traumas and imprinting and conditioning—and so bam! Your light gets the projection of something you have that they don't yet have. Or You're reflecting to them the actual need to go within and they don't wanna. So, it's resistance being projected on to you again. It's not that you have to necessarily do something different other than reframe it.

Student 4: OK, so yes, we could reframe it, but what can we do if we are actually being bullied? Is there like a tip or a trick or something that we can do with our vibration? I mean we can call the police. Is there something that someone can do to help shift that out of their energy or if this is happening should they come and seek coaching?

AJK: First, get some tiger's eye and some carnelian around you—or tell them to. Next, it depends on the extent of what they are experiencing for bullying. IF in any sort of physical danger then obviously do whatever it takes to remove yourself from that physical danger. Do not be afraid of it.

And you reframe it, and you understand that this person is not stronger than you, they are actually weaker than you and they are looking for the strength in you. They are looking at something within you and looking for that for themselves.

And sometimes they just want to give in to the sexy allure that the dark side has that many give in to, and they want to see if they can squelch your light. Especially if You're a free, sovereign woman shining her light. Men love that conquest game. See if they can capture and own that strong, free, sexy life force. So, if You're doing a proverbial dance with a guy like that, then remove yourself asap. That's a dance of darkness that isn't going to lead to you evolving, ultimately. Possibly some good sex, but that'll likely turn.

That reframing I spoke about can help you shift out of that dynamic of "They're more powerful than me, therefore, I need to be afraid of them," into actually having compassion for them. When you start to engage *that* vibrationally that will shift them automatically. I know a Chinese Master who says Love dissolves all blockages. I get that. And the higher vibrations do dissolve or entrain the lower ones on up to higher ones. Love is so powerful and weakening. For sure.

But you could also ask yourself if this is karma. And if it is, work with someone who can help you clear it. Because think about it; you'd be engaging compassion just to soften up someone with bullying tendencies. Would you want to stay with that, ultimately? That takes a lot of intense, concentrated focus to dump compassion on a bully to the point where they shift. It's possible. But again, you always have a choice.

And to be clear, I'm not saying all of a sudden, their desire to beat you up will have stopped by engaging compassion. Love dissolves all. Love absorbs all. Those are great sayings and to a degree this does work, yet it's so not overnight, especially where karma is involved. But once you can get yourself into that position of compassion— and I don't mean to have pity, these are entirely different vibrations and perspectives—You're on the way to ceasing your power leakage.

Student 4: No! No! No! Pity and compassion are completely different, yes.

AJK: To be clear, I don't mean that if you realize it's karma, it's your job to remain in a situation if you are now out of the household and safe. So, building on the understanding that you've remained because there has been no threat to your physical safety and well-being, if You're remaining and you spend a half hour every morning and every night meditating on that person, sending them love and compassion, that's still a lot of work.

The ho'oponopono is brilliant. It really is the Hawaiian prayer of love and forgiveness. There were studies done, for those of you who don't know, with folks in a jail in Hawaii and they said the ho'oponopono repeatedly and a lot shifted. They were able to get out on bail sooner. They were able to become more productive citizens. There was a higher ratio of early release and higher rate of productive life afterwards without a return to jail.

After a certain point, within this dynamic if you've chosen to engage tools to help your boyfriend, spouse, whatever, shift and you see that they're not participating in the lightening of the situation at all? Well, everyone is expected to do their own work, you know? I say that after a certain point, if it doesn't shift, then consider that could be containing Karma, right? Karma has its own timing and a way to dissolve karma I talk about, but this is not the place here. I spent tens of thousands of dollars in being trained in how to clear karma. It's tricky! I guess what I am attempting to get at here is to understand that if somebody is bullying you it doesn't mean that you've done something wrong.

It doesn't mean also as I suggested that you have to apply compassion in a concentrated way to have it go away. You don't even have to continue to interact with that person. After a certain amount of time if there's no behavioral change if it's a spouse or a partner or intimate friend or lover and the change hasn't happened, it's likely not going to.

You know, I feel that it's even impossible to go about the idea of approaching a potential romantic counterpart with the "let me change you." If it's a marriage, then it's your spouse's *choice* to change. But it's not your job "to get them to change." That never works!

I feel like when somebody shows you their behavior when you first meet them, that's pretty informative and indicative. Heed those red flags and notice the color of that flag! What does it mean to you when You're in traffic, and lights and signs are that red color? It's the same meaning here with "red flags."

Unless you are in a dating situation where people are putting their best foot forward and they are hiding and you don't have enough intuitive sense to suss it out, or it's just pure karma and you have to go through it. Meaning you date, possibly marry, have loads of stuff come up and choose to evolve. Please note, karma is by no means an excuse to go against your inner knowing nor your safety. But karma does tend to have a pull all its own; yet working with that pull consciously is what I mean.

People will show us in the beginning who they are and so we'll know by their character. Really listen to what you are observing at the start. Don't dismiss it, *don't hope it away, don't think it will get better,* don't approach the beginning of a relationship with anything other than neutral observation to see who the person is. Then *let them show you who they are.* I don't mean to be super critical but if you get any of those red flags kind of feelings you must pay attention to them.

Student 4: Yeah, that's a really good point.

AJK: If it's beyond the relationship and it's somebody in your intimate field then just get away from them. Ask to move to the other end of the office. Ask to be moved to another floor. Leave the job or fire the employee. There is compassion but there is also being like a doormat.

Many of the spiritual people in the spiritual community I have seen expect to just sit down and say the ho'oponopono or concentrate on compassion or ask me, "How do I get my ex-husband unchorded from me?" And "How do I stop getting triggered by my ex-husband?" Or "How do I get my husband to see what I'm doing with this spiritual stuff?" And "How do I get him to eat better?" Or "How do I get him to change?" Or "How do I get that person (boss, colleague, adult child, adult sibling, or adult parent) to change?"

If you are ever finding yourself asking that question—stop! You are going down the rabbit hole. You can work on yourself.

What I have seen historically is when I have clients working on themselves and working with me regularly and making a lot of progress, their vibration is naturally rising because they are clearing out blockages. Then the pheromone exchanges affect the spouse who is sleeping next to them that are now emanating out a higher light.

An example: One woman I was working with got her level one and two attunements back when I was just doing Usui Reiki Attunements. After her second level attunements, I was working with her—also as a weekly client—and during this time she went home, and her husband started to have ankle pain. It was an old injury, and she was unintentionally healing him while just lying next to him, being a stronger light, herself coupled with being attuned to the Reiki level where people can then step out and flow healing energy to others.

I've seen other husbands get triggered. I've seen wives want to go hide in a cave while they're going through a purging process because they're releasing so much pent-up stuff, including anger and resentment (like when the heart chakra is clearing, post breast cancer), that they end up in a lot more fights with their husband as they act out of their healing response, until I caution them, reminding them this is what I meant by a healing response! It's old stuff coming up that the healing light brought up during their session and it's lingering in their field as it's on its way out.

That's why a lot of this work has been done in caves or ashrams. But this awakening time nowadays is meant to not be removed from our daily lives but incorporated into those exact mundane levels!

The most frequently repeated coaching I do around this, when one of my clients or students really has their second profound—foundational—shifts or so, and their vibration is really upgraded, and they start, inevitably, to ask me how to deal with their spouse who has not yet shifted . . .

Wait, here's another example that'll really be helpful: one of my female student Masterminders has shifted entirely out of any lack vibrations and has really, fully stepped into the abundance and even the abundance for all vibrations and her husband is still in the lack mentality.

The strongest tool here is compassion.

And in this case, it *is* easier *both* the said and the done, because your heart chakra, from being in this program, has become much more open and able to, therefore, actually *feel* compassion and engage patience over the ego-mind's demands that their spouse hurry up and catch up and/or change.

But the bottom line is you only have the ability to get close to "changing" someone else by being a higher vibration yourself and working on yourself. You can send the violet flame. Thinking of changing someone even with this field and vibrations I have been both naturally blessed with and have chosen to cultivate and build all around me with the work I do . . . and now the work you do, my dear, and with the work You're now being trained in, it still comes down to *it has to be someone's choice to change.* Their own choice. The door to the secret garden shows up by making a choice.

Student 5 : Dr. Alison, now that I have my Vibrational UPgrade Practitioner certification and I am cleared to go work on other people, I was working on my website this weekend, as you'd prompted. I found myself wondering how best to frame my offerings. Considering that I also have that LOA training and certificate about attracting the perfect partner, while you've actually filled in the gaps with getting me cleared and attuned to be able to actually manifest using the LOA, should I include that in my marketing?

AJK: Well, what we came up with you framing it as, is that You're desiring and able to serve women specifically, and in all three stages around divorce: 1) considering it 2) having chosen it and in the proceedings 3) after the divorce. Right?

Student 5: Yes. So, what I mean is in that third stage, what's your sense or what does your guidance say to including the other certification I have in using the LOA for attracting your perfect partner?

AJK: What does *your* guidance say? To switch the offering entirely off of finding the perfect partner to self-nurturance, or to change the focus just a nuanced bit in the wording of it, while still including this aspect? What I'm actually hearing behind your question, based on what else we've been working on, is that is it possible you have an unconscious belief that in order for you to model a successful business as say a coach and energy medicine practitioner supporting folks through the divorce process no matter what stage they're at, that because you have certification to work with LOA to attract the divine partner YOU have to have attracted a divine partner?

I have spoken about this quite a bit, i.e., the weight loss coach not launching until she's lost that last 10 pounds. It comes across more authentic if you genuinely reflect your gig, as you've said before about my modeling of authenticity and vulnerability. You may have attracted the perfect mate in both Mike and Bob, but *you chose* not to go ahead with it as you allowed your priorities to become more focused on you and your desires and realized that right now that included more self-nurturance and self- care than a relationship.

You're a busy single mom, full time teacher, coaching girls' sports after school, attending your daughter's games, while also starting an additional revenue stream. In this process as both Mike and Bob presented a relationship to you, well you tried, but found the self-care you desired wasn't able to be compatible with the demands of keeping up a relationship with either of them, right?

Student 5: Yes.

AJK: So, you *did* manifest them—and yes to your mind's argument I can hear telepathically, " But then they weren't perfect for me, if

I didn't choose them because I viewed something wrong with them and their level of not giving me the space I wanted . . . "

This is not about them. It's about you growing and realizing more and more of what you wanted and growing into actually allowing yourself to speak up for it within the context of a possible deepening relationship. You can't get much more authentic than that. Frame it as such; it's what happened! So, you can include in your offering, if you feel joy around it and want to.

There's nothing you haven't accomplished that you're offering to others; there's nothing you're having to hide. Your truth is your recognition of while, yes, you could've "settled" for these men, and others would have termed them "divine partners," *you* are asking for even more than that. Right?

What if it's all just choice, summoned by our heart's—and 3rd chakra's—desires broadcasting out there? And the soulmate and twin flame thing, some of this seems pre-destined in at least the meeting of "the other," to work out karma, but I find the soul mate thing over worked by Hollywood and that any relationship as you know takes work no matter how romantic and mystical the initial meeting may be. So, "finding" (I would say magnetizing) the perfect partner is a fallacy. And you can bring this reality into your mindfulness coaching.

I think these terms, "soulmates" and "twin flames" and "perfect partner" all indicate someone seeking that "perfect fit"—cue dramatic music in the background—when it may be meeting up with someone from a past life who we were pre-destined, or contracted, to meet in this lifetime, so time and space collapse and mystical feelings occur, like déjà vu's. Hollywood and poetry and songs and literature have made it all really romantic when they were attempting to capture this mystical feeling.

Because once the band or orchestra stops playing, no matter the heart connection, a relationship is a relationship, and requires compromise and work. Yes?

So, "divine partner" *is a choice*—a choice to allow, to "make" another divine partner. Because there are many soul mates—perhaps you and I and everyone in the Mastermind are soul mates and "twin flames." (This usually has even bigger, more intense romantic connotations, especially for those into kitch online spirituality. We then end up having even more of a hook for them, or attachment than "soul mates", making it even trickier to have clarity.) We have all contracted these challenges before incarnating, to work through as a part of our connection and karma.

And from everything I've seen and heard and researched, typically people we marry or have long term, intimate relationships with, and our immediate family, we've been through other lifetimes with in another relatively intimate arrangement, so we frequently have karma to work out, some more than others, and it can be thorny and labyrinth like to navigate through.

I've heard and seen and experienced myself that these definitions or labels and expectations don't take into account this biggest possible picture: of it being a relationship pre-destined to clear karma. And for couples with that particular configuration of "twin-flames" and/ or "soul mates," it requires that much *more* work, as it's even trickier! I've read some research a colleague, a fellow PhD, did on soul mates and out of many, many couples who had to consider themselves "soul mates" in order to sign up for this long-term study focusing on a lot of couples, only one chose to marry, acknowledging the inherent challenges to their relationship, even as they did so.

Don't get me wrong. By no means are all close relationships all about work! Some soul mates bring more fun and joy out in us due to the way we resonate. Other soul mates are "business partner soul mates" who collaborate together to build something special. I've also seen people have sweet, nurturing, healthy, growing relationships (like my parents) while romantically referring to themselves as "soul mates" yet still doing the work while also playing a lot and describing each other as their best friends. It's not all work. So, in making my point, god I don't want to overstate this! Light and fun and laughing uncontrollably and making good love and dancing and adventuring . . . all good!

The bottom line is there's choice as you've described with Mike and Bob, you *chose* that they not be divine partners, whereas someone else would be so grateful—as you yourself said about Mike, "Well shouldn't I just accept him? Who knows who else will come down the pike? And he has these qualities x, y and z which look good on paper. . ." But still you evaluated and chose, based on that evaluation, he wasn't for you at the time, both times. You gave it a good chance and you consciously chose he was not for you, and same with Bob.

Others would claim, in their lack thinking—which is part of what we had to clear out of your unconscious, right? Or in their low self-esteem thinking, these *need to be* the perfect divine partner(s) and so they give it a go with them.

I have a really, really different view on relationships than most, it's that neutral mind again. Observe the choices, observe how that makes you fly or plummet, observe the level of lightness this man evokes in you as your natural response. For example, "Do I smile naturally or feel a smiling cell or two or 20,000, most of the time I correspond, speak to, or see him?"

Some choose to *make* a person a divine partner, out of the unconscious influence and conditioning of not wanting to be alone on Valentine's Day; wanting to fit in with society so that "they too feel normal"; wanting to show that someone has approved of them, that they're accepted by another; that they're doing what everyone else is; or that they're doing what's expected of them by society/ parents/family. And they make compromises in order to have and be that which are all choices. Some are made with less awakened consciousness, if it's from this list I just gave. Those are unconscious and subconscious level beliefs, for most, conditioning the choices one feels able to make and constricted to not being able to make. Some consciously choose to enter into a clear bargain of, "If I marry him/her, then I'll get _____. While I won't get _____, it's more important for me to have what I'll gain by being married."

Like right now, I'm helping out your fellow Masterminder, as you have seen, who came into working with me, having already made the choice to end her marriage, where they have two tween age girls, and asking me to help her with the strength to do so. It has required—and still is—a load of work to break what seems like a spell that he has over her, when really, it's just a controlling man and she with a load of conditioning having grown up as a woman in India, in an arranged marriage then moving to the States, learning how to step into her power.

So, it's clearly the level of a *samskara*, that soul-evolving lesson she's choosing to pull through this life changing event, and she's choosing to move through this in a clean way, so that once done, she's done and can live free of this pattern within her, then also within all relationships. Yet there's karma there too, and it's taking a bit to wind itself down with her ex. So, I'm helping her to speed this all up, while having the best possible outcomes occur within the various proceedings and acclimating to life after the split and learning how to thrive now.

Including, passing the lineage clearings for the female line down on to her two daughters, while breaking old, crushing patterns running back in her lineage, and imprinting from her Mom, and conditioning from the society of her childhood.

I don't believe in divine perfect partners, sorry. I believe these can come in at the perfect time for us to work through karma with a huge love, and if it's workable and causes us to feel the way we want to and live a day-to-day life within the energy we desire, cool. Over time it became clear to you—and me—neither Mike nor Bob afforded that for you. So, you said no. That's what I mean, it's a choice. So, observing how we feel when we're interacting with the man, and if it's light or heavy, constrictive or expansive is a great measurement. But then we can still choose to shut down or allow that expansiveness to grow.

. . . I trust this helps.

CHAPTER 4
The Land and The Goddess

SATURDAY DAY

INTRODUCTION TO WALKING THE LAND WITH A MASTER

SO, ONE THING I desire my story here about this retreat is to bring out is how it is to be around someone who understands the land etiquette. There is a lot about working with a spiritual teacher, things like respect, listening and not interrupting, and basic courtesy.

Then there are parts like not hanging on their energy, or asking them to do what is actually your work for you, being courteous to fellow students, not stirring the purity and integrity of their teachings by bringing in loads of other stuff You're googling out of curiosity that your wondering mind may want to know about the Universe's workings, respecting the high-vibrational state that the teacher is in after performing work or clearings or blessings, offering some space there, and lots of types of etiquette.

Dr. Alison is like a land guardian or something. She is respectful, in turn, of the land and the elementals. She also has all that training with native cultures' spirituality and earth energy, and also a ton of reference information—like a human Wikipedia. Going out onto sacred land with her is a whole different experience than going out on your own, or with someone lacking the gifts.

So, here goes. This is my first trip to an ancient stone circle.

We got into the over-sized passenger van and I was sitting next to Arabella. Yay, a new person, someone I had not spoken to before in person. But we had connected online, and I was fascinated to hear more about her idea for her soul-based business that she's been developing during this program. So, we shared with each other during the drive. I didn't know where we were going because when it had been announced I didn't catch the very unfamiliar name.

I watched out the window as I listened to Arabella's marketing plan. I remember Dr. Alison working with her on this on quite a few Mastermind calls, because some of what was said really helped me. I saw more hedges as we drove along, and many fields, and an ancient Roman aqueduct which may still have been carrying water. Then we were in a forest of some kind. Arabella eventually asked me about my own business plan. I responded with what I was up to. So, I missed the twists and turns around and around, and deeper into this forest world.

Then we were turning into a small street. Is someone asking for a potty break, I wondered? We were parking close by what looked like a farmhouse. Were we going for tea or something? "Wear your field-walking shoes, those cow and sheep dung friendly shoes," Dr. Alison said into the microphone from the front of the van she'd hired, along with a driver.

"I hear you. I don't want to take home any surprises from any animals," I said. Dr. Alison flashes a smile my way, while also confirming something with the driver.

Oh, we were getting out. Wow I was feeling a little disoriented. Is it just my eyes or do things look a bit different here? And somehow, I notice there is a kind of ringing in my ears. A tickly buzzy sort of ring. I am not seeing any bees. What is that?

Everyone is putting on shoes and coats, so I follow suit. And I see Dr. Alison and the driver walking up to a silver gate. Both come back to the tour van. The driver gets back into the driver's seat, while Dr. Alison speaks with us all in a circle, once we're all suited up, and gives us a sense of where we are, the folklore of this stone circle, how it may have been used before and why *we* are here. She also surprises me by talking about its connection to one of my favorite constellations. Wow. I had no idea these, well, that there was that much to this all.

She then walks us up to that silver gate. We all follow. I am feeling energy, almost like my hair is starting to stand up on its ends. I hear bells. And these are actual bells, not just in my head?

"You all are going to want to not engage in any conversation, please, as we go along this processional path that leads out to the stone circle. Really have your sensory-perceptory equipment engaged, and Observe it as best you can, because it will be engaged!" Dr. Alison laughs one of those big, hearty laughs. "And get ready to have an experience of a lifetime. Your intuition is going to be giving you messages." Dr. Alison continued for a bit to guide us on how best to work with our intuition at this site.

When she finishes, I ask, "Yeah, is that why I'm hearing this buzzing?"

"You've got it, Maggie. Yep. Are any of you feeling tingling at your feet, despite having the leather soles on them from your shoes?"

No one responds.

"OK, it's already starting," Dr. Alison laughs as she finishes saying this, and gives us just a few more tidbits about this processional path leading into the stone circle. And then how to approach the stone circle before entering it once we get there.

Then she conducts a bit of an activation, but I'd not seen her yet do this form. I guess I could say it was some kind of a land initiation. But then she does something else new, again. Some other stuff too, but outside of the retreat and our group, I don't know that I could translate it.

And then we begin the processional walk. I look right and left to notice the nettles, hawthorns, roses, foxgloves, blackthorn, and oak that line the path. Such vibrance and so many colors! Another two minutes and another gate. Dr. Alison opens it and pushes it wide open so we can all pass through. Then there is more path, with even more brightly colored flowers. Butterflies are dotted across them. They seemed to be singing. Then, I look up because the person in front of me had stopped, because the person in front of her had stopped, because Dr. Alison had stopped. She, and I'm not kidding, was pointing up into the sky. She was pointing to a rainbow, and was laughing, giddily.

We all just stood there, sorta mesmerized, as if our feet were planted in that spot. And it felt like the entire group exhaled together. We walked on in what I can only term a sacred silence for a while. Then we reached another massive silver gate, which Dr. Alison opened, and held for us, smiling at each of us as we walked through, nodding.

There it opened up. There is a large field with a river at the bottom. There are cows, many cows. And there is a ring of standing stones. The cows are eating the juicy grass all down the sloping land. There is a fence around the stones. But there is no one else there. And the ringing and energy current I sense seem to be coming from the middle of the circle. I am immediately drawn to the center. But I see Dr. Alison going to the right, across the top of the field and stopping, so I follow the rest of the group following her.

I don't want to give everything away, so I don't ruin it for you when you go. Yet I have to share some of it. We walked to one of three circles there. I hadn't seen the other two at first because my eyes had been so drawn to the center point. We went to a small ring of stones and followed a process Dr. Alison lead us through to open us and our intuitions' receptivity more, so we could tune into what this stone circle's possible function was in ancient times. She also brought us to what had become known as a fertility stone and did some really cool activations for abundance and fertility. There's a whole lot more to tell about that, but this is not the place.

While people took turns connecting with the stones, I was drawn to stand out in the middle of the long grasses nearby. Dr. Alison just let us play, interacting at times with us individually, but most of the time she was observing us. Yet she took some time to also connect in with the stones. I could tell which was her favorite, and I could feel it whenever she connected in with a stone, and not talking with one of us. I'd just look over, knowing she was with one of the stones and each time she was.

The energy I was feeling reminded me of when Dr. Alison has done an energy integration treatment on me, during my 1:1 session. The energy in this part of the field was so soothing and yet energizing and invigorating at the same time. It was as if I could feel all my cells being magnetized into the correct configuration. If you have ever played with a magnet and iron filings and seen the way they line up with a pole then you are seeing how that energy made me feel—all lined up. Someone had to call me over to take a turn feeling the energy of the big rock in this configuration. Everyone was very peppy and invigorated from this circle. Most even played with the cows who came up to us in one of the circles.

When we went into the larger field, Dr. Alison stopped for a second and seemed to look at the land with a distant gaze. Again, it was as if I could feel the hair on the back of my neck.

She said, "Go around and feel the stones. See if you can discern the different energies here. One of these stones is supposed to hold the masculine pole and one the feminine. See if you can tell which is which."

I got to walk into that circle center I clocked right as we entered the site, at this point. I wanted to just sit down and not move. It was a strong feeling of being pulled down by my feet. It felt kind of grounding but also not quite as good as near the stones. Laughter started as some of our group chose to interact with the cows instead of the stones. It was really fun to watch as each woman walked up to stones and appeared to greet them. I went around and felt the stones myself. And one of them I really liked. I liked it so much that I thought about climbing up on top of it. Leaning up next to the stones was electric. You could really feel the life force coming through.

"Go ahead, Maggie, you can climb on them here." Dr. Alison had appeared out of nowhere. So, I did. And wow, did I buzz.

After an hour of sampling the energies we all walked back toward the cars. Dr. Alison pointed out a church built very near the other side of the circle. She said that old churches were often on top of ancient earth temples. And that she'd seen this especially, in Ireland. And that much of the time when this was done, it was to snuff out the transmission of energy currents that was traveling out across the land. I could well imagine it.

I felt so charged up. Really like I had been on vacation for several days. Dr. Alison *had* said that we would receive charges and life force and be storing power by going to these places, and that we would receive an evolutionary boost by going there during this retreat. Huh. Wow. I guess so.

"Did you all enjoy?" asked the driver when we got back and silently piled into the big tour van.

"Yes!" We all replied, nearly in chorus.

Feeling a deep connection, I plunked my rooted butt down onto the seat, much more aware of the feeling of the leather under my hands.

As the driver pulled out of the car park, there was not much chit chat. I was grateful. I watched as the lovely pasture lands and hills and their wondrous emerald green rolled by. I felt pulled in by this land, as if it were somehow talking to me. I realized yet again, how Dr. Alison was up to so much more than she directly spoke about. And how focused she is on delivering an embodied experience, rather than just talking about it. That woman, the Beast, is so action oriented. But I get more-and-more nowadays why she has such high energy levels.

I found myself really deeply moved by how it is so much a part of the energy of our teacher, this sacred land and its heightened life force. And how it's such a match for the brightness of our teacher.

It's interesting, in how her style can be this soft motherly love, or fiercely protective momma bear over us, or frank and unadorned, or inspiring, to name but a few. And in that moment, I got that her motivation behind the style she must intuitively choose at different times is that she wants you to sprout in the best way possible for you, according to your own internal design. And she pulls out the requisite delivery mode that'll be the best conduit for the impetus to our sprouting. This land guide, or land guardian, this was an entirely new configuration of Dr. Alison. I'd never seen nor felt her energy, nor her delivery as it was, guiding us and playing with us out on the land.

She also, in her clearings and activations and coaching around the "Abundance for All" concept that she speaks so frequently about, and the work she has us engaged in with our own bodies and then with connecting to the goddesses in the unique way that she brings in for honoring of the feminine, and how she from day one, has worked with me and all of us to connect us with the field of unlimited possibilities, and now this experience with her on the land . . . It all lead up to Fertility, and connecting us to the essence of it. Huh. She is sly.

Heather, who is now sitting next to me, asks, "what are you smiling at?"

"This fertility we're being inducted into. It's brilliant."

"Indeed," she responds, and turns to look out the window.

Female Teacher—Loving

Student: Love means a lot of things, especially attempting unconditional love in a conditional world. In your international, #1 bestseller, *Reasonable Dragons,* you said The Feminine (Goddess) needed her own chapter.

You spoke about masculine—feminine balance coming into being. And about how the patriarchy is starting to show signs of wear and tear.

By now most everyone knows about the tie between the physical form and system of the planet and the bodies and life systems of all the beings and people living on Earth. It has always been connected and yet it seems like people have forgotten a lot of the truth of that.

How do you train people to connect to the land? I understand there are many rules of respect and what you might call "etiquette" about working with natural energies.

It is our birthright to be here, to connect to the land, and maybe lately also a duty? Are there ways that cultivating an appropriate relationship with the energies of the living Earth support our own spiritual path? Besides the obvious good karma we earn by being good stewards of course.

AJK: Well, *all* of that is in great part what you are going to be both taught and given specific attunements for—particularly at the

Dragon Master level. That includes learning about the element you asked about . . . and as of lately, do we have a *duty* to connect with the land?

Your first two levels and first retreat were still focusing on clearing yourself to the level of being well-equipped to take in the experiences on the land at the sacred sites we went to. You were shown how to interact with the land and the elementals, the stones, and the sacred sites, and more. Then you had your formal training and attunements on how to contact, connect with, bring down, and then work with the vital life force energy first for yourself, then how to on behalf of Serving others, in one-on-one sessions and group workshops.

At the Master level, this became more about mastery within and over yourself, and typically rebalancing how and when and why you give to others and help others, while learning how to bring that into balance with allowing others the space to claim what is their responsibility, for a more compatible VUP Practitioner-client relationship, so that it's a way more aligned and effective Service. And you were trained in your formal trainings how to step more into the role of a Master, to be able to attune others, and have your own students. All of this is occurring while You're clearly raising your vibration. So, your higher vibration and freer heart indirectly helps the collective uplift as well.

At the Dragon Master level, You're introduced to the dragons, so that you can more directly help the collective and our beautiful Earth. You learn how to interact with the dragons in a way where You're cooperating with them, never commanding them. So, You're taught what I've come to understand and research about the proper etiquette so that they want to Serve with you. It's quite nuanced and so special! This is also contained very much within your attunements at this level. This way, You're better positioned to have the dragons actually approach you.

In fact, in great part, many of you while at levels I, II or Master, have had the dragons showing up a bit in your field as you get closer to Dragon Master level. And they're very much in my field and *this* field of this program. It's almost like you can feel them calling, because in part of my connection with them and then your desire to meet up with them too, with the undercurrent being *to Serve*. As well, many of you come in already having your own connection to dragons. It's all so totally cool!

You're then taught beyond what you were taught in the first three levels about how the vital life force energy flows within the human mind-body-spirit system and what it does and why we need it to flow and how to engage with it and increase its flow, and how to direct it so that it flows as intended.

The dragons are so much a part of the Earth, and so all of this is then applied to the Earth. Her meridians, energy lines, what chi is called as it's applied to the Earth, how it travels within the Earth, how it works within stone circles, how it works at sacred sites, natural springs and wells, power spots, standing stones and other megaliths, and megalithic sites, how to work with the dragons to work on helping clear these spots, and flow the energy so it travels out and along the Earth to help both the Earth and humanity. And then how to work with the dragons to help infuse more light into the collective, so You're no longer working "only" in a one on one or workshop capacity, you are now helping at a higher level, in a bigger way.

You're taken out on the land during the Dragon Master Level retreat, and each given these sweet, handmade copper dowsing rods. And you'll be shown how they work and how these little copper rods can be used out at stone circles, power spots and megaliths, and along Ley lines and energy lines, to better work with the energy there for the benefit of the Earth and humanity, and to increase the embodiment of your intuition, dropping it down beyond your head and heart.

What I can say is, the dragon master level, well, all of it is geared towards us helping the land, humanity, and ourselves shift into our highest and best possibilities, evolving forward.

Regarding your question about your own spiritual path being able to advance—I specifically have tuned in for guidance for where to take you all. After doing nearly two years of research and from going out to *these specific*—and the *sheer number of*—sacred sites and power spots and megaliths all together within so few days—that is the nature of the design of it all. Your answer is a resounding "YES!"

Now, when You're taken out on the land, specifically at the Dragon Master level, this is when you will most directly see all of this coming together. What we've done on previous retreats has been building you and your mind-body-spirit system up for it. All of these retreats have included this same rigor of research and then intuitive work for the Guidance of the best places to go to, which ones to do together and when, and in what order. So, you've been moving through a sort of progressive learning and experiential growth program.

And of course, I've allowed this all to be directed by my Higher consciousness, and brought in *through* me, rather than my ego-mind strategically planning. It truly has been this divine orchestration that's turned out better than my mind could've logically pieced together. It's a combination of that Mad Scientist mode I get in with Hansel and Gretel following the bread crumbs gig I've said I've been doing my whole life. It was much the same with the creation of Magic, Manifestation and Money Flow. Like what was needed came through me. Because I asked what will bring about the most robust results for _____ intention, and then I was open to receive. Ask and you shall receive, right? (Laughing)

Student: Yes, you have and do model that for us a gazillion percent! "It's an ask and you shall receive Universe," some great teacher of mine told me.

AJK: Ha, ha. Don't get your nose too brown there :) And thank you, yes. Wow, that felt weird using that sarcasm. Kind of like a cactus' spike, pricking or stinging. I don't typically use sarcasm anymore. So, I notice it when I do. And it feels so off. It seems I was deflecting some of my very own receiving of your compliment right there. Hmmm. Anyways . . .

Much of this has been focused on increasing your embodiment, while bringing your increasingly higher vibrations and purified consciousness *down* from just lingering up and around your head, *down* into and distributing throughout your body. So, you are becoming more-and-more a bridge between heaven and Earth. And then we use that higher and purified consciousness, which then and only then can work cooperatively with the dragons to benefit the Earth.

Yet what also has been happening is you've all been dropping, progressively, out of your heads and more fully into your hearts and bodies. As well, you've participated in certain ceremonies and have received specific clearings, activations, and attunements to increase your connection to your intuition.

And thus, we've been increasing your connection to the feminine. We've been doing that by increasing your connection both to *your* body and our mama's body, *the Earth*. And the Earth benefits, as does the feminine, as does your body, and ultimately as does your heart, and overall mind-body-spirit system. This has also included serving humanity with your light; first through working with others in one-on-one sessions, then collectively, through what we're doing at these sites and with our beloved dragon companions.

There will be a sense of culmination and understanding of this all coming together, as well as further evolution of your own spiritual path. All of it! Meanwhile, you'll also be catapulted forward in your own abilities to bring down more light, on behalf of yourself, the land, humanity, and the Earth as a whole.

So, you seem to be, yet again, sensing some of what's coming. It's likely you've perceived some of what I've been doing in the overall Mastermind program's field leading into this next retreat—your Dragon Master level training—as well as what we've done on previous retreats as it gets called back up in you by what I've been doing. The intention is for you to have further integration so that you are ready, and can make the most gains from the experience!

Much of what you ask for are pieces of wisdom that demand respect, and to be demonstrated in action, while out on the land. It's how I learned from the Wisdom Keepers and teachers before me. You will be given further clearings and activations, as well as specific attunements within the more formal part of your training to help move you into the "best" consciousness to interact with the dragons, the land, and get all you can from it, while also contributing as much light as possible to the sacred places and land we'll be going to, then intentionally flowing it out beyond the sacred sites to the Earth's distribution centers and along its meridians.

I have specific methodology I'm applying that will become more clear once You're out on the land and I explain what to do at each site. You will likely end up perceiving the overall "mad scientist" design behind it all, that came through me and my Guidance, or *my intuition*. Again, it's me modeling learning to live on the cutting edge of the newest possibilities just beginning to come "online" so to speak.

This process I've discovered, or followed my intuition and the proverbial breadcrumbs to create, could be called what one of you has given me for a new phrase, a "Maverick Moment." And it's where I'm saying, "So, what if it doesn't exist yet? I'm choosing it anyway and by that choice I'm helping to create its existence. I am honoring my own magical being as an individual and free-being, choosing to create beyond what currently exists while also Illuminating the choices in front of people—a wide road ahead—*which is full of choices.* Always, I am being the one to say, 'What would it take for xyz to *be* possible? And then on top of *that*, what *else* is now possible? And then again? And again . . . Paving new ground may take longer than going down a road that already exists. And yet, I frankly don't know any other way. Nor do I believe I'd want it any other way. But all of this with grace and ease, please!" So, that's what You're getting the benefit of, all that culminates in this Dragon Master level of retreats. And that's what Vibrational UPgrade System has been created from as well. I'm grateful for that phrase, "Maverick Moment. Thank you." (Laughing)

So, yeah, back to the Earth. You'll also be taught how to basically walk the land and receive the messages it has for you, in silence. I remember one of the priestesses from Glastonbury telling me that part of their initiation for one training was to walk around the nine levels of the labyrinth around the Tor in silence. She said it took them all day. So, then I hired one of the priestesses to walk the land with one of my groups to see how she did it. That was interesting to contrast that with my previous trainings, while bringing in what the sacred land there called for and offered, particularly, from a more feminine approach.

And what'll also be occurring is you'll be either learning or deepening your ability to connect in with the fairies, the elementals, and all that sweet play that *I've* been connecting with since I could walk. I've had to reverse engineer this, in a way, to be able to articulate it out to teach in words, while you'll fully experience seeing me do this, by being with me on the land, at these particularly alive places I've chosen.

So, you'll be able to, even more than you currently can, perceive the interconnectedness of you, and your field, and the elemental kingdom, and the natural kingdom, and ultimately, divinity. Because you'll be shown how to perceive the vital life force, or chi, that's in and behind all existence. And so, you'll be able to feel the connection, overall, to all of life. So, it'll be opening up your heart chakra even more, increasing your coherence, and dropping you even more down into your sacral and root, perceiving how your body's wisdom interacts with the Earth's. As well, you'll be perceiving the flow of life force not only in you now, but all around you.

In your female body, you have the wiring to drop eggs monthly, right? The terms "menstruation" and "menses" come from Latin and Greek words meaning month (mensis) and moon (mene). The global average menstrual cycle length is 29 days and the lunar cycle lasts 29.5 days. You know how the tides are affected by the gravitational pull of the moon? Well so are our feminine bodies, right?

It has been known for a long time, meaning ancient wisdom, that if you bleed at the new moon and ovulate with the full moon, you will be fertile and attuned to the moon and her cycles. If you bleed at the full moon, You're meant to couple the fullness and potent power of the full moon with the let-go of your own menstruation blood to manifest something new, so you co-create outwardly, for the collective.

Further, the folklore goes that if you bleed during a new moon, you're being called inwards, to nourish yourself in some self-care practices, while you have one foot in this world and one foot in the metaphysical.

You wanna hear something fascinating around this, that's personal, that matches this ancient wisdom? So, I've been serving in this bigger way, both with clients plus the collective since I came back to the States from my decade in Asia, in 2010. At that time, I was menstruating with the full moon. By half way through that (2015ish) it seems my body was saying, hey now your regular gig is as if there's a full moon all the time, so we need you to start menstruating at the new moon. And I do, every new moon, moon, or bleed. (Laughing).

Apparently, it's a thing now, for women to attempt to get themselves to menstruate under the new moon. This is part of why I chose to become a vegetarian back in 1993, because I *knew* those artificial hormones would mess my system all up. Plus, it's electricity and light from our tablets, laptops, phones that off-set our natural bio-rhythms—and the earth's, right?

Yet this Vibrational UPgrade work that You're doing, both before we ever get out on the land, when we're clearing your systems to run more vital life force energy through them, keeping in mind that each and every chakra corresponds to one of the major glands of the endocrine system, so as you increasingly clear out the distortions at every level of consciousness, in every chakra, it'll readjust your system, bringing it back into rhythm and natural harmony, and in harmony with the Earth and the Universe.

And then, we take you out on the land, a higher vibration and aligned, attuned, and balanced with your natural biorhythms restored, you'll help the land too. That too, is part of the intention, or the "mad genius," I've been guided to see, following the breadcrumbs, while I created the space and the proper context to perceive and receive, integrate, make choices, and co-create from. And voila! There is *so* much more possible beyond the average level folks are satisfied to live at. But you already know that—that's why You're here.

So, our bodies have wisdom that is completely connected to our Earth. It's a symbiotic, or synergistic relationship, yes? And then beyond our beloved Earth, to the planets around it. The stars, the celestial realms have really been increasingly talked about since around 2011. I've noticed it by even starting my practice of standing out under the stars each night asking to perceive all that I can to help humanity move forward with grace and ease. As well as what comes through after doing so, as I integrate it. This has become much stronger with my studies of many of the ancient civilizations and visiting some of the very impressive sites including the Mayan ruins, stone circles, and megaliths personally.

We are meant to be a bridge *between* heaven and Earth, more now than ever before. That is in great part, the design behind eventually bringing you out to the specific power spots, megaliths, and sacred places we visit by the time of, and then specifically during your Dragon Master training.

So, you know all land is sacred, obviously. But some land has more wisdom in it, is more alive, and/or is older than others. Some of that is simply because it's been above water longer, and so more life has been experienced on it.

Some of this is because there are power spots around the world. Yes, there are chakras of our planet, and then the Ley lines—originally called d*ragon* lines—act as the meridians or nadis for the *planet's* energy distribution system, building on what you now know about our own bodies' energy distribution system. So, yes, there are simply places where more energy lines and Ley lines pour into, and or cross, like at sacred holy wells—natural ones.

Part of what you'll learn at the Dragon Master level is how to use the dowsing rods for a multitude of purposes and gains. Some of what you'll be shown is that energy currents tend to gravitate along fault lines and where natural water sources flow, as there is much conductivity there. I am not talking about Ley lines; these have a different definition.

Basically, when three—some say five—or more sacred sites built by humans dedicated to the same saint are there, and placed in a straight line, this is considered to be more than a coincidence. So, for example, the Mary line has churches dedicated to Mary—and we're not clear which Mary, Mother or Magdalene, and there's been much speculation as to which one. The Michael line has many churches dedicated to him, while those are higher up, due to Michael also being about protection.

To learn how to open up to be receptive enough to receive the Earth's messages is only one part of it. To then be respectful enough, and of a certain vibration to get the ancient wisdom within a stone circle to *want* to respond to and communicate *with you*, or an ancient site's ruins, that's an entirely different story.

The bottom line is that yes, of course, first starting with respect and humility towards this green and blue ball that remains suspended in our galaxy with gravity on our side, supplying us with all that we need to live, is obvious.

Building off of that quiet, deeply embodied reverence and humility—not false, ego-mind forced pretense at "I must feel humble, so I will act it,"—just go sit anywhere in nature. And then shower that respect out onto the plants, trees, and birds, and critters, and water bodies—if you happen to also be by any—by emanating out this reverence and softness of appreciation. Watch the shrubs or the leaves closest to you begin a little bit of a wave. Remember that video I gave you in module three of Magic, Manifestation and Money Flow? Re-watch it.

OK, so You're now engaged with the elementals. Next, open up your heart even more, allow it to flow out a happy feeling and just Observe what nature does all around you. Don't do the kind of a thing where you demand a sign from god in the form of some bird, so you have proof this all is "real" or god exists. That's not from an open heart. Really, watch your spirit that is your essence that contains life force to it, interact with the life force all around you in nature. That's enough for now.

So, you asked about being stewards of the land, having a duty to protect it. In part, this is what I'm doing by taking you all out onto the land and introducing to you a deeper embodiment and connection with the land, so you feel how alive, embracing, supportive, and nurturing it is. Then you'll want to interact with it even more.

So, of course, a natural outcome of that is then protection. You don't want to throw plastic bottles onto your sleeping mom's or infant's belly, or pile up plastic bags or if You're no longer using those then pile up empty metallic cans or basically your trash, OK, (laughing) on your sleeping spouse's chest, do you? I know that imagery is crazy, but that's what it's like for me to see the trash strewn about our mama's body. It's just so incongruous!

So, check this out. I was watching the news on the BBC last night and came across these statistics quoted by an environmental protection specialist from Australia. These stats have just been published in *Nature* magazine. You can check out in *The Guardian*, US issue, for Wednesday December 19, 2020, the article entitled, "Human-Made Materials Now Outweigh Earth's Entire Biomass–study."

"Production of concrete, metal, plastic, bricks, and asphalt greater than mass of living matter on planet, paper says." And to give you more of a feeling of this: "Ron Milo, of the Weizmann Institute of Science in Rehovot, Israel, and colleagues examined changes in global biomass and human-made mass from 1900 to the present day. They calculated dry weight estimates, excluding water.

Anthropogenic mass is defined as the mass embedded in inanimate solid objects made by humans and does not include waste.[4]

The basic take aways from this study:

- Human made materials now, *already*, exceed, or outweigh living things

- Estimated weight of human made objects 1 tetratonne

- Building and roads make up majority of human made mass

- Weight of living things falling mostly due to plant loss

- Every 20 years for the last 100 human made weight has doubled

- 1950 seen as a breaking point

Part of what is being brought back into balance now is the balance between the feminine and the masculine yes. So, you can view industrialization as yang, or masculine. While you can view nurturance, or understanding the holistic approach, whether within medicine and healing, nutrition, and health or holistically how our earth supports *us* and our lives, as feminine.

Yet the rebalancing that is also occurring now is that between spirituality and materialism.

Student: Gloria Steinem is supposed to have said, "God may be in the details, but Goddess is in the questions." You do so much around asking questions and living from that childlike wonder, as you call it. I see a connection there between your training us to see what it's like to co-create when living more with asking questions and coming out of living with so many beliefs.

---

4   Website, theguardian.com; https://www.theguardian.com/ environment/2020/dec/09/human-made-materials-now-outweigh-earths-entire-biomass-study The Study itself first appears in Nature magazine December 9, 2020, with a super long link; authors Emily Elhacham, Liad Ben-Uri et al, from the Dept. of Plant & Environmental Services, Israel

I deeply appreciate all the illumination you've brought to my consciousness when working with clearing out unconscious and subconscious beliefs, that while I don't know they're there because I don't hear them, I *can* see the block in my life. And I can see how, once you intuit what the block is and clear it, it's been locking that undesired behavioral pattern I'm wanting to change, in place. So, I see how having conclusions and beliefs kinda weighs us down and slows us down. And how you speak and work so much with the feminine and helping bring that balance back in, as did Gloria Steinem, in her own way.

AJK: Well, geez, I'm deeply honored by that massive tribute, seeing commonalities in the work of what I'm up to and to the great Gloria Steinem, for god's sake. What an honor. Thank you.

I know that for me, having worked with my own mind and learning about how the mind works, whether in my Western Psych background or my own meditation practice or meditation and yoga teacher training or teaching meditation for decades—the act of "figuring something out" using logic alone feels glompy, clunky, slow, and frankly an outdated tool or strategy, left on its own. And it feels similar to the industrial revolution, full of pollution and cumulative affects that's become out of balance.

I mean that kind of mechanism, mechanicalness, motion/cognition, and belching pollution uncaringly, and mining, leaving deep holes in the earth. Mechanical, polluting and leaving deep wounds, while also feeling invaded. While yes able to create outward physicalized items both desired and much of it required, there's also deep irresponsibility.

I also know that figuring something out to arrive at a conclusion locks something down as solid and real.

Whereas energy is a wave. All subatomic existence is energetic and is sorted through vibrations. Once there is a solid conclusion—after spending time with more random thoughts that don't come together the way a conclusion does—it stops that flow of energy and locks down, or *stops*, the flow. And a particle is formed; the beginning of something becoming physicalized.

The intuition works within that flow. The flow of all life force that, when unhindered by blockages or the dominance of logic and reason only, our consciousness is able to join up with. And our Earth's waters and land are able to be fed by this flow of energy or vital life force energy too just the earth's version—not too different, really—when not invaded by mining or irresponsible environmental impacts that take up the—Earth's energy to heal, rather than keep flowing so it can flourish. So, energy in its pre-matter state is yin, as is the intuition; while "figuring something out" using mechanical thinking like logic is yang, as is the outward manifestation, as I've said before. We need the balance of the two, and both in their healthy states for our optimal potential to become realized.

Evolution is a constant flow. So, if we want to continue to evolve, logically, we'd want to live more from questions than conclusions. Because questions don't lock something down; they allow for flow. In fact, they engage the flow. I know when teaching workshops in public, I've done that thing where I'll close a door in the room while everyone watched and ask, "What does a conclusion, or a belief do?" And then, after receiving responses, I'll open the door, asking, "And so what does a question do?"

Student 2: Dr. Alison, I feel pretty strongly that nobody else can do what you do on the level you do. You are that unique, and you are that much of a maverick, and you do deserve to be paired with the level of revolution that Gloria Steinem has been for the feminine.

You just seem to prefer being understated, not that Steinem didn't as well. But the point being, yes to that parallel. Plus, I know you've talked about how much your nose has been to the grindstone, pumping out healing sessions, energy medicine workshops, books, and talks—basically serving, more than paying attention to building a big name for yourself. So, I just wanted to offer that to you, as someone who has actively said yes and paid for receiving your work for years. I've not found anyone else out there who brings together so many different, divergent understandings of the metaphysical world together in the comprehensive yet understandable way you do, applied to day-to-day life here, now, on Earth. We so need what you do, and I, for one, am just so grateful you've chosen to not go live on an island quite yet, lol, as you've mentioned you'd do if what you did didn't work, but that because what you do works, you continue to do it.

AJK: Well as much as I'm "out there" in the public's eye, and speaking about myself when asked to on interviews, one would not consider that humble. Yet you can see me, when being asked, "Tell me how you got to be this way," so many times I respond with, "Well who really cares," and I say that with a laugh, "That's not really too important, considering what folks out there are needing in these times, so let me just go into clearings." But the way interviews are structured I just have to, in some way, give them what they're asking for and talk about myself in that personal story or bio form. I have that English blood in me and that decade of living amongst and integrated with the Chinese. My soul definitely likes to be more low-key and keep things on the down low. Again, a great part of me is that natural surfers' and ex-pats' "no worries, mate" flow-with-it mentality.

Yet, in order to follow my mission and Service, I've chosen to be this seen, in order to fulfill this mission. And I love, love, LOVE seeing you all get freer and freer. That's my greatest joy. So, by being so "out there," meaning so seen and so in the public's eye—well, if I had my own personal preference, I'd be a lot more private. But I prefer this mission over it.

Student 2: OK. So, you, serving as you do that causes you to be more in the public figure sphere, and speaking a lot, is yet another example of one of your most frequent teachings: "The ego-mind typically construes things to mean the exact opposite of what is actually meant, at the soul and Universe's level of meaning"?

AJK: Ha! Yes. Thanks for pointing that out.

Student 2: And I've been out on the land with people who do this spiritual retreat leading thing, not classifying what you do as just that. But well, you know, my first master opened up most of California, um, to the guardians and that was his job. And I was one of the first people to go out on the land with him. So, I witnessed it waking up. And I'm getting such a full body response telling you this.

Um, you know, I've seen you do these things where you're, you know, just that story you tell about being, I think it was in Chichen Itza on December 21st, 2012 and you told us you could feel the land's aliveness shooting electrical impulses up through your feet, when the year prior to that you were there taking VIP clients on retreat, the land did not do that. And that you were there on 12/21/12, on the job from being one of the experts on that Mayan Galactic cruise, I think you called it, and you all had that special ceremony with the Mayan shaman. And somebody saw you on TV as far away as Poland?

And, you know, just, well, that's a part of your story. And I think it's just getting more, like I'm feeling very much more, this energy coming in for this next year, it's energy coming online with you and really, um, stirring up the electricity. You know, mother earth is needing people to start putting energy back into the ground. And yeah, I'm bringing up electricity. There is some awareness of mine too, that electricity in the life force form is, uh, is going to become increasingly important for either sacred technologies for in green technologies as well as health.

AJK: Yeah. There you go, now You're starting to sound like a professional VUP practitioner and Dragon Master, bringing in the electricity half of chi, or the vital life force energy. Well done! And so, while we're at it, let's review. What's the other half that makes up chi?

Student 2: electricity and, um, magnetism, right?

AJK: Yes! We have a winner. Ding ding ding! (Laughing). Because bringing forth spiritual and new green technologies is in great part what I'm up to with you all at some of the stone circles. I've just not said it out loud, *yet*. Rather, it's been in the activations of your latent keys and codes . . . and voila! Here it is, now showing up! Excellent.

And you know, if you look at something like that beautiful little place up in Scotland, Findhorn. And you know they've been doing a sort of energetic nurturance on a certain level for a while, to the earth there. Permaculture.

Student 2: And then on another note, scientists are noticing that the trees, for example, are not as robust. The leaves of trees are not as robust at the moment. Or that there are as many insects . . . so that the energy of mother earth, she's doing so many things right now.

I'm about to start asking people, OK. So, you've got these crystals, are you putting something back in exchange? You know, you might be buying them from the person, but what are you giving back to the mother in exchange? And that's the bedrock of my crystal prep program. It's basically sending love into the ground where the crystals came from.

AJK: So, loving and so lovely! Great, have you set a date for that and begun marketing it?

Student 2: Um, well I offered it for free first, to give a trail run.

AJK: How'd it go?

Student 2: Good, um, it was good. Got to play with crystals while being with some lovely people. I saw a few things I could revise.

AJK: So, yeah, have you set a date for the next one? And what will you charge?

Student 2: Um not yet. But I will.

AJK: OK, so by our next mastermind call, please have both done, and then also have the write up for it so you can start marketing it, OK?

Student 2: (Smiling) Yes!

AJK: Yeah, so that permaculture gig, where we live in more communication with the land and the plants and what we're harvesting, it reminds me of some of the most recent research coming out of how agriculture grows when close to certain types of megaliths. I'll tell you more about that on your Dragon Master retreat. But what we're talking about is along those same lines, to the Native American training I had in wildcrafting.

And I remember when I lived in Taiwan, I used to take my scooter out, sometimes with friends on theirs and sometimes alone, out to the river and the mountains away from the city, on Saturdays. We'd see people nearly all the time, stepped onto the mountain side just there to the side of the asphalt road we were riding along, collecting herbs into cloth bags. And I remember seeing a woman holding her palm over the plant before picking it, which was the exact same thing I'd learned from the Native Americans before picking off a flower or tree branch. I began to see the aura of the plants and trees and ask permission to first take the flower or branch, and if it said yes, then after I would place my palm over the area, I'd just taken part of from the mother plant, and channel chi onto it, until I perceived the aura had sealed back up.

And they do that in Cornwall—the U.K.—too. There's a specific mustard blend in Cornwall that is splendidly growing there that people wildcraft for their salads and cooking. I've seen them doing so when there and asked them about it.

Student 3: Dr. Alison, I know that your work with goddesses totally comes into play with all that we're up to. And especially with what we do on the land. Can you talk about one, please?

AJK: So, whenever I was participating in Native American Medicine Wheel trainings and ceremonies, we'd work within the wheel. It contains all directions, not just the cardinal ones, but also the ordinal ones. We would get smudged with sage before entering, then handed a palm-full of loose tobacco, that once inside the ceremonial wheel—we had to enter and then walk to the left, so clockwise -we'd say a prayer over our tobacco in our closed hand, then open it, blow on it, and allow the tobacco to float into the flaming fire in the center. The smoke would then carry our prayers up to Great Spirit, is the premise. Then we'd start to walk around the ceremonial wheel, choosing naturally where our bodies were guided to sit.

I would always—and I do mean *always*, it was just uncanny—gravitate to the Southeast position, unknowingly that first few times. So, the southeast direction, I came to learn, encompasses the energetics of childlike innocence. In a reading I had done for myself—which I don't do frequently, yet at key times I am particularly selective and will get one—this reader said to me something along these lines. And this reader is very steeped in the goddess traditions, is a practicing Druid living near one of the main stone circles in England. She said you have a childlike innocence. So, she brought that up too.

Student 3: Well, it's a sunrise. You have a lot of sunrise energy.

AJK: Yes! Exactly. And so OK. So, that's part of the triple goddess Brigit, when she's in the Bride form, or the maiden form—the one I most connect with of her three, and always have. And I've visited Kildare where Goddess, or Saint, Brigid's eternal flame and natural healing spring are in Ireland. I've come to understand, after my second time working with her from Imbolic to Imbolic, that she's actually permanently a part of my field. One of you already sensed that, seeing as you bought me that Brigit corn doll last retreat here in Glastonbury.

So, she's very much about that maiden sunrise, new beginnings, childlike innocence and also joy. But there's a whole other part of her—and my—wiring, and that's the healer element. And you know, I don't refer to myself as a "healer" typically, save for when I first got back from Asia and started my Facebook business page, which I've never been able to change, conveniently, lol. So, Ok . . . This part of me I refer to as "my healer's seat." I have no idea where that came from; but it made sense as soon as I used it.

Student 3: Well, you invoke Brigit on a daily basis. You know, that's like a priestess level embodiment tool. You know, it seems to me, you've obviously made vows, too, to embody Isis. There's no way you'd have the level of facility with her that you do otherwise—and Brigit as well—in this life.

You've really taken Brigit into your heart in a huge way. I guessed Brigit, even before you said which goddess, remember I even said, I said, Oh yeah, well you have so much Brigit energy because anyone who knows that energy knows that it's just there. So, you know, she's claimed you and you've claimed her. Yeah. Yeah. So, you know that those are your two. Those are you.

A lot of people think you just have to have one. I find one as very patriarchal reduction, ah, no offense, but women can handle more than one.

AJK: Laughing

Student 3: And in fact, we tend to do things in two's. I remember in the year 2000, the United States issued its first coin with two people on it. And it was the Sacagawea Dollar. People said that's just one person. I said, no, she's got her baby on her back. Very rarely do you have a woman who's just standing on her own. There's usually some sort of, you know, we're created inside of our mothers. So, even if we don't have children, there's still a literal part of our mother's body, still in our body, that endures until we pass away.

So, you know, anyway that I think you have this Isis inviting in some of the people who work with you, especially the ones who become Masterminders. There's all the other goddesses as well. Of course, there's, well, I won't name them. Don Juan would say, "I don't have enough power to name numbers." I'm not going to name them. But the other, those two, I know them. They are known to me in a way that I can acknowledge.

AJK: Then one more who wants to be brought in is Kuan Yin. Any place you look in my house, you can't glance anywhere without seeing a Kuan Yin statute I brought back from Asia. Or the one on top her dragon I bought in Glastonbury. I spoke about this in one of my talks in Glastonbury, later, and wrote about this in *Reasonable Dragons*. So, I don't want to be redundant.

OK. So, when I reached for her, it was because I wanted to soften. I felt really dominant in my masculinity, post Masters graduation and job hunt and placement time. And once that was settled, I was like, it feels so aggressive. It feels so hard. I want it to stop. I feel out of balance. I want to soften. And I reached out, asking for help with this as I do. I ended up with a book on Kuan Yin, and I started reading about practices with her and how she was the goddess of compassion.

So, the softening began and then I ended up within a year at that point, moving to Taiwan for a decade. It's considered, comparative to the United States, a feminine culture. While, comparatively, the United States is considered a masculine culture. So, over there, massive ten story high statues of Kuan Yin are all over the island.

OK. Hold on please. (A few minutes pass.) So, I don't like to exaggerate. Hence, I just googled, "tallest Kuan Yin in Taiwan" Up came: "Keelung (Taiwan), has a white statue of Guanyin (the Buddhist goddess of mercy). She stands 23 m high on a hill in Zhongzheng Park, with a view over the city and port." Thank you, Google.

So, the very first weekend I was in Taiwan? The only other ex-pat and colleague who was already there was the college entrance/guidance counselor, prepping. I went early too, so I could ground in this new country I was to call home, before starting my job. Besides, I wanted to get to know the island. We became best friends; he became my traveling buddy.

The first city outside of the one I was living in, for my first adventure in Taiwan. I chose it, Keith was happy to go along with my choice. Guess where . . . ?

Yep. Keelung. That very city—I feel it's safe to not google this to confirm—before saying that in Taiwan every city and nearly every mountain town or village no matter how small has at least one Kuan Yin statue there—is where I was drawn to go. I also got my very first reflexology treatment there, by a blind trained Taoist massage therapist—they all had to be blind at first—and have a picture of me screaming out loud, it was so painful. (Laughing)

AND wait there's more! Just to round out the experience: Keith and I arrived via train at night. The street market was the first thing. Then the reflexology. Then we emerged back out onto what had become the night market. A Taiwanese special grilled squid on a stick later, and Bon Jovi's "Living On a Prayer" was being belted out of some speakers down the Night Market's street. Up on the hill, overlooking all of this was that 75-foot-tall statue of Kuan Yin. Five stories high!

So, we walked up to the statue, because there were clearly loads of activity and the lights were on. It was my introduction to night life in Taiwan, and in Asia overall. It exists, to begin with. So, while we were up there, by the Kuan Yin statue and temple at this high altitude? I got my first professional I-Ching reading from a local. I'd been doing them for myself since discovering the I-Ching book in Chinatown when I lived in San Francisco.

OK, so Kuan Yin is the third, who is at embodiment level. Compassion, mercy, and softening. If you want to know more, you can go to my previous book, *Reasonable Dragons*.

Student 4: Dr. Alison, I totally agree with what my fellow Masterminder just said, about how no one else does what you do at the level you do it. And I realize I've gotten some of my biggest joy throughout working with you, when out on the land with you. I mean I know your first career was in politics, and about environmental conservation, and that you got a masters degree based on that. I just feel like there's more going on with you when out on the land than I currently understand. And I know that the way I responded to being around you on the land was unique, unparalleled, and stellar. So, I will jump and go in an instant for any chance to be out on the land again with you. You've already spoken about, at least as much as you can share with us, what You're up to when out on the land. So, would you talk about your love of the land?

AJK: What a great question. Thank you. Um, OK. So, I know that growing up with my older brother, Alan, and walking through the woods every single day after school and on the weekends are my earliest childhood memories, starting at about age six. We lived next to and backed up to the woods. I grew up through elementary, middle school, junior high, and my first two years of high school at this house. And then we moved my junior year of high school to this other new development. So, Alan and I used to tromp through all these woods that were undeveloped and had a creek. And as I've said on interviews before, and you've heard me say this, you know, he would go out in front of me and jump on the dead wood and break stuff that was dead. He wouldn't kill a live tree.

Meanwhile I would be busy connecting with what really felt like the elementals on the forest floor—literally a *ground* level introduction. My specialties were the water elementals, pixies, and fairies. And really just being out there totally feeling the interconnection with nature. Like I was a part of it all, immersed in all of it, in a totally magical land. And day in and day out every day after school, we would do that. Um, until later towards high school, I think before we moved, there was a new neighborhood put in. And so, then we would start to go into like, we'd go through the woods, but then we ended up at a new neighborhood and we'd end up like going in partially constructed houses.

Student 4; Yes, as one does. Right.

AJK: (Laughing.) Apparently, yeah. So, I mean, the woods around my house were so much my haven and I trusted all that went on out there, feeling safe and held, that even to the point that one winter time there were—so I don't want to give the name out of the street, but it has a street name that recognizes that there was a creek crossing it. And, um, that creek that I'm talking about had our road require a little bridge to get over the creek. And it was right there.

Like once you reached our street right outside our long driveway, you'd go to the right. And it was just like a hundred yards. So, the creek was right next to our property and was basically a part of our property. And there were stone walls there, like you see in England because this is New England's Massachusetts. So, it had to have been there for a while.

Uh, OK. So, there were a lot of boys in the neighborhood. Um, and girls, not so many. But I had my best girlfriend from the neighborhood and after she moved off of our same creek street in middle school, we would bike to meet each other halfway, at the working farm that sold milk. We'd go there to get those school lunch sized cartons of chocolate milk and walk around the barn mostly.

So, I remember my hanging out with my older brother and some of the neighborhood boys one day in the winter, it was either late winter or early spring and the ice was melting. There was a patch of ice on the other side of the bridge, again the bridge was our road. So, in the pond part that didn't flow quite as much as the creek part, ice had formed. And then when you cross under the bridge that our road is, it became the creek. There wasn't ice there.

So, the boys—early teens at this point—are all like, "Hey, somebody, go float on the ice and float under the bridge." My best friend, as I said, was not there that day. I was the only girl, hanging out with my older brother and his neighborhood friends.

And none of them would do it. Cowards! (Laughing.) And so, I did. And I remember like just sitting there as the only girl, like on the patch of ice and looking up at all these boys looking down, watching me, as I approached the tunnel to go under the bridge/road and get to the other side of the tunnel, where the creek really began to flow.

And then I went under the bridge into the tunnel, this like steel tube with ribbing on it, and rather than yell to make echoing noises or to respond to the boys yelling up above on the road, who'd run across the road to the other side of the bridge to watch me emerge out of the tunnel, I found myself feeling like I was in my own little world of water, and dragonflies, and nymphs, and all this life. I don't know how to explain it, but it was almost like something told me that I had done perfectly by being the one to get on the ice, to trust the Universe, the creatures all around me and the magical land itself, that it would never hurt me, that somehow I was protected and even nurtured by it and that it seemed to really make certain I understood that.

So, I emerged from that steel tube a more independent, yet interconnected version of me. And I came out the other side. Then I looked up at them, all, and they're like, kind of did some form of showing mild surprise but I had earned respect, the wooses, that much was clear on their faces. (Laughing.)

Student 4: (Laughing too.) Woo cool.

AJK: It really was. And I was like, I was just sitting there, like, I kind of felt, I don't want to say princess, but I kind of felt like I was perched on the ice. And just like, of course I'd be fine. Like, that's why I didn't hesitate. Of course, this is nature. I can trust nature. I can rely on the mama. I'm part of it. Um, and those guys were all like afraid and disconnected.

And just my understanding of how my body was so connected to the Earth, as if we're living extensions of each other. And my reason for becoming a vegetarian, uh, in 1993, was from understanding how much of the earth producing cows that I then ate the meat from was draining the Earth—and I loved steaks, medium rare, which my dad grilled every weekend when I was growing up—how much that production, how much extra consumption of the Earth's resources was happening. If I ate low, then would it be happening if I ate lower on the food chain? No. It was as if my body was rejecting that idea—on behalf of my friend, the Earth.

My health purposes were secondary in motivating me to cease meat consumption when I realized, you know, what they were pumping in for the bovine growth hormones and all that artificial stuff from greed to make more profit. When I became aware of that I also got a really strong bodily reaction too. Like my whole body responded with, "Your body does not want that in its hormonal system; it'll mess you *all* up." Yet that was secondary, after helping the planet not be taxed. And it was really strong. My body, like my spine shot straight up and that awareness was, you know, I couldn't deny it, but the first one was, I don't want to hurt the Earth.

It's like as soon as I learned it, I'm like, of course I wouldn't do that. So, there's this love of the mama and I've wanted to trample, and play, and climb, and roll, and ski, and fly, and explore all over it. So, why would I do anything to hurt it?

So, exploring being in the body and exploring being on planet earth, yeah. Fun! I mean, I'll never forget when I was in South Africa, I was going to connect again with my best friend who was a fellow ex-pat over in Taiwan with me. She was from South Africa. We had both moved back to our home countries by then; ironically, that was the year my other ex-pat best buddy from Taiwan, Keith, died.

So, I was also feeling really excited about getting my bare feet out onto the land there in South Africa. Like I was aware that I was walking over crystals. While there, I went to a Rose quartz mine. I have a picture of me sitting on a huge Rose quartz outside of it. Honestly, it felt like I was walking on amethyst at times. I am barefoot as much as possible. Always.

While I was in South Africa, there was a story that a girl told me. She was in her thirties. And she said her grandmother got them to eat dirt, that they grew up eating dirt because of the amount of the, uh, value of the minerals in their soil. And that was a little riveting for me. Like I couldn't imagine having grown up where I grew up in

Massachusetts, about a half an hour south of Boston, scooping up a handful of dirt! Sure, I scooped up handfuls of water from the creek. But wow their soil must be so much cleaner! And it is, that's the point. I could perceive the crystals I was walking over while there. The ground is so rich! I understood the minerals thing. I mean, I take a mineral supplement every day 'cuz our soil sucks so bad after industrial agriculture has raped it of its natural mineral supply.

I have never really felt a separation from the Earth. Then there's the sacredness of water in natural springs, which I love, love, love! This has come in as, um, I lead these retreats to Glastonbury, understanding the historical importance of pilgrimages to sacred wells and the cleansing and purification of water. And very much making sure the first place we visit is that sacred well here. I travel all over the world, for natural mineral springs.

Um, but I mean, even if you look back to the Audubon Naturalist Interpreter internship I did, that speaks for itself. I was being trained how to see, identify, and point out the birds for others on tours. Woohoo! And then before that, my first career in protecting the environment through political work. That political work was getting legislators elected who will write laws that will protect the Earth. It wasn't canvassing legislators who are already in there. It was really incredibly logical. Let's just get people in there who are pro-environment. I feel like that's enough, yes?

Student 4: OK. But honestly, I could listen to more stories from you like this for a lot longer. Thank you.

Student 5: Dr. Alison, OK, so now, why is it that you connect abundance work with the Earth? I mean, sure, it makes sense. But then, that "Abundance for All" you do so many clearings and activations

for and talk about so much. Why, when everything is just a choice, do you work on that, knowing how many people are choosing to stay stuck in lack?

AJK: Well, because of exactly that. And it's a human, dare I say "man-made" creation—lack, for power and control. It has been an abuse of power. And we're moving into the new paradigm, the new golden era, where the playing field is meant to be leveled, and equity takes over the inequities, and abuses of power blow up in the abusers' faces. Meanwhile, the rebalancing of the spiritual with the material in this new era also involves what I just said, the rebalancing of where there have been abuses of power and inequities; it's just not going to be able to exist within the new vibrational backdrop of this new paradigm. So, I'm helping to bring in the new paradigm by bringing in the "Abundance for All" vibrations. You know? Everything is changing.

So, another fun thing that I love to do and that really helps me shift people, albeit at a very initial stage with money, is the understanding that money actually *does* grow on trees! And that prior to the paper currency, even coexisting with it, were coins made out of minerals from the Earth and before that were shells and beads. *All of it from the Earth.*

Our abundance is tied in to our Earth mama and she's so giving. This reminds me of the message that I've been saying for years now, increasingly, about looking under the surface of our ego-mind and of our physical existence, *to the nurturance behind all life.* And whether that's life force—energy—or consciousness, or it's our mama earth. Or it's our mother's unconditional love or our spouse's or our friends'—to stop taking it for granted, that which sustains all life.

Student 5: Yeah, no I've been in, you know, I've been around quite a lot of very wealthy people in my life and the ones who made it themselves without exception are extremely grounded. Um, some of their kids not so much, yet wait, some of their kids are grounded, but the ones who may have made fortunes in one lifetime, it's not simply hard work. It's not simply, um, you know, skill. It's not simply opportunity.

Somebody made a joke to me the other day that if hard work was all it took to be wealthy, then the women in Africa would all be millionaires because they are some of the hardest working people on the planet. Um, but you know, all of the ones that I know who actually made money are, I mean, you could just kind of go off here and please do . . .

But Dr. Alison, You're—and they're—just extremely grounded. You know, the market is catching up with you a little bit in some quarters about where money comes from. I wonder about bit-coins' role in all this. I mean, you know, even just, if you look, I worked in the stock exchange for a while in the commodities exchange.

Um, I wasn't in the actual exchanges, but I was working with the brokers, who were in the exchanges and, you know, they're, you know, making $40,000 in five minutes betting on copper futures, you know, or wheat futures or bacon or orange juice or, you know, nickel or what have you—wheat. Um, and so they're still, it's still one of the backbones of wealth.

One of the things that I'd like to see change is status quo-based economy instead of a growth economy. So, the idea that I had the other day was for people to, you know, to have shares in the rainforest to protect it. So, you would, instead of owning it, you could sell your shares because the local people need to make cash or, you know, buying the mine because people need to sell crystals or oil or whatever. Some people could buy those mines and then not mine them, you know, that the premium would be on preserving the Earth. Or the economy would be based on, you know, service to each other.

AJK: That's exactly what I'm up to within Vibrational UPgrade's certification of new practitioners like yourself! And what I'm doing myself *for and with you*, prior to the certification. Service to service. Value given for something desired that does no harm, instead cherishes and preserves, uplifts, and protects life. Right?

I've been talking about this for years—it's that patchwork quilt concept, where everyone is living up to their potential, bringing forth their own unique magic, and humanity is shining, overall, all its different qualities and colors, with everyone thriving.

Student 5: Yes, I know. That's in part why I'm saying what I am. Or at the very least, our economy is something other than, you know, a certain person using, um, Mother Earth, like for food or minerals, which are again, precious and some irreplaceable and then monetizing it, with the motivation not only for profit, but for greed. So, what would it take for the economy to start to shift into something that was sustainable and generative to the planet and repairing to the planet? You know what I mean?

AJK: Indeed. I do. For sure! Clearly. (Laughing) And it is what we're in the beginning stages of now. It just has to occur faster! This is also, again, one of the many aspects I'm activating to come forward through any of us from being at these sacred sites—any ancient, clean technology or spiritual technology that was once used, that wants to or can be brought back in again, for this to awaken in any of our consciousnesses, to help humanity and our Earth now, evolve in a more harmonious, preserving way.

Like some of what has been found more recently at some of the megalithic archaeological digs, the field of archaeology is going through a revolution of sorts, in my view. I was actually scheduled for two archeological digs this year of COVID-19, so of course they were cancelled. But I was going on them as a citizen archeologist; one to a megalithic dig, and one to one of my favorite English eras, a Tudor dig. So, there have been questions around how some of these massive mantels and stones have gotten either where they've gotten to, or how they've been positioned so stably to have endured for thousands of years without mortar. I'm not talking about the blue sarsen stones at Stonehenge, either.

I mean the holes in certain megaliths that engineers of today have been brought in to attempt to explain how they could've been made without electrical drills. No explanation for it, is the end result. Or as I said, the moving and lifting and stabilizing of massive multi-ton stones to then stay on top of each other, whether in Peru or the Mediterranean.

And then the absolutely massive sacred geometric and mathematical and astrological insights and understandings that ancient man, let's take the Mayans, had that exceed our current understanding.

I've stood on Mayan observatories that they'd use to study the stars at the ancient ruins; there is just some phenomenal energy there! Or in Newgrange in Ireland, best known for the illumination of its passage and chamber by the Winter Solstice sun. There is such massive knowledge around the stars from ancient humans, where these megalithic sites tie into some of the key astronomical events for Earth, whether Solstices, equinoxes, Beltanes, full moons, new moons—I mean one of the aspects to Scottish megaliths that's nearly unique to them are these stone circles that have a special horizontal lead stone in the center of the circle that lines up with the full moons coming up on the horizon. So, much of this exists that it has required a new field: archeoastronomy!

How did they know this stuff, without telescopes? What ancient wisdom did they have, that would help us here, now, at the stage we're at, with the needs the Earth and humanity have now, that if we were to remember it, to tune back into it, could help?

So, as I've observed my consciousness, upon returning from massive trips, where I've visited quite a few of these sites all together and have integrated what I'd gained from being on the land there as me, with my consciousness as it is with the intentions I have to Serve, it came to me. This idea to not only continue to allow that asking I'm doing as I go to these sacred sites, stone circles and megaliths, to be carried in my field and consciousness, but to actively cultivate it, setting me up in such a way so that someone with the proper training, time, and space—the proper context—and attunement within their consciousness, could perceive these intentions and whatever solutions the sacred sites offered that I took in within my consciousness and field, and take it from during a clearing and activation I'm doing and run with it, so to speak, serving humanity and our beloved Earth, ultimately. Not that any of this occurs at a conscious level, at first. I talk about how to work with these "downloads" of consciousness in my last book, *Reasonable Dragons.*

The stone circles, so many of them, and the sacred sites and megaliths, whether Mayan, or Incan, or on Easter Island, or on England's Salisbury plain, and in Wiltshire county—where Avebury and Stonehenge are, amongst others—or the Southwestern desert of the States like Sedona and area 51, have this history of folklore of having been where many sightings of UFO's have taken place. Some say that many of these ancient sites, including some around the Egyptian pyramids, were possibly started from other galactic beings; that Earth's humans started from visitors landing here, from other planets, using technologies that were way advanced beyond what we have now. And/or technology of a different sort. I don't know how to properly term it, other than that.

But if the stone circles or some ancient sites have a "known" or studied and suggested connection to extraterrestrial origins—like the stone circle we go to whose central stone is understood to point to the Pleiades—or ETs of benevolent intelligence who got here with green, clean advanced technology and we've forgotten that—then what would it take for this to be brought back, for humanity's and the Earth's highest and best good and potential? I know this may sound out there; it is!

The serious, comprehensive study of the society, knowledge, and achievements of ancient Homo sapiens is worthwhile even if extraterrestrials do not exist.

Reality Check: Due to rapidly advancing human science and technology, especially astronomy and synthetic intelligence we should make contact with advanced ET in a couple of decades, possibly in our lifetimes. The current degenerating state of humanity does not indicate a happy outcome for that event.

But who really knows, beyond all that conspiracy focused stuff, when truly looking into this with an open, clear consciousness, what else is possible?

Look at what Tesla is up to. Mind you, looking at what Elon Musk is creating and has tapped into, at first made others guffaw at him, right? Or at least judge him. But it's those advanced ideas that humanity typically ridicules at first, or back a few hundred years a person like Galileo could be executed. These fresh, clean perceptions that can then be worked with into creating something of value that is helping us evolve are what we need more of as these are the types of times we're living in again, yet I sense with an urgency that may not have been present before in any other historical era.

But remember, I'm following the bread crumbs, and some of this has emerged from being within these sacred, ancient sites and power spots, with my consciousness and intention being what it is, framed the way it is to Serve humanity and the Earth moving forward, evolving with as much grace and ease, and thriving—and as little struggle as possible. Living on the cutting edge of what else is possible . . . open to all possibilities. This is that.

We just need to Observe when this idea came to me. It was after a year of intensively visiting loads of Mayan ruins at equinoxes and then stone circles and megaliths all over England, Scotland, and Ireland for Solstices. And that was after taking you all out on the land, each level, consecutively, having two retreats each, that year. While I've been going to power spots all over the planet since my early twenties, it's been increasingly since 2011, *increasingly*. I've been Observing what my Guidance has been for indications of what's going on; that's one of them. To actually visit these sites at these times *and* take people who are attuned out too.

Meanwhile I say yes to following my intuitive guidance, taking the steps, (i.e., "be *there* for solstice this year") and then Observing the results and effects on my consciousness, with it cultivated capacity to receive and perceive information intuitively. I then work it through a balanced hemispheric environment within my brain, so that I can have some higher order of logic help me eventually unravel what has been perceived while out there on the land. This is that integration phase you hear me speak of. That last bit may not make sense, and that's just fine that it doesn't. (Laughing) Holy cow, did a red-tailed hawk just totally start to cry out, in a tree right in front of me! And now it just flew overhead as I began to tell you this!

So, I've been asking for that to come through me or anyone who goes out on the land to these sites *with* me, so long as it's your choice and in your highest and best to bring it forward, obviously. I can't do what I do if it's not. It doesn't work that way. Remember, the light, or energy, or chi or ki etc., has an intelligence of its own and it prioritizes what is most needed within a system, when we're say focusing it on someone when they've asked for the help and are a paying client in one on one sessions with us, to say come out of chronic back pain, and the light/energy goes first to their knees, because that's where the support is most needed first, in order for them to come out of the issue. And yet we're initially surprised because it's not knee pain they're complaining about, right?

Well, that's what I am talking about. I went into this at the end of my second book, *Vibrational UPgrade: A Conspiracy for Your Bliss—Easing Humanity's Evolutionary Transition.* Where I was asking Gurudev, the founder of Kripalu Holistic Center in the States (the first of its kind), if prana is the same as soul force, and he said yes. Then I asked if prana is the same as unconditional love force, and he said yes, smiling and nodding at me on that last one.

So, that's what I mean whenever I say we are living in a world that has as its underlying motive as unconditional love, for our highest and best, and that the support is always there, should we ask for it. Behind all of life, sustaining us. And you've been learning how to open up to it more through your work with me, as you clear out the blocks within, let's say here for the first time, "your lower self." (I've never used that term before! Feels like it's coming out of 2020 . . .)

And this is what I mean when I say I came back from that decade in Asia with my mission to professionalize the field of energy medicine, because in doing so, in helping folks in the West stop ignoring subtle energy, we'd be able to reduce so much of the suffering; that so much of the suffering isn't necessary, if we'd just learn how to work with our minds, consciousness, and thus subtle energy system.

I've also asked that my consciousness activate latent keys and codes of listeners out there when I'm doing other shows, on interviews, my YouTube videos—esp. those "Q and A with Dr. A" ones—or even more on my monthly free Vibrational UPgrade call, where more of the masses join in—that if anyone out there has a consciousness that can take in or have any of their latent keys and codes activated to bring forth new clean technologies to help advance humanity—including my client who has been an environmental impacts assessing scientist now focused on global warming—and they're in agreement and all is for the highest and best—then let's see what else is possible!

Look, we know stuff changes when working with me. We see how accurate my intuition is, over and over again. I had that filming when I spoke at the L.A. Conscious Life Expo and had my booth there, giving mini-sessions. The guys with the special filming equipment, beyond Kirlian measuring of auras, caught on film the positive –healing changes when filming me work on a volunteer. Interestingly, that CD that I bought from them filming me, was never found afterwards, by them. I suppose I wasn't meant to have that "proof"?

So, I am literally living on the cutting edge of possibilities. I don't know what else is possible, do you?

But again, this has been done in such a way, just in case anyone is getting paranoid—well, let me put it this way; Einstein came up with e=mc². But anyone whose consciousness was open at the time to have brought through this idea, would have. This is contained within Carl Jung's theory of the collective unconscious which I'll paraphrase here. An idea that's timely for humanity sits there in this field. Think of it as a grand net encompassing all of humanity and floating in space until the right conditions for the right consciousness (person) to bring it forward into alignment, and then a person brings forward that concept.

Copernicus and Galileo were seemingly doing this as they spent approximately a century perfecting and explaining their theory that would revolutionize our understanding of the relative motions of the Earth, the Sun, and the Moon. I've written about this before, I believe in my second book.

Another example: When I came back from Asia, and began to have my first book, *What if There's Nothing Wrong?* edited out of what I had written it in, "Chinglish", from having been immersed within that bilingual context for a decade, into American English so it was easier to read, I realized other American authors were bringing forth some of the concepts that were along the same messages I was presenting in my book—to move more into the holistic model and/or to understand how our consciousness plays a key role in our lives. So, I could see this "collective unconscious containing an idea" dynamic at work—that when an idea is ready for humanity, those who have created the proper conditions to bring forth this new idea, will. Where this idea first comes from, or who or what is responsible for the timing of it . . . I don't know . . .

So, if someone is the right consciousness, they receive the "download" that's lingering around in my field from visiting these sacred sites with this intention and my own work with my own consciousness so that I can be somewhat of a "broadcaster" of this into their consciousness and they can then "unpack" that, into an integrated, conscious, and meaningful way that may help them see, from whatever they'd been currently working on, a new tweak to a new green technology, for example.

I do a version of this with folks' businesses all the time, right? That's one of the main intentions, in fact, and outcomes, of Magic, Manifestation and Money Flow. Yet I'm thinking right now of me sitting in that lovely Ganesha room at Yoga Village where I taught at first my yoga and meditation class before being moved to the bigger room. I had a female student show up for the first time for my class the week before. She didn't ask any questions—not that it's a big Q and A environment, it's a yoga and meditation class, for god's sake, (Laughing). I mean before or after class, mostly . . . But then she came in the next week, and as she rolled out her yoga mat before class started, she exclaimed, "Oh my god, Alison, what you said about us possibly having more energy and possibly more creativity so that we may end up staying up later than normal and to make the most of it, rather than resist it?"

This is really typical of me to say, particularly after that class or any event where I'm running clearings and activations,

"Yep, I sure do."

"Well, I left last week's class and couldn't sleep. I was up for hours, really hyped up. So, I remembered what you'd said and there's been this particular problem within my business that I've been wanting to solve for a long time, and I did it! In one night! And then I slept like a baby afterwards. I haven't slept like that for years! Thank you so much!"

"Well, I'm super stoked to hear that occurred for you, Lisa." Lisa became a regular student after that.

But that economic model you were speaking of reminds me of the whole co-operative model, right? Like those were the original health food stores I used to go on. My very first health food store was when I was in college, you know, and it was a cooperative with wooden floors and cooperatively owned, so we in the community could buy more organic produce at a cheaper rate, by acting like a co-operative, or cooperating to pool our money together to be able to purchase more organic produce in bulk, because organic was so crazily overpriced at the time. Um, and it's finally started to come down because there's more demand for it.

Yet it's also happening at other levels, as the spiritual and material begin to come more into balance. There's was a millionaire. Like I posted it when it happened on my Facebook page from, I think, one of the Scandinavian countries. He bought up a track of forest to preserve it—in the rainforest. So, while some of that has been done for gaining good PR and tax write-offs, nowadays, there is this different feeling to it too, at times, of genuine intention to use their money for good.

Um, one of my favorite long-term weekly clients is a scientist focused on global warming. And he was just talking about how we're in the feedback loops. Now, the feedback loops have started where the Earth is crying consistently from global warming.

So, we're starting to, like the Siberian forest is now burning because it's so dry. And they're having a hell of a time. I've seen video of this on the BBC of how they're putting out the fires. They have these little water tanks on their backs. Like I said how I saw how they sprayed pesticides in Taiwan, they had those little silver tanks on their backs and then a single little hose with a tiny nozzle, spraying? They're doing that with water in the Siberian rainforest.

It's not like huge hoses with trucks like we have for the western fires here in America or they used in Australia for their ravaging fires. So, we're starting to see all of the feedback loops beginning that's been kicked into gear because of global warming, right? We have to hurry up! So, I'm open to any and all possibilities for that to show up, what will help us ASAP help the Earth.

Because it's beyond the Earth crying. The other day I posted something, again, about how the old paradigm, or model, was about destruction and how this new paradigm is about construction. And if we work with our own destructive interiors, like our ego-minds, and the motivation for massive consumption that mirrors the nature of the ego-mind, then we're doing what we need to be doing, to help clear the Earth. Each of us doing so. Remembering what shows up in the physical first has to exist in energy.

And that shows up too as the consumption of information in the marketplace. I see it—as does my team of enrollment coaches nowadays—with people when they're in "researching" mode, to see about working with me. That's typical, when looking at the stages people go through when changing a behavior—remember that I have specific certification in addition to my personal trainer certification as a "Behavioral Change Specialist,"—and so this is understandable, at times, in the beginning stage of considering changing a behavior or pattern. So, we have questions to help folks qualify themselves to self-assess what stage of readiness they are to change and then direct them to help match a product or service to where they're at, so no one's time is wasted.

So, now add to "researching mode" typical consumer psychology, then they're in the research *and* consumption mode of, "What can you do for me? What's in it for me?" Which totally results, one could say that's even the formula, for the ego-mind! And yet what I see frequently is this "researching phase" is covert for self-sabotage, when it goes on for too long and action just simply needs to be taken. But the ego-mind pushes away that change, by perpetuating more "researching" rather than just stepping up, at a certain point.

Remember, the ego-mind prefers status quo, and for example, with traumas: traumas that are shoved down, they linger in the subconscious, and so get intimidated by the actuality of coming to the surface to safely be cleared out, as I do with this work. So, this is also at play, when people see something that can help them, but they delay the action; that's the trauma, in this example, trembling and yet it's subconscious, so what shows up is the person just doesn't feel comfortable in investing in a program that'll actually change them, so they remain in that "researching" and "shopping' mode, perhaps with the delay tactics of some other expense, more related to tangible goods they can point to, that requires their money "more."

The trained, professional, best response to that when working within the field of supporting people in making desired or needed behavioral changes is, "OK, but how much worse will this get if you don't do anything about changing this, in this next year?" See the delay tactic at work? And so, then this is how crisis then comes in, in order to catapult someone out of their preferred comfort zone.

The spiritual path, or enlightenment, or however you want to term it, is like, well it's such, it's so nearly incompatible with marketing! Especially when the energy behind the programs with me, as a person is considering taking action, actually works! Because then there's more resistance, because the actual ability to change that comfortable yet undesired behavior, is perceived. And the ego-mind shrinks back.

And this all translates to our approach to our Earth. What is, what must it feel like to her, our ever-giving Earth, with all of us saying, give me, give me, give me? While we only make changes that are comfortable for us towards helping her? Hence the increasing crises across the planet due to the feedback loops of global warming now kicking into place more. Hence the increasing fires, floods, hurricanes—*crises required* to get us to take different actions!

Student 5: You know, we've had this conversation, you know, about, money and how what you just said, well that was part of my rejection of money, as you know, back when I was first in Magic, Manifestation and Money Flow.

I'm from mining people on one side. And I was like, absolutely horrified to think that somebody is taking that out. And I still, you know, I still have trouble with it. Um, I remember the first time I was a girl and I, the first time I saw them paving the road and I just was screaming. Cause it was painful. How could, how could they do that? You know? And, um, I just, you know, I was sort of, um, reformatted quite specifically to not keep having these outbursts.

AJK: We are so wise as kids. There has been so much conditioning to shut that right down. But it has awoken again in you—your natural feeling state and that wisdom. Thankfully. And it's awakening for many now. It has to! And again, it's part of the vibrational backdrop we're moving into, within this new paradigm.

What we're talking about really smacks of the need for folks to go inside and manage their ego-minds. To engage in that self-management, I returned from Asia talking about. And that's the marriage of my earlier planet-saving career in politics that transitioned into my work with consciousness. If we'd just recognize the invisible forces at work and rather than run from them, face them, and learn how to work with them, it'd be *so* much lighter, in all ways, including our impact on each other and our earth!

And I mean consciousness and energy, which result from the ego-mind's own innate tendencies—hence the requirement for self-management—and then become more capable of directing ourselves and thus our energy and thus our creations into more constructive means, rather than such self-destructive ones or destructive ones.

I know the suicide rates have been increasing since around December 21, 2012, as has been the amount of people waking up to being able to perceive more, or "those who have awakened," (not my language) or "have realized how sensitive they are." So, rather than understand how to work with their consciousness, well there's medication and there's increased suicide rate.

But there IS also an increase in mediation apps. But it's *not* meant to be just for reducing stress. COVID-19 hasn't done what it's done just for people to have the space and proper context to learn how to manage stress.

It's to go inside. And face one's self. And realize that it's not all about work, both literally and this with our own minds and consciousness and subtle energy system. The sheer amount of joy that is there, meant to be experienced, once you clear out what you're carrying of other peoples' energies, beliefs, and conditioning, recognizing your own sensitivity rather than self-destruct from it, and learn how to allow it to be your superpower. I created that product back in 2013, "Your Sensitivity is Your Power" due to this, and it's the free gift

I give the thousands of people as they come into the free Vibrational UPgrade Facebook group.

So,—SO—many of our societal problems would not be there if we would stop running from going within. And not turn to holistic or natural healing or "this spiritual stuff" only when we're either in crisis or we feel like it's only an "extra" aspect to get to when we have the time and money. Rather, the recognition of how fundamental to our existence a healthy consciousness and subtle energy system is, needs to replace where we've taken it for granted.

Student 5: So, this is what was coming through before were two things. When we talking about, um, female spiritual teachers and how you're so valuable to people and how, when I was, when I was blocking, tackling, and glued down, just taking a thread back to that, the thing that came up was the consequence.

So, the reason people, um, in some cases, their animal bodies respect the teacher up on the pedestal is because the teacher is *on* a pedestal. That's sad. That's again, functioning well, but it's a facade, but it's also the animal. So, the animal and those are mainly the male teacher, um, thing. So, this is why the female teacher, nonhierarchical thing is that male teacher King of the mountain, all that, but then people have done it, it has been very, um, useful and very effective.

The thing is, if you want that, for example, then there's nothing wrong with that, but that's not you. People may still not a hundred percent know they're handpicked. You say that, but not everybody gets it. And I think that that needs to be articulated a little bit more, how, um, that it's not just the money. That comes in—the money—it's the exchange, but it isn't, you know, it's priceless what the people get with you, and that's the truth. And so, the money is there, sure.

What they're getting for that money is not the teachings, though that's priceless. The money is, is exchange for your time, but the *actual results* are what's priceless and those are a completely different animal. And that's the difference between, um, for example, um, buying a pair of shoes and buying a personal transformation because the personal transformation requires that each party be a hundred percent committed.

And many times people will throw down the money. The participant is a hundred percent committed, but then the teacher is not. Or the detective, technician, practitioner, expert, whatever you want to get, is not. So, the person doesn't get the results. So, they're putting the money in the wrong place or in this case, people might be putting down the money, but they don't understand the process. Right?

So, match the process of the actual thing. But this isn't. This is in respect to working with a spiritual teacher. So, this is the misunderstanding in, you know, in esoteric teachings. One of the vows you take is to not materialize the elements. And basically, the essence, what that means is you cannot put material rules onto something quintessential.

AJK: Yes, like I said, it's a quagmire. But the material and spiritual are coming into balance, and so eventually this quagmire will get sorted.

CHAPTER 5
The Lightning Bolt

SATURDAY NIGHT

THE EVENING TALK Dr. Alison gave to the Glastonbury Positive Living Group was about how spiritual people can create more wealth for themselves. All of us on the retreat attended, while folks from her Magic, Manifestation and Money Flow who lived in southern England drove in as well, to meet her personally, and attend the event and receive the clearings and activations in person.

The talk appealed to me because I had often thought it important for good people to have more money. It can't continue that only people who are willing to destroy the environment, exploit child workers, or abuse the power having money gives them, have a lot of money.

The talk vanquished what feels like *all* of those negative assumptions about people with money. And what else surfaced that she then cleared were so many hidden blocks for all of us around why we don't have the levels of money we desire, where we have the power to believe differently, so we can shift our material reality. She gave many examples of how stuff exists first in energy, in consciousness—so in our beliefs—that then end up creating that material reality in the physical. She especially focused on where spiritual and creative people deflect prosperity, due to unconscious beliefs and conditioning, that to be "spiritual" and to be a "minimalist" who cares about the Earth, or to be an artist, have caused us to push money away. Which money then hears and responds to. So, she did a whole lot around increasing our receiving capacities.

I'd heard much of it before, while being in Magic, Manifestation and Money Flow, but it was different, receiving her clearings around money, in Glastonbury. It felt like she was reaching into a blockage and opening up a distribution channel so that more flowed out to the masses. She said as much, before running that specific clearing, joking about feeling Robin Hood'esque in this land that birthed that myth, just a bit further north . . .

After the talk I wanted to go out for coffee with some retreat folks but there wasn't anything open except for that haunted hotel's pub. That didn't appeal to me, so I went back to the B & B to make some notes and get some sleep. And I knew I would sleep well that night. And dream of crows. And golden coins dropping from the sky, which I was left feeling during her clearings and activations. Plus, I knew to work with the clearings and activations after an event or group call, especially one that had so many clearings that felt so completely relevant for me, with getting a good night's sleep, so I could wake up with more possibilities that my conscious mind would then have "as ideas." I slept like a baby.

FEMALE TEACHER—INTEGRITY

Student: Women live it all the time—integrity e.g., Moms—so I see how the few female spiritual teachers there are, are more integrated, not only as a "role" but a "being-ness." Like no sexual deviance or abuse of power due to their position, right? And so, I see this in your own field with its coherence, your consistently higher vibration, your actions—especially that "Beast mode" you get into—and your motivation, and how much you live all aspects of your life in alignment, with you and your mission.

Of old, spiritual teachers may have come through a specific pre-set system and so would achieve an authorization due to lineage, study, and so forth. Another way which has been widely practiced in the East is to recognize someone as the reincarnation of a teacher from the past. Either way these authorizations have come from outside the teacher themselves.

Increasingly, people are waking up to parts of themselves which do not fit into the usual descriptions we have of how to be in the world—whether this is as a creative, a sensitive, an empath, an energy practitioner, way-shower, priestess, or shaman. Or teacher.

Owning the designation of Master is something to take seriously— holding oneself accountable to the years of discipline, practice, study, purification, refinement, and service. A Zen Master once said that one is not a master of subject . . . one is mastered *by* it. And I've been learning this since I became attuned to the Master Level within the Vibrational UPgrade System. Interestingly, that's the retreat that precedes the Dragon Master level retreat.

So, part of this is also part of my description of this role, namely that you, Dr. Alison, have the personal mastery and self-management, cultivated over decades, to throw yourself continuously into the flow of what is highest and best. Amplifying the power of The Divine, the flow, the highest frequencies, while also attenuating the influence of the personal ego-mind. So, I feel you provide a trustworthy foundation in your ability to serve from the purity of what you've referred to as your Healer's Seat.

Do we refer to you as a Coach or Teacher?

Well, let me first tell you what I found, OK?

AJK: Yes, please!

Student: So, according to the etymology-word-origin site (etymonline.com) the word coach is from a European term meaning, "to convey in a coach" or in fact to the four-wheel vehicle itself.

AJK: (Laughing.)

Student: (Smiling) And then in the 1830's it came to mean, "instructor / trainer" who would, "tutor, give private instruction to, prepare (someone) for an exam or a contest," which does describe one of the activities and style you employ to empower those whom you serve, like me, to step into our highest possibilities. Yet it is only part of what you do.

You have created, transmitted, and trained Masters in the use of your Vibrational Upgrade™ System of Energy Medicine and Mindfulness. In the Vibrational Upgrade Container, I genuinely see miracles begin to unfold. As part of your system, *I see,* and I really want to give you this as a gift, my perception of this, people begin to:

- trust themselves to be the divine creators
  they truly are
- develop the balance of health, vitality, and strength
  in their physical body regardless of their current
  state of health
- tap into a deeply supportive, infinite vortex of
  abundance and prosperity to fuel every desire and
  resource they could ever want or need, and actually
  feel this so readily that it helps to encourage us
  as we see the results of this, to go for our bigger
  dreams and goals
- deepen spiritual connection to the universal source
  of all possibilities and miracles, activating their specific higher mission to catalyze change for themselves
  and others.

Yet, you are also a Master of mind-body energy medicine.

And why a Master?
- Lightning bolt = vajra
- Light-heartedness
- Humor
- Energy and Allowance and Following
- Plus, *practical,* Inspired, Aligned Action
- You are modeling a new way and cherishing us into full form
- Maverick / Pioneer
- Political to help the world, then individuals. Teaching and enormous skills. Then the new system of energy medicine
- Meanwhile You're a completely unique person

You operate in the self-actualization spectrum where we focus on being and growth, plus our motivation increases as our needs are met. Which you seem to completely know, hence the design of it. Again, your "mad scientist" gig.

Always asking, how does it get any better than this, and what else is possible? Always jumping into the unknown for the very best reasons of joy and freedom for all, then always the ceiling is reached, and exceeded, in a constant expansion. And you keep going!

You are an inspiration, and I'm not sure you ever, ever built that into what You're up to here.

AJK: (Laughing) I've only realized that recently, due to reflections like this.

Student: That it was never going to be about you personally inspiring people, that it was never about you as a human woman, but rather the mission of the elevation of consciousness. Yet you do, oh human woman you, YOU inspire.

AJK: Mmmmm. Received. Thank you. Your intention has been received as you can likely see from the smile on my face. And a wee bit of liquid in my eyes.

I know I'm so focused on the task at hand that I do not typically consider that last bit you mentioned. It also feels deeply, Idk, not transcendental? Lol. But I hear you. I began to tune into the fact that I had people who wanted to be more like me, or that just by being me I was inspiring people, at one of the talks I gave in Glastonbury some Masterminders were there on retreat at the talk and I asked them to name in front of the room of about fifty people, something they'd done that they were proud of.

I had been in the midst of illustrating the point of how naturally people slide into listening to the inner critic, and how seemingly uncommon it is for folks to listen to the inner cheerleader. Hell, most people only have the first one! So, I knew I could rely on my Masterminders to be able to respond to that with something.

And as I called on them, two of the women said they were proud they'd traveled internationally without their husbands, one of whom was recently divorced so this was her first time traveling internationally on her own. I stood there in a bit of shock for a moment, that they'd actually felt that, or well that it was even possible *to* feel that way, because I just do it and have since age 17—naturally traveling internationally. Yet one of the women had said, "Like Dr. Alison . . . I too have traveled internationally now alone as a woman. And I'm damn proud of it."

So, I began to understand it more at that point, something may be happening that I'd never intended as a part of what I'm up to. It's sweet! It's such a compliment, and honor. (Laughing.)

Student: Dr. Alison, your clients and students span the globe. You clearly have sought to help affirm the positive and beauty in this world, especially when your clients and students have been struggling with the serious worldwide negativity we have in our reality now.

And, you have a particularly unique ability to somehow have people feel safe almost instantly with you. So, then, with this trust, the process of opening up to one's highest potential begins. And it makes this all so much easier—this trust you so naturally gain because it's so obvious we can.

Journeys with you can go through physical ailments, mental turmoil, emotional pain, spiritual seeking—and it typically *does* touch each of these levels—as the healing is holistic. Yet the outcome I've seen—and it's part of why I've gone for training in the Vibrational UPgrade System so that I too can help more people feel this way—is that people remember how to relax, feel safe, and expand into peace and bliss. People feel like they have come home, in a way. So, they can more easily ground into their bodies and the present. I know this too, is part of your overall intention and design.

AJK: You're making me think of how I've been saying for decades now as my mantra, "Universe, please help me increase my tolerance for bliss."

Student: Yes. I love that. I mean who thinks to ask for *that, in that way?* And beyond this nurtured feeling, people are then able to go beyond the tense limits of the ego personality so they can experience the freedom from living from this higher perspective.

Because, Dr. Alison, you help people transform their consciousness, by assisting them within their "everyday minds"—hence the holistic mindfulness coaching you support us with, after we receive energy medicine whether in one-on-one sessions or your verbal clearings and activations. Yet it is so clear that You're doing this all so that we can transform ourselves *at the daily choices level,* where the real change is needed, and desired. And we do. And it does.

Like I know you've talked about how you approach your weight training and workouts and nutrition from that holistic, mind-body and vegetarian approach. And you share that with us, some of that longevity geared nutritional support. In fact, I love the nutritional support you give; it's one of my favorite parts of being in the Mastermind. It's such different knowledge that is so much more about thriving and not many other folks are sharing the stuff you do there. It's not just about healing a disease or fixing a problem.

You know so much there, like from both India and China, yet you don't talk about it as much until, well at least starting a bit in Magic, Manifestation and Money Flow.

And all the time you talk about having to go eat and then exercise as you end a call with us. I get inspired by that. And like, when you talk about recognizing You're sitting more than normal, how you work through that with working your body in yoga postures. I love that. You're not meaning to inspire, but you do. You don't realize how different you are, and so when you talk about your-self, which I know you don't like to do—it actually supports us.

And that I know, this self-care you do not only inspires me to do more with my own body by at least first becoming more grounded in it, but I also know I gain from your practices. And I'm sure it's part of what gives you your edge in your energy medicine practice and healing practice, as You're accessing what feels like and seems like more, or a new level of power. But you don't talk about that much.

AJK: Thank you for that feedback. That's because the longer I've been in the States, the more I've gotten pigeon-holed as being within the "spiritual" marketplace because of working with energy. These don't blend easily within marketing here. Meaning . . . energy used not for healing nor even medicine, but for positive, proactive applications, like the human potential field. Same with the meditation teacher background. They're entirely different professions and fields. It's like energy medicine is still typically considered as natural healing, assuming there's a problem, like IBS, that needs healing.

Whereas the endurance athlete, the chi gong teacher, the yoga teacher, the personal trainer, nutrition—whether raw foods, vegan, vegetarian, or healthy omnivore—and longevity fields are clearly more about potential, it seems, within the current collective consciousness. I know many have taken the first steps of understanding how their diets affects their physical bodies, which I was speaking a *ton* about when I first got back from Asia. So, that's good. But I'd like to move us beyond only using a vegan diet to heal IBS, for example. And it has taken off more, especially as more people begin to be impacted by the changing vibrational backdrop we've been increasingly living within since 2012, and they want their bodies— *which circulate consciousness,* to correspond better with the lighter consciousness they've been perceiving. This is great! Plus, it helps the Earth so much, eating lower on the food chain, which is also why many folks are shifting there too.

But again, what if there's nothing wrong? What if there's nothing to heal? What if I can and am applying the understanding of using energy and consciousness in a way that helps me—you live up to my or your highest potential, and be who I/you are most fulfilled being, while making great money and serving others, too, helping uplift humanity and the Earth in some way? Whether that's a chef of clean healthy food, installer of more electric car charging stations, or what I'm doing.

Yet in the way it's currently conceived of within the marketplace, still, it seems in its neophyte stage; marketing energy and consciousness not as something spiritual only, nor for healing as an alternative or complimentary modality to go at health crises. I've been working to bust that, but it takes time. Again, learning to come into "What if There's Nothing Wrong?" and possibilities-living requires new stuff to be created. We're still watching the old paradigm, of destruction and problem focus, die off.

But marketing energy medicine and mindfulness coaching for reaching one's potential—that causes about 20 double takes before someone gets it. (Laughing.)

Never mind puzzles the hell out of my Facebook ads team member, 'cuz the targeting is just so different that it's not even there yet. But thank you, Maggie, for bringing this all up and saying this, reflecting to me what you are. (Smiling)

And god bless those of you with the eyes to see what I am actually up to! Rather than approach me for health concerns only, which I still help with, or wait until a problem hits crisis mode before investing in your inner transformation, but to really *see* this bigger, master plan I'm up to and we're up to—it just elevates and brings in so much more joy!

Student: Well, with so many options out there for instruction and spiritual training sometimes I feel like it's almost like making a lottery pick to guess if you have chosen a good one.

I know you work very hard to ensure your consciousness is dependable, that you show up and are in the highest and best version of yourself. From the methods you teach it is clear that we can each have much more choice than we think we have now. You are one of my really important teachers; did you have favorite teachers? What are some stories about that?

AJK: OK, so I remember in India, the yoga school founder and director who taught us the postures and ran all of the Ashtanga sessions as we ran through Sri Namaskar A and then Sri Namaskar B—two hours in the morning and two hours in the afternoon. He is Indian and is married to an Irish woman—and they've produced beautiful children! (Laughing.)

So, he was more "used to" Westerners and interacting with them. However, I remember the teacher he brought in for the Yogic Philosophy units was Brahmin, dressed in a traditional white robe as the Brahmins traditionally did, and still do and I remember the difference between these two Hindu's teaching styles.

And so, then we had a western (either American or Brit) teacher for the anatomy units of the training. And then we had a local India Hindu again, for the Ayurvedic Units, who I went to see for a personal consult later because I was so intrigued by what he taught us and wanted to know more. And that's how I came to Chyavanprash, a longevity tonic which is blessed with sacred Sanskrit chants sung into it and something like 400 medicinal ingredients (joyful chuckle) put into it. How cool is that?

And I remember how the Ayurvedic doctor was like if we think of steps, it was like the founder and director of the school was Lalit. And—I never realized this until years later—we were given spiritual names at the end of our intensive training and he gave me the name Lalit. And when I looked it up it means, "spiritual seeker" and I was so turned off by that because it was so obvious. (Laughing)

I wanted a more glamorous, full, substantial wahoo wow shooting stars explosion of a name. (Laughing.) I just wanted it to mean something that wasn't so obvious. But then last year I came to find out that Lalit means, "spark" or "awakener and with special powers"—like a lot of light, as an awakener, *as a lightning bolt*. And only in the last year, nine years later, that I realized he had given me *his first name! Duh!* (peals of joyful laughter.)

On my Facebook Business page there is a video of where he is making fun of me. I had asked him to sing a favorite chant we'd been introduced to during the teacher training that I just felt echoed joy throughout my body, and he did it on our last day. And you can see on the last day, he brings me in and says, "Alison." That's when he lovingly made fun of me, with what he said afterwards. Such playfulness!

He did such a great job teaching me as a student. He made room for me, with all the power that he saw being expressed in and through me, free of ego. As well as in the different questions I would ask him. Different than what others would ask. Different in part I think because I was a westerner who at that time was in my tenth year of living in Asia. I was living in Taiwan and had become "more Chinese than American" by that time. Whatever.

It was just this beautiful combination of humor and seeing and honoring and giving me space to bring out that which he saw in me. And the use of just that heart-centered humor where I felt seen and understood, as a student of these sacred teachings, that unspoken dynamic (and sometimes spoken, like when he makes jokes with me on that mentioned video, where we sang together in a circle on that last day, as a closing ceremony.) You can see the joy in the dynamic between us or from him to me.

That meant a lot to me because I had also had the perception from working with the local Taoist and Buddhist teachers back in Taiwan and even the Buddhist ones in Thailand—where I'd typically go for my Chinese New Year holidays between semesters—that masters work with humor. And I had also started to begin channeling information. Not just for clients about loved ones who had left their bodies and who would want to get a message to their loved one who was my client. But overall channeling of higher levels of consciousness, that I was learning to work with, and unravel, that contained bigger messages for the collective. The point here is that I had begun to discern and understand the playfulness which the spirits have. There can be almost a trickster element to them. And so Lalit, modeling that in his teaching style, showed me what a genuine teacher he was, how connected he was. And thus, how he walked and lived what he was teaching.

When I say "trickster" I don't mean like the Native American symbolism attributed to the Coyote. That ensnarement where you just can't get around yourself, and the lesson smacking you in the face that you need to move through, and yet you just keep hitting brick walls until you face yourself and that lesson. That trickster kind of tripping up, I don't mean that way.

But like the playful trickster kind like the Middle English word, "Tomfoolery." And so, I know that in America in particular we are quite frequently, serious. And students come to me with such ardent fervor wanting to learn these universal laws and these ancient secrets and ancient wisdom and it *is made so serious.* I remember as I was teaching from different texts during my course I'd created, "Global Psychology" in the classroom, prior to moving into teaching AP Psych, both from the Dalai Lama and from Osho, the amount of humor that they both use and express.

So, that teaching about using humor, was really valuable. As opposed to the Brahmin philosophy teacher in his white robe, who would stand a lot of the time with his hand over his heart chakra, with his eyes closed and communicating to us almost as if downloading some of this secret, ancient wisdom. And with that, a bit less of the eye contact and the direct interaction than with Lalit as he interactively taught, or even the local Indian Ayurvedic doctor.

So, these ancient teachings are meant to be respected, and so the Brahmin philosophy teacher kept his distance, I got it and get it. Yet, when he wasn't teaching, he was lighter and did interact with us a bit, but still he was pulled back. And possibly that could've been a bit of personality stuff, just more shy. But it does feel related to what content he was teaching, and where that content had evolved from.

Whereas Lalit, and to a lesser extent the Ayurvedic doctor, made himself accessible, so you could ask questions, while there was this sacredness with which we were shown to approach the Brahmin philosophy teachings. And it is almost like Lalit, in understanding the western mindset due to his marriage to an Irish woman and having taught enough westerners by the time I got to him, it was almost like this understanding of respect that is built in towards the sacred teachings that make the teachers of this wisdom relatively unapproachable, he had come to understand Westerners don't typically get that. And it seems too, he'd made a conscious choice to allow that role to be played more by our Brahmin yoga philosophy teacher. There is an element of "you can't badger with questions as your ego-mind produces them," the teacher who is "downloading or espousing these ancient secrets or wisdom"—like you can't approach the master.

And I know that, now going over to another anecdote, when back in The States and I was within the ashram that Gurudev Yogi Amrit Desai has established who I speak about at the end of my second book, he too, had lead teachers surrounding him, to do the block and tackle. And then I worked for quite a few years with a world-renown Taoist teacher up in Canada and he too, had the master level students doing the block and tackle for him. So, that neither of these male teachers, like the Brahmin yoga philosophy teacher, could be approached and asked just any old question our minds had. Distance, discipline, and respect had to be in place.

Student: Interesting, that those are all male teachers. What about a female teacher for you?

AJK: Well, I have one who I remember being my first teacher when learning about the chakra system. She was American and fierce, a no-nonsense kind of a teacher. (Laughing.) And that makes me think of how one of my long term one on one clients, from Asia, who grew up in boarding schools in England, jokes about how English men sometimes require a good telling off from the head-mistress. And I get what she means by that! Perhaps because in the States, we've not yet had a female head of state, whereas in the UK, they've had female queens for much of their history.

So, on the inner realms, I know that a great inner teacher of mine who I bring forth on 3M and MM calls is this one strand or brand of energy that has this particular quality of fierceness. That comes in from my connection to the goddess Isis. I don't know how I know that it's Isis. And I feel like, I feel it's likely that nickname of light-ning bolt also speaks to this quality of bringing down a command with a certain level of that fierceness to shoot out the command in that certain vibration that causes it to manifest.

One of my earlier energy medicine modalities I was taught (Tibetan) had me learn how to make a command with my heart chakra. And it's the energy medicine modality that I used, before creating Vibrational UPgrade System for all physical ailments., So, it has a real cutting ability of cutting off the old pattern and establishing a new one, yet from the depths of the center of my heart. Interesting, right? Because we typically equate the heart's qualities with softness.

If we are going to put it in a language of goddess, let's classify the fierceness as Isis, I know it is because when I am, in particular, doing clearings for women on their power and especially when their female power has been particularly squandered due to male abuse of power (and remember, that's also directed at the collective, *always*) or they've been sexually abused—and it's not the official stat of one out of every two has. Every woman I've spoken to or have had as a client—so now we're talking tens of thousands of women by this point—has been pretty much, if not sexually abused, then at the least had some sexually inappropriate behavior projected onto her, so I don't agree with the official stats that it's one out of every two women, especially if we include the classification of "undesired sexually inappropriate behavior thrust upon her" that it's not even one out of two. I find it one out of 1.5.

Meaning, even women who haven't been inappropriately touched by some male, they've been given some sort of weird conditioning about their body, which was sexually appropriate, you know what I'm saying? Like all the way down to those catcalls walking by construction sites. Or not being safe to walk on a city street at night if You're dressed to go clubbing. It's, as far as I'm concerned, all sexually inappropriate behavior thrust upon women to deal with.

Um, so the claiming of the feminine power, it feels to me like a lion's roar. And now I'm seeing the Sphinx. Like, it feels to me like I am taking a rod and I am going like this. (Makes a hand motion as if has a sword and is striking down) Maybe that's why, I mean, I've been called the lightning bolt in part.

Um, I had always thought it was about the amount of energy I can channel down on behalf of somebody. But somewhere within the past four years I've realized this other meaning for that lightning bolt nickname.

And I'm seeing it now. Cause that's what it feels like. It's almost like what is that? A scepter, it's almost like taking a scepter or maybe it has an arc at the end of it, like that image of Isis where she has the tools of a scepter and crook and flail. Right? And so, it feels like I'm bringing down alignment for this all within the collective even when I'm going through one person on a group call. The VUP Clearing and Activation itself, every time it's said, contains this element of clearing on behalf of the collective. So, when I'm doing this for somebody when they show this is what is needed, when I'm doing the verbal clearings in that Isis mode of the command for women to, you know, line up with your power and cast out where you've been distorted, it feels fierce, and it feels like a command.

Words can't really get to it. Yeah. You know what I mean 'cuz you've experienced it. That's why I'm speaking of it now. (Laughing.)

Student: Yeah. Coherence is definitely an Isis jam.

AJK: (Laughing) OK. What a great sentence.

Student: Yeah. Um, sometimes now I see you also as like goddess Brigit, wielding the hammer on the forging, like sometimes when you're working with someone's ego-mind, it's like Isis, you know, but sometimes you're like, OK, we're going to hammer this out. And it's, it's, it's a hammer of love, but it's like, Nope, Nope. Whack-a-mole, yeah. So, the shaping gets done more in this wielding than on the force of the hammer. But the good news is you also give the people, you're giving her lessons as well. You're saying if you liked it, if you'd like to do this at home, you know, this is how. And I love that because when you were talking about that part of goddess Brigit, the metallurgy part of her, that also fits here, you know?

AJK: I have a strong connection with metallurgy. And so, Claire, my skipping sister from another mother, um, (Laughing) she's wanted to do welding for like her whole life. And I resonate with that. Although if one of us was more inclined to actually go to that local (to us) studio with the female welding teacher, it'd be her. Like when her sons graduate.

I have an appreciation for all of the traditional crafts, like the rebirth that's happening within English crafts now and leading into Brexit and the, um, like all of the traditional woodworking and the met-alworking and the leather working skills, all of that. I have such a deep resonance with. And so, Brigit's relationship with metallurgy completely fits in here, yes, with the sense of shaping what was once hard and seemed fixed and solid, with the fire.

And I feel like we have brought this not just into discipline, but also into a workable functionality, frankly, while yes, the ego-mind with all its causes of us to make the choices we do and continue to not make the choices we don't—there's especially the male ego, where it has gone out of balance. Like with the abuse of power, that requires not only the lightning bolt fierceness of Isis, but also Brigit's connection to the metallurgical welding for re-shaping of what seems like iron, but then also the compassion of Kuan Yin to aid such massive, seemingly, confrontation issues throughout these times of humanity's greatest evolutionary shift.

And I say specifically the male ego in this context for where the male ego has gone out of balance and caused much destruction. And so, if you look at the overall categorization of where we've been living from a destructive force, we also need to look at all of the inner work I do with every single individual, where their ego minds are turned inward with self-destructive thoughts. And then self-destructive behaviors being brought back into balance, yes. The ego mind balanced with the heart. I talk about that constantly, right? It's not just about coming out of the mind dominance. We need to then bring the heart more online, with all its gifts and skills.

There's this beautiful example I just saw of "Operation Nightingale," started in conjunction with Wessex archaeology and the UK's defense department to help returning soldiers, particularly from Afghanistan but also Iraq, who've been suffering physically and/or mentally, to recover. Their official mission statement: "Operation Nightingale is a military initiative developed to use archaeology as a means of aiding the recovery of service personnel injured in recent conflict, particularly in Afghanistan." How? Through the calming of digging in the Earth, out in nature, discovering archeology through active digs. This happens particularly on the Salisbury Plain, one of the richest archaeological landscapes in Britain.

And so many of these vets report restoration from this project, where they're able to be given perspective via the historical implications of archaeology, and a sense of calm from being out on the Earth. This calming and nurturing and *helping them feel safe* by being out on the Earth and methodically digging into it, replaces where they'd been traumatized from the hazards and destructiveness of war. This was in part, I think, started by a returning vet, seeing the need, after being soothed, once he'd returned from Afghanistan, by repeatedly watching, in pajamas on his couch, the British TV show, "Time Team," a 20-year run of what's become a classic, that's helped in great part, to reinvigorate the field of archaeology, particularly in the UK.

And so, with the over worshiping of the intellect, seeing the intellect as *the* tool to gain the glories of the external material gains that using our intellect trained at Harvard or Yale or Stanford or Princeton leads to, and then the ensuing material gains, that too is needing to be reined back in, to come into balance with the heart. Even that like a statistical analyst doesn't have something better than say, a fireman or policeman, just due to degrees. Everything that's been out of balance, and especially that's been causing destruction, is being brought back into balance.

So, we're also talking about the rebalancing of the inner and outer. It's the rebalancing of the physical and metaphysical, the spiritual and material, the ego, and the heart, the masculine and the feminine. So, any of those categories where there are behaviors that lead to destruction, they're being exaggerated in these times to that healing crisis level of the fever needing to peak before it breaks such as with COVID-19. We're seeing this exaggerated presence of authoritative regimes, for another example, because that is the healing crisis that always happens before something breaks and becomes a new, higher form. So, yeah. That lightning, and the fire to shape iron and compassion that's required to move through this all with as much grace and ease—and speed—as possible, these are all extremely helpful now!

Student: Can I offer how it looks to me as well? So, because I was going to ask you about this with respect to how you work with people individually. You're not trying to turn out cookie cutters, because there are a lot of women still doing the masculine formulaic thing.

AJK: But female teachers, well—there's a predisposition to raising children in a way that is going to work for that child, ideally, right? They're all nurturing plants that are going to express whatever their particular flower is, as I spoke of as a classroom teacher—another traditionally historically "nurturing" profession, the first that women could do outside the home . . . of seeing humanity as a quilt of a bunch of shining individuals living up to their potential and what a brilliant quilt our unity, each working their own inherent genius and passion zone, naturally fits together, as our humanity.

I guess those who are still modeling themselves after what men in authority positions do, well, I don't really consider them feminine teachers. I can sit with them. I maybe will consider them teachers of their tradition, but I wouldn't necessarily say they're female spiritual teachers.

Student: What about females not only acting with that nurturance, but also with the authority men have traditionally garnered?

AJK: Well, it seems that this is in process, right? In the States, I know that we have a particularly hard time with women in authority positions. Bitch or tough come up as names to call a female authority figure here when she's fierce. So, how to do it, without a negative connotation? I feel like more has to shift, frankly, with the mass consciousness "out there" rather than with women. And we just need to have more women in authority and leadership positions. And we need to stop being so hard on women. Women are more judgmental of other women than men are. If a woman is wanting to wear heels and show cleavage and acknowledge the power beauty has and use it, well, hell, why would we judge her for that? Because she makes intellectual women with degrees look bad? Why is it naturally assumed that there are those two different categories?

So, if I show cleavage then I'm uneducated, but if I don't then I'm educated? Showing cleavage is unprofessional?

Well, I know from my own personal experiments, when I wear makeup I do not get listened to the same way as to when I do. When I show cleavage, I do not get listened to the same way as to when I don't. We've got some more work to do on what women in leadership show up as, and accepting women in leadership positions, rather than tear them down.

I also know that there are more male hosts on a particular well watched documentary cable TV show in the States. When I asked one of my Masterminders who had a friend who was a frequent guest expert on one of this channel's shows, why there were no female hosts, the response she got was that males just naturally garner more authority. I'm sorry. What? But that then makes me think of the "Wait 'til your father gets home" old school threat. So, yeah, we have more work to do with this.

Student 2: Dr. Alison, I feel like one way you do this differently, as a female spiritual teacher, is you don't do the hierarchy thing, nor do you do the development of "dependence on you" thing. So, that is, uh, I think that's a real hallmark, you know, people don't leave as groupies. Do you know what I mean? When, when victims, yeah. There's a lot of people who come out as victims of this, of the path. Like I have not had that experience. So, I'm, I am blessed to have been spared of it, but I've heard stories.

AJK: I can give you some, I have many that show up on OTD calls and talk about that. I mean, this is from many: they went to the more well-marketed male authority figures in this field, on the spiritual path. Like one just because he *looked* Indian and all of a sudden was given some level of, um, fame on all the summits when he was not delivering anything different or new, and started having packed live events in hotels' banqueting rooms. And they'd come to me afterwards and say that they were messed up from what went on there. Or that they were told they would get x results and did not.

I've had other people work with psychics, who've told them something, or other practitioners who they got traumatized by, in the process of working with them. Um, so I have a lot of what would you call it, picking up after other practitioners' pieces, or getting their job done. Yet, it's also that I feel it's that mismatch of the marketing and the spiritual paths. Perhaps the people had inaccurate expectations? Or the outcomes weren't phrased in an understandable way? This is a different track, though, than folks out of integrity with their practice, while gaining popularity for superficial—or egoic—reasons.

I think this is important. I had no idea it had been going on, until enough people came in with some element of this and I've worked on clearing it out and getting them able to move beyond it—once their conception of this work and the spiritual path was restored to a healthy one. So, you're absolutely right when you're helping to bring out the distinction of what does make me different. Thanks for that. I appreciate it—and you. 'Cuz it does take an extra level of output and energy to toe the line, so to speak, when folks come in hurting and/or distrusting.

Student 3: I feel like you have had certain expectations of me, Dr. Alison, to understand when you teach things in story form or indirectly, for me to understand it. I apologize for that, but I really just so want to understand the nuances of what you say. I'm so happy to be working with someone finally, who I can ask this stuff to.

AJK: So first, I hear you. I know that the Asian tradition of spiritual teachers teach in that parable, and indirect style. And it can be annoying when you just want the bottom line, for sure. (Laughing.) But if you consider Don Juan with Carlos Castenada, that's from the South American shamanic tradition, and he too, taught through indirect means. The student has to work things through so they can embody it, and have their consciousness expand correspondingly, in order to make sense out of these massive life teachings, based on ancient wisdom. You can't expect them to just be instantly understood, that's not the nature of it. And if you are experiencing that with another teacher, then perhaps you might want to have a little think about that.

That's only for intellectual fodder, and theories. And theories, well they're meant to be tested. And this stuff I teach is meant to be applied. So, you gain that ability to apply it to your own life, rather than my doing it for you. It's more effective when your own consciousness has to work to reach a new level of understanding and integration.

And I get it, from an absolutely untrained perspective, fresh out of average American life, as a customer, we're used to being able to ask for what we want and get it. This has been an interesting navigation for me, balancing between this wanting to serve the customer dynamic, the ego-mind, and balancing that with the integrity to how this spiritual path progresses in order to keep you safe from frying up your circuitry, as in too much too fast, or kundalini rising too quickly.

Yet then also from the Asian tradition, well, from the beginning, for live events, I've had people volunteer to do "block and tackle for me" in that live event setting. Claire, god bless her, and then before her, another woman gave that kind of support when I was speaking and administering mini one-on-ones, at expos. The protocol is just so foreign here. But it's becoming better known. Look at you, you eventually understood.

So, here's a setting to help. Once I was back in the States: when I was sitting at Gurudev's feet and I would ask a certain question, we were on the floor, on meditation cushions. We're obviously at an Ashram, or in a yoga setting. And there was an energetic quality that permeated of sacredness and that translated into what we would allow ourselves to say and do, *especially when in the teacher's presence.*

Now I'm by no means asking to be treated as a guru, for god's sake. (Laughter)

Student 3: Yes, we know that (Laughter)

AJK: Right? Certainly not my style. I'm much more informal and enjoy that play. However, what I am speaking of, yet again, is that sense of self-management over the ego-mind, that can and does translate into the spiritual path, out of the marketplace, as a customer. Meaning having a feel for the room, or the setting, and not asking outlandish questions. And understanding when the teacher does not give you an immediate, direct response in the style you were looking for, that perhaps it's meant for you to work through it yourself with what was the response, so you ultimately gain more from that initially resisted response.

I have been fielding, well I've been, at times asked for things like when someone is at stage B and they ask to jump to stage Z. And there is just this safe progression and natural progression with a soul's evolution and with the way the ego-mind let's go of control, that takes time and is a process. There's no two ways around it.

Otherwise, the entire field of yoga and meditation would not have lasted for five thousand years. I've seen that ego-mind, cause a person who is at that just freshly starting stage B, without understanding, to ask to go all the way to Z, rather than understanding that they have, there are certain steps that have to be done, that they have to go through *in order to get to* that more advanced stage.

It's like when I imply something and expect students to infer it, like there is some mismatch with my indirectness, especially with Americans because, well for example, as you probably recognize, the Brits are less direct than us Americans and the Chinese are all the way to the other end of the spectrum of indirectness. And the Indians are in between the Brits and the Chinese. And Americans are, comparatively, really direct.

So, like when I was doing a video two weeks ago and I found myself saying, this is not going to be, I had to preface it with, there was going to be a story that I tell here. So, this is not going to be a direct, linear teaching. So, just sit back and relax, and then I talked a bit about how the Asian masters deliver teachings—not to say that I'm an Asian master, obviously—that's how I prefaced the video. But this was typically the way I was taught, and I had to work it out for myself, without being able to ask the teacher every little question I had. Monks in monasteries spend a lot of time in silence, as well as discussions, to work these kinds of teachings out.

So, there was this impatience when led by the ego-mind within a culture that doesn't recognize nor value at a cultural level, the disciplining of the ego-mind. It wants to "get to the bottom line," asap. I don't mean to say it's like the Wild, Wild West here; there are many patient people, increasingly so, in the States. But people dig bullet points here. (Laughing.) And I get how inundated we are as Americans. And I get how busy business owners just want their data so they can make decisions; I'm a busy business owner with decisions to make and tasks to cross off my list . . .

But there are, you know, protocols, when engaged in this kind of a learning curve. And thankfully, the people I work with nowadays aren't typically this way. But what I'm saying is when it's not, when you're allowed to, because you pay for something you then demand, what you want, or the unconscious collective conditioning is "I've paid for a service. So, therefore I should get what I want." It's a bit of a mismatch here too, with the work of the spiritual path because you can't demand your way through, into enlightenment.

CHAPTER 6
Becoming Whole Again

Sunday noon

TODAY WE GO up to the top of a very big hill and look down. I write this in my journal, a little bit grumpy today. Chewing my cereal, quickly, as I've woken late and need to get out front to meet everyone ahead of the walk. Dish in the sink and grab an apple and my coat. Launch.

Outside, waiting for stragglers, I overhear Laura saying she is very grumpy this morning. Apparently, this isn't 100 percent unusual on the day before an attunement, according to what Tiya then said, who was standing next to Laura.

"Yeah, didn't you hear Dr. Alison explain that on the first day? It's likely You're going to have a day on the retreat where You're grumpy or a bit off, due to how much new, higher energy You're receiving. So, You're shifting through and clearing out a ton of the old." Tiya said, looking at me and Laura as we're kind of bad students.

"Yeah, she said she's always working on the people when we come to these and our evolution can be sped up by being out on this sacred land and receiving the activations she does there, as well as those attunements—especially those!" Sam slid up to stand next to me, as he said this.

Wow we haven't even done the attunements yet, either. Holy cow. OK. So, OK, my grump is OK. It is just a byproduct of moving fast down my evolutionary highway. OK I will give myself the benefit of the doubt and go on this hike rather than staying back and trying to de-stress or make myself more pleasantly positive.

As if being able to see my internal decision making, Dr. Alison is all of a sudden there, pats me on the shoulders and says, "Great choice. Just let yourself be as you are," smiling and turning away from me, she spurts "OK, OK, let's go!"

We walk as a group, over to the tall hill called The Tor. Apparently, there is a connection to Archangel Michael and Mother Mary in this area, as Dr. Alison has explained on our first day, when she took us to the sacred well. I can't believe I totally forgot about that. Dr. Alison says it's her favorite place in Glastonbury. Well, that and the Abbey.

But this is our first time experiencing the Tor together, and it's a big deal, apparently. I mean, I can tell. I feel it and we're not even there yet. She posted pics of the Tor in our private group, and that sacred well come to think of it—why do I keep forgetting about that sacred well?—frequently, in the month leading up to our retreat.

"So, there are some special energies available here. Make sure to tune in. This is going to be different than any of the other sites so far!"

And Dr. Alison is going to use her land-whispering skills to introduce us. As we start to walk off the road and out onto a wooded path, she calls us together. "Be aware of elementals, which you may catch as flashes of light out of the corners of your eyes." She has been here every day since arriving and apparently this is where she always does her daily runs when here. So, she has made friends with the land. She tells us the tale of the red and white dragons, that is related to the red and white springs she took us to that first day, when she took us to the sacred well. Oh yeah! I get it, that's why it's the "red" dragon—that water was so "red" due to the iron, and

"Dr. Alison, you know how you told us about that white spring? Where is it again?" I decided to just ask.

"Basically, right underneath where we're walking now. I'll show it to you when we come down, depending on the time we have."

So, we walk along through a field and over a stile and through a gate, and suddenly there is the mini mountain. There is a tower on the top and the people look like insects from all the way down here. I see switchbacks half way up the side. I am glad I wore my athletic shoes for this.

We walk as a group at first, but do not go straight up the walkway that I'd seen.

"We have to obey the flow of the energies of the land. My body has never wanted to walk straight up that path, it kinda cuts off the flow of energies, and feels disrespectful to the land as a whole. It requires a bit of a gradual initiation to be able to get the most out of the energy present. This way too, you won't get knocked out by the climb, because you'll have gradually adjusted to the stronger energies here. I've seen people get headaches from how strong the energy is here. Besides, it'll be an easier climb for you, you'll see." And then she steps off the paved path and off to the right, onto a natural path that kind of hugs the side of the steep hill.

So, we wind around the hill of the Tor, as Dr. Alison explains the labyrinth and then goes silent. And then the line thins out according to pace and fitness. I am last. As we walk by this patch of massive oak and yew trees Dr. Alison points over to them, without saying anything. I guess we're just supposed to take that in. Then we're winding around a corner and she points again off to the right.

Oh, it's an apple orchard and a ton of sheep are below that. "How lovely!" I hear Jan say right in front of me.

I am huffing and puffing, looking down at my feet and then I hear Jan call my name. I look up and she's stepped off the path, to the right, with her arms on a gate, apparently following Dr. Alison's lead. So, I follow Jan in through the gate. Everyone is sitting close by each other, on these horizontal, low hanging tree limbs in this apple orchard.

These apple trees look ancient. They are twisted and gnarled, covered with moss and lichen. It is a magical grove where witches and priestesses, and nature devotees have come for ceremonies and practice through the centuries, I'm told. And it is of a feminine energy in here, whereas the Tor is masculine. It is a really nice place to take a short rest. Dr. Alison does a clearing and activation round for us and then a blessing for us, linking us to some secret aspects of the place. Ooh that makes my body shiver, and I shudder.

Sheila, who'd been sitting to my right, notices my shudder once the clearings and activation and then blessing was done, and asks, "That's from the energy, from what she just did, right?"

I nod my head, unable to formulate words and just wanting to be in silence.

Sheila holds up her arm for me to see and I can see she has goosebumps. Wow. What is going on here?

"Ok, so what do you feel, lovelies? You good to go to the top now?" Dr. Alison is standing now, looking at all of us sitting on the low tree branches with a different look on her face than I've seen before. And her face somehow seemed longer, and she seemed taller. I blinked and looked again and still she looked the same, in this new and different way.

We all look at each other while we're getting up.

"Yes!"

Dr. Alison smiles, then says, "Cool. Let's do it." And leads us through the gate, out of the orchard and up some steps. Then the path winds, and we've somehow met up with concrete stairs and begin to climb them.

It seems easier to go up the hill after this, although the slope out of the orchard is almost vertical. Perhaps it is the special energy, I doubt it is my imagination. Can't really make up this stuff, I've learned by now. I focus on my feet, so I don't trip. And I lean forward a little bit to use my weight as forward momentum. And I walk up a bit more. Next time I stop I see Dr. Alison at the top and she has her hands above her head in a cheering motion as she calls my name. That encourages me and I keep going.

About ten minutes after everyone else I arrive at the top. The view is so vast. There is a flat metal map at the top that looks like a sun dial that allows us to identify what we are looking at. Some people—not our group—are standing inside the tower and singing with drums and recorders. The tower looks at once both smaller and bigger than it looked from the bottom. It must be a trick of the light because the people at the bottom don't look as small as the people looked up here when I was at the bottom. It shouldn't make any difference because the distance is the same. This area is full of contradictions. Or maybe it really is magic like they say.

We stand as a group and look over the sacred geography that we have heard about during our tours so far and from the drivers and locals. So, much legendary stuff has happened here. So, much history and sacred tradition. Dr. Alison shares some details about less well-known legends and features of the mountain itself. She shares with us that these tours she's doing now are the best of the tours she's ever given. Remembering . . . oh yeah, I recall what she's talking about: she was actually a tour guide at the happiest place on

Earth world famous theme park, (Disney) and also for the biggest international birding organization. She is actually a great tour guide because she gives the info you want to know and then lets you have time to go around and digest.

As she pointed out features of the rolling sides of the hill, including the wild hares and their homes, as well as where the two springs, red and white were—seems like that was for me, 'cuz she said that bit while looking at me a troupe of women in black flowing robes began to ascend using the ridges and natural features instead of the path. Meanwhile white sheep with black legs and faces grazed on the same ridges. Several people nearby pulled out phones to capture the moment. A strong breeze struck our faces and it looked like the day would change. Clouds were slowly mounting up in the sky.

"Shall we descend?" She asked, and took us down the short way, straight down to whence the women in black had appeared. Near the gate out there was a big tree, covered with ribbons. Apparently, people were remembering themselves to the place by leaving something behind. Dr. Alison had told us ahead of the trip to pack ribbons and then last night to bring ours today, so she paused while we tied our ribbons there, those of us who wanted to mark our gratitude to this place as sacred for us. The wind whipping through the ribbons and the leaves made an unusual sound. And I felt a shiver. Magic indeed.

FEMALE TEACHER—LUMINOSITY

Student: I would define luminosity as the renewed innocence and purity of being whole.

And I feel like feminine [energy] is often a matrix wherein stuff is seeded, fertilized, gestated, birthed, nurtured, fed, taught/brought up, and released to life and/or to the natural ending/heights. Lately that seems to be something many are trying to use (materially) or even abuse? Rather than respected etc.

What is your definition of wholeness?

AJK: My definition of wholeness. Hmmm. I used to spell Holistic with a W and it caused too many problems with autocorrect, so I eventually had to drop the W. I mean you know that fight you sometimes get into with autocorrect? God bless autocorrect! (Laughing.) Like I wonder sometimes, well I used to, I guess I've gotten more accustomed to AI being more prevalent, but I used to ask, "So, who *are* these programmers who program autocorrect? They certainly don't think or speak the way I do! They don't even know that word I'm trying to use, instead they keep forcing it to be something I don't mean. Man do we come from different paradigms, trying to get me to spell that word when I'd never even use that word . . . ." Yah, you get the drift from my tangential rant. And then autocorrect with Gaelic, when traveling in Ireland or Scotland . . . whew! (Laughing.)

OK, so "holistic" is that approach where you are not in that scientific paradigm of reductionism, you are doing the exact opposite. The holisticness of everything, how it interconnects and interrelates. The coordination of the interrelationship of everything. And that's seemingly in part why I would have been led to learning about the chakra column to such depth. Because I've come to understand it as the way to unravel anything or create anything. And as the quickest way to get in there and get things shifted into the positive direction. Why are the chakras the quickest route?

They're the intersection of the mind, body, and spirit. Through the spirit element, that's how I can get to Karma. That's how I can get to so much of the past lives stuff. The DNA is partially in there too, containing the past lives and ancestry. All of this is in the cellular matrix that seems to be in the grey mist seen when a soul leaves a body (dies.)

Wholeness implies that there's not a ripping out or fragmentation, either at the mind level which includes all levels of consciousness, nor at the body level which stores something toxic (like a trauma) being stuffed away (in the subconscious, but because it relates to an aspect of life, say sexual abuse, that chakra that covers that aspect of life, sexual abuse, is most directly related to the root and sacral chakras, then this trauma also corresponds via the relevant chakra, to a part of the body, so that trauma is also stored, then therefore, in the body around that chakra; body trauma is also when the body part itself has had an accident and there's actual physical trauma, because its being ignored, rather than cleared and dealt with.)

Nor is there fragmentation at spirit level when wholeness is present. This fragmentation can occur where there is a carryover from wounds from past lives or karma carried in the cellular matrix. If all of that is working cohesively together, without traumas or blockages, we are able to function optimally. This is why the subtitle for my second book is "a conspiracy for your bliss." We are innately designed to be blissful.

Meaning, going to the solar plexus chakra's aspects of the inner child, joy and manifestation all being there; so that implied in that is the solar plexus gets more functional the more joy we have with what we are manifesting. We activate our full power, or we become whole. In this definition of wholeness, it an activation of our whole power. It's not just, I'm not wounded or I'm not sick or I'm not having pain at any level of my existence. It's beyond that. It's full activation of our potential.

To be clear, for me, I feel also the wholeness implies that level of beyond woundedness, beyond fixing things and problems into, not only, what if there's nothing wrong but the full activation of what we are designed to be able to do and having the courage and capacity to choose to co-create (5th chakra) based on our heart's (4th chakra) desires (3rd) and intuitive guidance (4th, 6th, and 7th chakras.)

This I say, as I am especially considering the vibrational backdrop we are living in now, where the field of possibilities is much more omnipresent. When we are sorted throughout our chakra column meaning at the mind, body, and spirit level there has been not only clearing out of fragmentation, catches (like a skipping cd) or blocks or stuffing down traumas.

To be clear, stuffing down of something is done out of trauma because of our conscious mind—read that as ego-mind not being able to deal with it at the time. The ego-mind when fielding the new couldn't process the trauma, so it gets stuffed back and down into the subconscious, or under (prefix of "sub"). It's not something we consciously tend to deal with until we start to do this clearing work so that we have ourselves come back into wholeness.

In that is applied coherence. We are moving from woundedness or having something to clear out, like parental imprints that life is hard, or we have to work hard for everything we get, or unconscious—and in this next example it's both unconscious in its effects and conscious that it exists—the belief that as a woman, I have to work harder to make sure I prove myself more alongside what a man has to. So, once we work with limiting beliefs at any level of consciousness, and we come out of them, replacing them with the positive, or affirmative behavior that frees us up to actually continue to co-create what we actually desire free of self-limiting beliefs, choices, and thus behaviors (whew! A mouthful, I know, but hang with me here, I'm doing that holistic thing by tying it all together), we get to this threshold where it seems like the mind-body-spirit system is functioning at optimal potential, where we're self-actualized.

Then what do we do? It seems like in that self-actualization, according to Maslow's hierarchy, the top part of the pyramid is the heart charka coming into its power of coherence and beyond that to organizational capacity. Remembering that even with all the neurological firing of the brain's synapses, from that raw level of one synaptic jump to very advanced intellectual conversations, all the synaptic jumps that are happening there, or here, right now for you, all of the brain's electricity is nothing compared to the electromagnetic power, which life force or chi or prana is—electric and magnetic— that the heart has, when we are in wholeness.

The heart chakra is open and the vortex in front of it is able to be a vortex instead of closed down or inverted as I've seen with some people. I've seen that dysfunctional inversion of the lotus petals especially with the solar plexus chakra's petals as the solar plexus' gets with overly empathic people who have no boundaries.

The petals of the proverbial lotus blossom create the vortex. These petals surround the chakra. If they are not folded over halfway in weakness, nor one or two of them not damaged, or five of them not damaged, or the petals aren't all inverted, then these petals are all open, and helping to shape the vortex and flow out the life force.

When all of the lotus petals are open and healthy that then creates the vortex in front of every chakra, *that's when* you can sometimes feel people's energy as they step into a room but are still far away from you. Because all their chakras' vortexes are flowing out energy as it's meant to be, and that's the communication to the outside world.

So, if you think of the chakra—there is the internal world. There is an internal vortex turned inward, facing me, going within me. The spinal column is what the chakra column runs down. They are in the front of the body as well as the back of the body. If we just divide my body in half and we go to, let's say the heart chakra: on the front of the chakra, it has a vortex pointing inward and it also has a vortex pointing outward.

Once we are cleared of blocks—like the conditioning of because I'm a woman I must over-give—then that chakra relevant to those wounds is able have all those petals whole and open and singing. That vortex is naturally there to carry out the emanation. So, half of it churns the vital life force out of its vortex to inside of me—the internal facing lotus petals—while its mirror image of lotus petals outside of me churns vital life force when it's open and flowing.

We are designed to be able to work with or signal and activate the field of possibilities we are living within to then bring in further wholeness to then bring in further cohesiveness and cohesion or unity. There is a harmonic of the universe. I can connect to it naturally and effectively, with the coherence of my system once I've created it.

So, because I'm cleared, I'm not having a thought that is able to stick, or trigger me, so that I pay attention to it, e.g., "I don't really want to do this while I'm doing it." Rather, I'm in agreement with doing what I'm doing. There's that coherence. There's that alignment. I'm able to work with, live with 60 times more power, not only with the electricity but with the magnetism of the heart muscle and then the heart chakra more powerful than any other chakra, in its ability to organize. And by organize, I do mean, create coherence.

It sings out through the open petals in the lotus blossom around the vortex—that electromagnetic life force—chi, to the environment that it now has flowing, or *emanating* as only the heart chakra does. And because it's a match—flowing electromagnetic life force, or chi—to what is in all of life, in nature, at the base of all cells and in between all cells, it is able to then communicate more with the life force of the greater field of possibilities. Because it has that heightened electromagnetic power, and it's the heart chakra, and it's now coherent, *it organizes.* That organization happens because of the coherence created *within you, first.* Cohesiveness is a synonym in this context for wholeness.

Then greater wholeness is able to be created because once I'm in cohesiveness within myself where I'm not running from myself, or any back of the mind thoughts, or that "back of the house consciousness" as I've come to term the unexplored, log jam of unexamined consciousness, or I'm not hiding from anything that I really feel, or I'm not lying to myself. Instead, where I'm in clarity and alignment and wholeness within myself. That then naturally corresponds to my chakras *doing most of the work for me in consciousness and in energy.* And that is without the forcing, the making it happen gig, the figuring it out gig, or the forcing stuff to come together, when it just keeps showing up as blockages, or hitting walls.

With their natural power that they are given through the vortexes emanating out that level of wholeness—that level of cohesiveness so that there is more coherence of my field, and *coherence has an organizing capacity of energy,* I'm more able to live within harmonics with everything in my environment. I am able to create more harmonics in my environment. *I am therefore, able to manifest with more ease.*

If somebody comes to me and they are feeling down or low, and they interact with me and end up feeling lighter—when I've not done any active clearings or activations—that's in part the *entrainment* that happens within a lower vibrating field with less coherence, to the higher vibrating field of alignment, coherence and thus organization. There is all that silent unconscious communication (unconscious to us, but the Universe is picking it up), remember energy is our first language—that goes on under the surface of what's considered physical matter.

In today's times sometimes for some people its conscious communications. Like what I'm up to and some of the examples I've both explained here and you've experienced. You can feel you are in somebody's field who is coherent or has this coherence or you can feel if you are in someone's field that is all fragmented. Some people can walk around with this assessment. I do, as it is extremely helpful with this line of work that I do. Right?

Student: Clearly. And that's one of the things I love about working with you. You're so fast!

AJK: So, I get automatically shown where the fragmentation is—the blockage, the non-wholeness, and where the defragmentation needs to occur, to come back into wholeness. That's my nickname, "Hawk Eyes," right? So, beyond all of that, when I'm now working in harmonics within my field it's not only affecting other people and creating harmony. It is also interacting with the greater field. And that greater field now is one of increasing possibilities because it's a new life. It's a new paradigm coming in from 2012 to 2032. There is a higher field of the new.

And so, I've been increasingly, intentionally, creating that harmonic with the new. If you look at what all the planets are doing and what planets are playing a major role from 2012 to 2032, you can see the new coming in, and it's one of harmony. We are being commanded to rise up into an increased level of harmonics. And eventually, coherence, at the collective level—which leads to unity. While we're still at the stages of most people if not learning how to do that within themselves, then learning that this is even needed.

The secrets that once were buried are being asked to come up to the surface. The skeletons are being brought out. Beyond each of us doing that, yes, it's happening collectively, but the more of us with coherent fields, the more we will naturally organize into our harmonic state. As well as being able to call out to or emanate out to the field of unlimited possibilities and to have more ability to collapse energy in a desired way that our heart chakra is calling out for, without us mentally having to focus quite as actively as we may have learned manifestation "requires."

Student: When you were talking about the field of possibilities. I think it's physics or chemistry where they talk about the atoms and electrons. There are the neutrons or whatever. The things spinning around the electrons. If they are spinning round with enough power sometimes the electrons can jump, and they can form a new organism. I think it's called a valence. The valence is like what it usually is and if it has a lot of energy it can turn into something else. I had this impression of all of this somehow may be actually quantum shifting that is happening in the heart. It's not only like it seems like these possibilities are present in your field. There is a sense of like a nuclear process of actually creating those possibilities. Is that true? Is that part of the heart too? The creative part?

AJK: Yeah, if we look at the wording that I have attempted to use for the free monthly call about what happens by just being in my field, it's become the word *entrainment*. If we bring it over to a one-on-one session, now, and say I'm going to help somebody with cancer or digestive issues, I'm bringing in the field of coherence. That's part of the usage. It's not just the hands directly on a person, whether a local or distant session. It's not just to bring more coherence to that individual's field, but it's also my field is somehow programming them, like reminding them . . . you know?

I have for a while now—I've been aware—it's not just about bringing in healing via my hands hovering over their body or in a distant session—and maybe this has come in more to help me considering how much more distant one-on-ones (non-local, not in person) and distant group work I've been doing. And interviews, and big summits and big calls; so, it's more projection than hands on, or one on ones.

So, I've been realizing increasingly it's also about what's in my field. My field is doing more of the commanding, nowadays. Kinda like I've become, after using my system so much in this same way, a finely tuned instrument. It has an organizing capacity. I've been calling it entrainment. I believe that is also why I have brought in the word keys and the word codes and activating them from that awareness of what I'm increasingly carrying in my field, around my body, so that I can have more robust results.

I was envisioning a big waterfall. I talk about the golden shower head of the 12th chakra up there. We talk about the fertility of the Earth and the water being such a primary need and necessity for the growth of anything. We are 80 percent water. I feel like what I was implying and getting at is that harmonic. In that coherent, cohesive *whole* field, that harmonic that is then able to sing out and have more organizing capacity to collapse non-harmonics.

Like when people come into 3M (Magic, Manifestation, and Money Flow) or with clients in their one-on-one sessions or VIP sessions, when they are in one on one's after like two sessions or maybe three, all of a sudden they are coming back with one of the most typical results—"I'm less triggered." On the flips side of that, maybe a couple of sessions later, days later or weeks later depending if it's 3M or one on one's, they report as religiously as the first outcome of "I'm less triggered," "I am having people be more kind to me. People are being more responsive to me. People are being helpful to me." It's always some version of one of those three.

First, yes, it's the chakras becoming less blocked, so as your unconscious and subconscious blocks get cleared, You're internally, less triggered. And then, as the next result, more chi is flowing out, as You're becoming more aligned within too, overall. So, that happens first. But then that becomes your field emanating out the coherence. And so that organization from you, well, that's eventually a harmonic that organizes people around me—and now you! to a degree—to collapse that which is not harmonic, as well as entrain up to that which is harmonic.

That harmonic also happens within the Earth. It seems like what we were talking about earlier about this damaging of the feminine and this killing of, or taking advantage of, that what sustains our life. The life force, which is what flows through each chakra, if the chakra is blocked because of karma, past life trauma, present life trauma, conditioning, or beliefs or any or all of the different causes of what blocks up the chakra and the life force, then it isn't able to flow through, right? That's one of your primary teachings. You get that by now, yes?

Student: I believe I do by now, yes. Thank god!

AJK: (Laughing) Woohoo to that for sure! So, that whole life force carries the term "vital" at the start of it. The English words, or phrase, that most accurately—and typically—translates what chi, or ki, or prana is, is "vital life force energy." It is meant to be understood nowadays as a golden frequency. Perhaps referring to Christ consciousness. We are talking about an emanation. We are talking about luminosity. If that is taken for granted . . . well, these destructive, disastrous results will continue to ensue.

This inherent life force that so many people walk around not even aware of and when they hear chakra, they check out and label it as woo-woo for the old school people. It's taking it for granted. Evolving beyond that, well beyond that now, is instead using this life force so it's focused on an outcome of something *having more* life force.

Think about a mother having that breast milk to keep a baby alive or a woman providing that softness for the man in the old paradigm's ways where he comes home from fighting a war or comes home from a competitive business or corporate culture, she provides the softness for him to fall into. Nowadays, sure that can be reversed, the genders I mean, sure. But that's not the point, the softness being provided to buoy up against that hardness is the point.

That nurturing underbelly. Whether it's the feminine, vital life force energy or our Earth's, which every single form of currency is still created from except for bitcoins, and always has been. So, the advanced state is what the industrialized, postmodern nations consider themselves, right?

Well look at those ancients! Why would they spend all of that time looking at the stars? Or look at those ancients they had such basic primitive tools but yet they are building places like Stonehenge and Avebury and the great pyramids in Egypt and Göbekli Tepe in Turkey. It's like that dismissal we do in this postmodern era where we have been conditioned to consider something more advanced the more we can measure it with instruments. When in fact it has led to an ignorance of the basics that keep us alive. Or an arrogant overlooking of the basics, of say the heart, and instead glorifying complexities, of the intellect.

Like the Earth, like our water, like the healthy soil with the full spectrum of minerals, to get us plants so we can eat or so the cows if we eat meat can eat. The air we breathe. The quality of the air we breathe. Right now, we have the West Coast of America on fire. The skies are orange at midday. Cars going over the Golden Gate Bridge during the day keep their headlights on. If you look at what the corona virus is, it's a respiratory gig. We are being forced to recognize and appreciate and preserve Mother Earth, and all that keeps us alive.

Student 2: Wow. OK. So, if we take the definition of luminosity as "the renewed innocence and purity of being whole", you've certainly illuminated that here.

Let me add to that definition: Luminosity is the measure of the total energy output by a star at all wavelengths from gamma radiation to radio waves. For example, the Sun gives out about 500 million, million, million MJ of energy every second so its luminosity is 500 million million, million MJ.

AJK: So, you're talking about emanation here. In another term, glowing, like someone glowing. Like it's said about a pregnant woman. Why is that said? She's glowing with the act of growing life.

So, growing life isn't only creating little people who eventually become big people. (Giggling) It's also the glow a person who is fulfilled has. And someone who is focused on creating, yes.

So, a story: I was watching Shark Tank the other night—again, going for some business coaching beyond my own business coach, (Laughing.) And the woman who started Spanx, the youngest female billionaire ever in American history, was on. She was on the panel with the sharks, fielding a person, a woman entrepreneur, who'd faced some battles over copy cats, when she'd held a patent for what she'd created and others were copying her. I don't remember what the product was.

What I was focused on, besides my high intensity intervals I was doing on my max trainer (Laughing), was that this entrepreneur and now philanthropist, Sara Blakely, responding to this newer female entrepreneur in the Shark Tank with her litany of battles, suing copy cats so that she was there in the tank raising money due to having spent much of it on these lawsuits as she was just getting started.

What Sara Blakely said, was, and I'm paraphrasing, so please forgive me Sara, you know, I had a lot of copy cats too, when I was still just beginning to build Spanx. And I had to make a choice, do I go after them, or do I stay focused on my vision? It was like—and now the other women sharks on the panel were nodding their heads, not the men though, interestingly, I could either stay focused on my vision, on what I was creating, or I could go into combat and defend. And I had to choose where I wanted to spend my energy and time and money and to me it made sense to stay focused not on protection and defense as it could have acted as a distractor, as much as on staying focused on what I was building and creating, to ensure that I reached what I was going for.

So, she clearly made a wise choice there. And she glows, this Sara Blakely. She's an inspired woman, on a mission, living a fulfilling life of her own choosing and making.

That glow I too feel. The glow of creating new life. Of helping other busy, successful women—and for me, and men too—who really want to go for their full potential, or at the very least, let go of what's been limiting them for living up to *more* of their potential. The act of creating new life causes luminosity. That glow happens from joy and fulfillment. And from giving good service, where you can clearly see how You're uplifting others.

Student 3: Wow, I love that. So, do you feel that on this track of "becoming whole" there are blind spots, perhaps where someone may be used to looking for problems?

AJK: Yes, that's precisely what I was just speaking about the and glow and luminosity that results from *not* doing that.

Student 3: OK, so then what about a possible blind spot, maybe you'd call this a block?—of labelling oneself as strong and tough because of what we have "been through" instead of being tough due to our innate wholeness?

Like here's a quote, it's an OLD thinking quote, but still in operation in the collective. "Women are like teabags. We don't know our true strength until we are in hot water" said by, I believe it was Eleanor Roosevelt

So, this is like where someone might be telling their story over and over again, with the "my trauma made me strong" kind of an ending.

And I know that in our training you say "NO" to that. That actually it's not about the trauma, but coming through to the other side of it, what's the now polished, shined up diamond, that had been all dirty during the traumatizing experience.

You know that thing you say about the gem being what's on the other side of a person's *samskara*, or biggest limiting behavioral pattern—challenge—they're working with you—or us now—to overcome?

AJK: Well, that first thing you said about women being made tough because of all they've been through.

That reminds me of the PR requirements I was presented with. They told me that there are two kinds of pitches, either where you are telling your story of suffering behind why you now do what you do, or some other framing that I don't remember.

But I didn't have a suffering story that made me who I am today. It was ridiculous, looking for some struggle to fit into that PR formulaic pitch. I eventually did, and it's in my intuitive development free webinar (on my website). But still, it was taken from the context of my looking for more possibilities, because I wasn't OK with settling.

So, one of my first teachers, that female one for the chakras, I remember her telling me a story about being at a luncheon, completely unrelated to her work, teaching about mysticism and the chakras. And she told me about how a woman plunked down at one of the banquet hall's kind of round tables that seats eight. She introduced herself with her name, and then that she was an incest survivor. No kidding, second words in her introduction of herself was about such a personal and deep trauma. They were not at any kind of AA meeting, I repeat, the setting was not for this kind of open confession or sharing.

So, this woman wore it like a badge. But I mean, how do you respond to that, besides choking on your water and possibly spraying it on your luncheon companions? It's something strange, her need for acknowledgement for having survived trauma, and then the expectation of receiving congratulatory approval for having done so.

It may seem harsh; I can feel it myself. I mean for god's sake, incest? That's just horrendous! And it happens more than I ever thought it had, now decades into hearing tens of thousands of people's stories as they come to me to clear out this kind of pain and suffering and trauma,

But announcing it like that, well clearly, it's over sharing. Beyond that, though, it is that thing You're asking about, that somehow, at least within American society, there is this badge of honor for being tough, for being a survivor. And that's good, you know? It's good we don't give kudos for being surrendered to trauma and giving in to it and being wrecked for your whole life. Clearly. It's good to be strong. I feel I'm "supposed" to say here "life can be so tough."

But yes, that leaves the resonant conditioning unconsciously that the more I pull through, the more I survive, the stronger I am. And being strong is a good thing. *Sure, it is.* But to require suffering in order to be strong is the lie, or erroneous thinking that is a block, that when cleared, would allow a person to make choices that are less resonant with the vibration of things they have to survive and fight through, and instead, situations that present more ease and dare I say, love? And peace?

I have a video on my YouTube channel: *How to Stop Being an Excellent Problem Solver.* Which is along these same lines. It's also, in part, why I don't label myself a healer. Rather than have things to heal, let's have things to activate, so you can live out a life of your greatest flourishing, that challenges you to allow yourself to be forced to increase your tolerance for bliss.

Student 4: Dr. Alison, can you talk more about what wholeness, or choices made from or for wholeness, rather than reductionism, might look like?

Because I feel like my husband is like reducing our budget down to expenses, while he's not seeing the whole picture.

AJK: Oh, we've spoken about this before, right? With how you've been growing even more into beliefs that support abundance, while he stays more steeped in lack?

Student 4: Yep.

AJK: OK, so I find it interesting in that element of conditioning. If you think about when you, or whoever makes the money choices or whoever made them grow up, what is said when there is a need for money?

Student 4: We have to tighten our belts, is what my dad would say. My husband says we have to cut down on our expenses.

AJK: That's exactly what I was going for, yes. But why is it that the lack, the cutting down of expenses is the cultural norm? Why isn't it, "OK let's see where we can create more money coming in?"

Student 4: Yep.

AJK: Yep. And wouldn't that relieve some of the burden on the "breadwinner"? Is lack of a construct that has been created by those in power, so that they remain in power? I don't know . . .

So, here's a story which I'm sure many of you will be able to relate to: I had a client that went up to level two training with me here locally. Not a Vibrational UPgrade Practitioner, but a Usui Reiki level II, so she was able to work on other people. She didn't go to that level in order to treat people, as she had a full-time job and was busy raising school age kids and just wasn't into it for that, but it did compliment her natural beauty products side revenue stream, so she was open to what came.

She was a happily married woman. I don't know for how many years, but I believe it was her high school sweetheart. And they had built a great life together. They were good friends, buddies, partners, and lovers. Really happy coupling, she had. And they had two kids, a boy, the oldest, and a girl.

She worked with me for four or five years. I walked with her through the changes as her daughter grew up out of elementary into middle school and started to get that hormonal sharp bitchiness and how to deal with that, and as her son began to get more liberated, out of a seeming ADHD label, into being a good student by high school. The whole time as the kids grew up, I was working with her weekly. It was fun, because I'd just come out of the classroom, so I offered her a lot of insight in that regard, during her sessions while I'd flow the energy medicine into her.

I remember at one point, in the last year of working with her, as I was cutting down on one on ones, her husband got sick with something and they didn't know what it was. She had been getting increasingly into the healing arts, also learning from me about essential oils, and then doing more on her own with that too. She'd been using all the frequencies and the chakra attunement audio series at home for years now, so she'd really morphed into an even fuller version of herself and her natural healing and intuitive capacities. She's a powerhouse and I totally enjoyed working with her; one of my all-time favorite clients.

So, her husband began to have digestive problems. He was having also having increasing irritability, which wasn't like him. They both were really easy-going, fun-loving people. Yet during this time, he was not fun to be around, even for himself, never mind my client or the kids he'd always been so close to and such a good dad to.

She had already been trained up to level two and was able to talk with him about it at the time of her training, and about possibly having some energy medicine sessions. Then he got sick and she suggested, one time, for him to consider what she could do with the energy medicine, and there was a resistance. So, she downgraded it to what essential oils he could use. Resistance there too.

Where he went to first, was the "science backed western medical system." She worked with me long enough to know not to push where there is resistance. As he went about the western medical community, she went to many of the doctor's appointments with him, knowing the whole time she could be helping him. Yet she remained supportive, clarifying at times, information as they went to new specialists, one after another. Doctor after doctor, MRI, X-ray after diagnostic tool used on him and it was never actually figured out. Instead, he was misdiagnosed, and put on meds. These made him blow up even more. Made the problem even worse and didn't solve it.

So, he got to a point where he began, and now I don't know how long, like maybe six or nine months before he ultimately began the research for an alternative. Now she remained backed off, he did this on his own. If you could guess—of all the places that a masculine American man would go as the most acceptable place after the Western Medical community, what tool do you think he looked at?

Student 4: You mean besides like the whorehouse?

AJK: Ouch. (Laughing) But yes, along those lines. What would you say?

Student 4: I would say a massage, some sort of massage. Getting women's energy into the solar plexus.

AJK: Interesting. Mind you this came up after four years of her getting weekly sessions with me and getting upgraded to level two—so you are not off. We did do massive amounts of work on her solar plexus, in fact. Yet, it was CBD oil he turned to.

Student 4: Oh, sure yeah. A pill would be the first. Oh yeah, You're right because CBD you can just eat it right? You don't have to do anything.

AJK: Yeah, I think he was doing the oil in food or he was putting it on him or maybe taking a pill. I don't know but that is where he got to. I navigated that with her. It was just such a revisit like originally of my dad, pre-Mom's brain tumor. Of where my brother used to be who just got his first reiki session with one of my local students and texted me last weekend, raving about it. His wife has been my client. She has been working with this student of mine because another student of mine has moved. And my older brother finally said yes to a session. Woohoo to that. But it's that male resistance, right, that I'm referring to.

The collapse that is happening from the old paradigm to the new, what the shifts are that some of our menfolk, particularly in the States, have to make to come out of that resistance and into balance—I go into this rather extensively in *Reasonable Dragons*. Like,

OK, I need to live with factual based evidence and information that is science backed to a degree for reality to get grounded.

Then there is all of the opening to all the work that gets done so that you can eventually trust your guidance and know that it's not making something up and projecting it into a situation so that's it's not your "wishes fulfilled" old-school thing. There is a certain population of our men who live in resistance. And nowadays, there's a lot of fear that has gotten catalyzed by the sense that this new world paradigm is coming in and they don't know what to do with it.

Let's go on to the hope thing. You responded strongly with that when I spoke about it before. What's your response when I say that "Women are the ones that hold hope?"

Student 4: I am somebody who is sort of anti-hope. You know what I mean? I always feel like, just like what men do about, OK, if I don't protect myself that means I'm not afraid. I often think that being hopeful is being wishful which is being weak.

AJK: I say the exact same thing. Don't hope when you have tools. As in like hope is weak.

Student 4: If the women can be a reservoir of hope, I would have to unpack that and say perhaps that is because she is willing to do whatever it takes to ensure that whatever is the hoped outcome occurs, especially when it comes to her kids or her loved ones. Right? The women throughout the world are the ones that are responsible for making sure that everybody eats. It might be the man's job too, right, but it is usually the women who are out there growing food or getting part time jobs when the guy can't work or he is off to war. Who takes care to the kids when the men are off to war? You know what I'm saying.

AJK: Who, historically, takes care of the kids when the men are home from war?

But there's this aspect of the wounded masculine that's coming to the surface as a part of all this clearing and purging that's been going on as we shift from the old paradigm to the new, from the non-divine masculine, or wounded masculine to the divine masculine.

I have had the men on my table and as distant clients who have come from the competitive business world where they made compromises to their integrity and they've done things to other people in the name of business and in the name of getting ahead that doesn't sit well in their gut. Meaning, they turned off how they felt about what they were doing, which was bad, in order to do it.

They have ended up with colon cancer or they ended up with digestive disorders or they ended up with high blood pressure. Where they've gone against their softness, their desire to preserve life, and instead have made choices to harm life. Whether that's on the battlefield or against someone within their corporation or a "competitor in their field" (look at that phrasing!) or against someone else in the name of competition. And I just have to add competition is a core requirement of capitalism.

Men who have been out to war and they have that hardened edge in order to do what they "had to." And so, typically, what they have seen doesn't get allowed to get looked at—that's in great part why so many vets have such issues—so it gets buried and it actually manifests into something later. I'm talking about PTSD sure, but really, beyond PTSD. Especially if they then also have habits of overeating or eating of certain types of carbohydrates that makes them feel better momentarily so that they get that big carb belly, but where their nutrition is poor, their foods are acidic, which doesn't combine well with the acidic of the toxic emotions, traumas, memories that have been stuffed down. So, some physical issue manifests later.

There are all these aspects of not only taking life for granted and the source of life for granted, if we consider it a spectrum, to all the way over to being suicidal. Then there is also that element of the masculine that resists that "going within." Where it had been considered the women's job to "bring up emotions" or "talk about the deeper stuff."

We are *all* being set up to look inside now. We are being set up to look at all levels, to stop focusing on just the external, and instead recognize the need to balance that with also going within. Ironically, our power lies within us, yet it's been historically, men who have abused power—externally—over others, while resisting going within. These two are not unrelated.

As well as, finding and discovering the source of life, which is Gaia, which is the feminine way of talking about the Earth. There seems to be like this hard edge of the conditioning and programming to men that makes them feel like it's not masculine or it's something they're just "not wired for" and aren't, therefore, "supposed to" be doing, by looking within themselves. And then conversing about it—especially with other men!

They have labeled going within as not desirable, or not "something that men do,"—while looking within *is a part of* the holistic health model—and have kept the pill taking and the external surgeries and all the cool equipment you use for that as what's considered OK. And possibly acupuncture as the "approved of" "alternative" modality. I don't know how much of that is related to the health care system in the States being based on a profit model, as a privilege rather than a right, within our capitalistic model, and corporations within the States being run so disproportionately by men. I remember traveling on the London tube, reading a newspaper there about their law requiring at least a 45 percent—something like that—of all CEO's to be women by a certain date. That's brilliant! And certainly not a law in the States.

There seems to be like some shaming that happens with going within and talking about it. I remember listening to a recent conversation Prince William had filmed, where he was in a professional football (soccer in the US) team's locker room, talking with professional male athletes. They were talking about this exact thing, as a part of Prince William's mental health program he started with Prince Harry and Princess Kate. And they were describing this sense of, "if I talk about what I feel I'm going soft and that is an absolute no-no." And, "If I'm upset, the only way to show that in the locker room is with anger. Certainly not tears." And they were all saying how this caused suffering. One to the point of feeling suicidal, another to the point of massive depression. It seems clear this is an element of the wounded masculine. As if going within or talking about feelings has been assigned to the feminine, only.

If you think of the example that you gave the other day about you being the one to help catalyze the men talking because they didn't know what to talk about, and then you saw them later at coffee shops talking. I feel like there is a redefinition that is needed here because I've met some real chatty men. (Laughing.)

You know where the men are quieter and the women are more chatty stereotype. What is that? Silent, strong type? Is that it? It feels like there is this old worn-out conditioning. That is so old and that has led to so much destruction. We are coming up out of the ashes like a phoenix. Coronavirus has been needed in order to get the masses attention because they are so busy not looking within so we need crisis. What else is possible? What if we didn't need crises or suffering in order to cause people to go within and deal with themselves?

Student 4: Yeah. Again, masculine and feminine. The thing I like about what you just said is because it really resonates with that topic of luminosity.

AJK: I'm hearing inspiration is a good replacement. It creates a leg of inspiration—which is luminosity. Or perhaps luminosity is the tree trunk and inspiration is one of the branches. Yeah, that feels more like it.

Student 4: Yeah, even if you look at these expressive behaviors you've got, there's treating something with awe and bliss. Accepting, letting go, awe and bliss so that's like OMG we are having the worst day we could have, but do you know what? Let's go out and have some fun anyway.

AJK: If the male is used going to the female for the well spring of nurturance, for the inspiration, for the luminosity including the metaphorical life from the milk of the breasts. Yet in the new paradigm, the divine masculine form is actual the quiet support. I don't mean to say he doesn't speak, but there's a sense of grounding in the lightning rod of support, behind the scenes. A bit different than being the burdened breadwinning martyr, with authority.

Student 4: Yeah, Yeah! I told somebody I was with recently, and I was talking about planet Earth having the same public relations issues at the moment as the feminine, because humanity—and that includes men and women—are doing the same thing to the planet as what has been done to women.

AJK: The feminine *is* the Earth! That's the Gaia principle.

Student 4: There has to be a sense of respecting the luminosity of the planet. And then respecting the luminosity of the feminine, and the feminine respecting themselves as well. When I finally realized that I was expected to be a battery within my marriage, which I never signed up for and that was not how it was at the beginning, I said no.

AJK: Yes, and that's both the divine masculine becoming luminous for himself, as well as the divine feminine being able to be luminous herself. And . . . stop using her husband as the projector of the cause of why she's *not* able to do more of what she wants to. I see that in the non-divine feminine form too, which is what you were talking about when you said the feminine, too, has to allow herself to be luminous. Well, she can't and won't if she's busy playing the victim-blame game with her husband, rather than owning her own stuff, clearing it, so she become luminous. Sex gets really, really good when both are in their divine form.

That's what is meant by tantric. Not the sex part, but the individuals each becoming their divine form with both masculine and feminine balanced within themselves. That is tantric. The sex part is where we took this Eastern teaching, once it got to the West, and made it *only* about sex. But there is that element, that then when partnering, the other is also in their divine, balanced form of consciousness. And then that's when the love making becomes tantric.

CHAPTER 7
Sovereignty

IN THE CAR on the way to the place where we would receive our first attunement. And as we're just pulling out of the parking lot, a conversation restarts, that had begun out in front of the B & B. Dr. Alison is driving some of us to where we are going to receive our attunements, while others chose to walk. It's a little chilly, so she offered.

Sue says, "So, sovereignty to me is being the choosing one. It is central to much of what we learn in this program." Dr. Alison looks in her rear-view mirror at Sue.

Sam says, "I think it has something, for me, more to do with the coherence vibe."

Jan asks, "Well, OK, Sam, but then, in this context, what do you mean by coherence?"

Sam responds, "So, I mean how we are taught to be mindful of what we are doing and yet also, using the observer, we are taught how to look into the next layer. To see if what we are thinking and what we are doing are going together, or *cohesive*. Or if we are doing something and yet at the same time thinking about doing something else instead."

"OK, I hear you. That makes sense to me. It also sounds like presence," Jan responds, nudging him in his elbow as we were packed in a bit tightly in this here vehicle. Good thing Dr. Alison said it's a really quick ride.

Molly then says, "I know what you mean, Sam. Or even how sometimes in the past, like I would just do something to keep the peace but be hating the task *and* who'd asked me to do it, the whole time. You know what I mean?"

Sam, Jan, Sue, Heather, and I all nod. I see Dr. Alison looking at us all and catching that.

Molly continues, "That is a lack of coherence. So, I find that since getting into the next level of this program, it's much, much easier for me to spot my motives. Or spot my underlying purpose in doing something. And then even lately I have figured out how to make a choice instead of just going along. It's so different for me!"

"Hallelujah!" Exclaims Dr. Alison, laughing.

I notice we're now pulling up to a house with dramatic lighting and Greek columns. The rest of our crew is all standing there, save for Laura.

We all get out of Dr. Alison's car and as a group gather around in front of the door. Laura walks up, just in time, with some fast food from the kabob place next door, attempting to woof it down.

"Laura, you don't have to hurry eating, no worries, " Dr. Alison says, laughing. "Why don't you, Laura, go on inside and eat right there in the entry way? There are a bunch of chairs there. And I'll get set up, so the rest of you take your shoes off right as we go in, please, and follow me straight back and to the left to the green room. We're going to be in the Brigit room for your first night of training."

So, we all follow her instructions. Eventually we settle down in the room. Dr. Alison hands out the manuals for that night but asks us not to open them.

"If anyone wants some tea, the kitchen is downstairs and you can help yourselves, just please be sure to clean up after yourselves. I'm going to go get the attunement room ready. We'll be starting in approximately ten minutes."

A few of us went downstairs to get tea. As we were selecting our flavors and the kettle was on, Sue picked up on the conversation we'd been having, "I have been there where I am almost ready to make a new choice that's me making progress and then I stop myself and question, well if I change right now who am I going to be then? Like what'll I have to give up? What'll I have to do that I'll not want to do? That's why I hesitated so long before finally filing for divorce."

Tiya, who'd joined us downstairs to get tea, joined in on our conversation, which I was happy to see. "What if the certainty about who You're going to become isn't important? Isn't that what Dr. Alison has called a trap of the ego-mind?"

"I guess, yes," I responded. "If everything is running smoothly, I suppose, theoretically, it wouldn't matter if I knew." Hmmm. Interesting.

Sheila too, was with us in the kitchen, as was Heather.

Sheila said, "For me it is like when Dr. Alison said that coherence within our actions is like having a strip of double-sided tape going up through our spinal column. It is like all of you is attracting in the same way. And then you have gotten to a stage with that, being so aligned that even saying well who am I going to be if I make this choice or shift doesn't exist at all because You're not fractured. So, you are not attracting stuff you don't want so you don't need to worry about who You're going to be. So, it's like the optimal state. All good, no worries kind of a thing."

The kettle boiled and we all were in silence as we poured the water into our tea cups. We then wiped up around us and made sure the empty tea envelopes were all in the right recycling bin. As we made our way back up the small, steep staircase, single file, I thought out loud, "Oh yeah, she'd said how people over-identify with all of this external stuff, and identity level self first, rather than going inside first. How instead we can be focusing and seeing how we feel about choosing something. And if we can feel that still small uplift inside to then choose *that*. Like being true to ourselves, right, but more so, understanding what we really desire, and learning to listen to ourselves, rather than outside influences."

"Right," said Tiya.

We got back to the Brigit room and settled in a bit. Tiya spoke up again, "The sense of a new model is needed. Like more than a modern-day female monk nurturing and hugging everyone, as beloved as that hugging monk is, or Mother Theresa doing nurturance. And then we have Maha Kali who is more like flashing lightning. But what if a new model is needed for modern female teachers?"

I found this compelling. I always dug when Tiya spoke up. That's why I wished she would do it more often. I should tell her that. OK. "Tiya, I always dig when you speak up. I wish you'd do it more. So, yeah, with what you just said, what about being an empowered person, or like in Dr. Alison's case a female spiritual teacher, guide, mentor or warrioress, or whatever? What if this new model of sitting in your sovereignty doesn't require over-giving, over-nurturing, or giving away quite so much? And that it doesn't involve fighting so hard for the feminine voice to be heard, coming at it from a place of oppression that we war against. Instead, if there wasn't something to fight against, then the fighting wouldn't be there. So, what if what she's been saying about how we're moving into a new time involves taking our seat of sovereignty means I am—we all are—safe going within to listen that voice, and then using it?" I leaned back in my seat and took a long sip of tea.

Huh. Wow. Dr. Alison had said I was almost there, to clarity, around making my "big choice." Maybe I am.

Jan pulled me out of my reverie, by saying, "There is a new way of being on the spiritual path, when applied to working with magic, or spiritual stuff or metaphysical stuff. The automatic shrinking back from that and maybe going into shame or hiding, or 'being in the closet, spiritually.' I'm done with that. My family knows I'm done with that, and I'm—we're all—moving on from that with, nowadays, surprising ease. I know my husband loves how much easier I've become, like when we have conversations. I listen more now and am more patient."

"Yeah, my husband too, he loves what I've gained from working with Dr. Alison. He's like grateful I'm working with her. He says that a lot. He even attributes his new business in a way, to my being in this program," Sheila said, smiling.

"Hey," Sam said, "Do you remember when Dr. Alison shared afterwards on one of our calls when COVID-19 was really ramping up, how she was actually crying about how much suffering humanity was going through. I think a lot of us were feeling really overwhelmed but then of course she actually did something about it. She said she is really impatient about suffering, like how can we do this stuff with her and get it all going where it could make it easier for everyone to get free? I love it too when they say that in the monthly free-call introduction. It's part of why I'm here." Sam finished what he was saying, and looked up, because Dr. Alison was standing in the doorway.

"Well, what do you all feel? Are you ready to begin?"

A chorus of "sure" and "yeses" ensued.

"OK, so we're going to step back outside to the front stoop, so I can sage you. I can't do that inside here."

So, everyone got up and walked back out to the entry way. Some people put their shoes on, while others went out in their socks.

On the doorstep stood Dr. Alison, holding a bowl with some burning sage. We all followed her motioning to stand over by the rose bush and wait our turns. She starts with Sam. "Sam, can you please step up right here, in front of me and face me, holding your arms out, perpendicular to your torso? I'll tap you on your right shoulder to then turn around so I can literally get your back, OK? And once each of you are done, you can return to the Brigit room, and open your manuals and begin reading, OK?" Sam nods and steps up and follows her directions to a tee.

Then, as we all knew to remain silent, she cleared each of us with the sage, even including under the bottoms of our feet. Murmers of, "Ooh I can see you have had a big heart opening" or "Yes there has been some clearing in your second chakra" or "nice grounding" as she gave each of us the once over with her critical healer's eye, looking at our energy systems and doubtless also performing upgrades during the cleansing as well. Like someone said earlier, "It's like that around here."

As I walked back in, I really took in the place. It was a dramatically lit hallway leading to a series of doors. One door was open, the room was lavender purple. Then another, and that room was totally full of crimson red. Long canvasses of goddesses in full vibrant colors lined the walls in the hall. When I re-entered the Brigit room, I noticed that what we had for chairs were without legs, comfy floor-backrest seats. And we also had a supply of blankets if we wanted them.

There was a mirror over the mantle of the fireplace on the back wall, and floor to ceiling windows with sunlight slanting in on the front wall, behind what appeared to be an altar. I wondered how old this building was. It seemed like at least 100 years. Palpable sacred energy vibes suffused the place. We looked around and at each other and each chose a seat. Some of us chose to sit in new seats than what we had been in when we first came in and hadn't really paid much attention.

"OK, so let's start right away with your first attunement. You are going to get two tonight. This is a sacred process," she said, "so please refrain from too much talking once you are seated here, in the teaching room, both before and after you receive your attunement. Quietly read your manuals and wait to be called by the singing bowl to receive your attunement. You can choose who goes when, or in what order. Once you come up the stairs the first door on the right is the attunement room. There is a bathroom halfway up the stairs if you need to use it. Please don't speak with me during the process, when you enter the room, and leave quietly so that the high level of energy can be maintained throughout. OK, here we go! I'll see the first person in two minutes." And she walked out of the room.

I looked down at the manuals for us to begin to read. We looked at them and began to read them. Someone started to check their phone and then we heard a loud, really deep humming sound. Later I found out it was an enormous crystal singing bowl. Dr. Alison was playing it in the attunement room upstairs. She later told us it was for the fifth chakra. And come to think of it, the attunement room was decorated all in blues.

So, I asked, ever the helper and project manager, "Who wants to go first?" And Tiya stood up. Wow. Each one left the room and came back. I had butterflies in my stomach. What could I expect? What is an attunement anyway? People I know who had received their Reiki instruction online or with other instructors in person had told me that it was no big deal, that it just gave you the authority to practice on yourself or on other people. I was really new to all this. Except for receiving energy medicine directly from Dr. Alison as part of my participation in this program. I was excited to be stepping into this!

My turn. I am last. Ugh, I am so nervous. I walk out of the room and up some winding grand staircase, to the top, the first door on the right she'd said. The door is white; they all are. I open it. The room is decorated in ocean colors, and there is Dr. Alison playing the huge white frosted crystal singing bowl. She looks up and smiles at me.

Take a seat she says. And I sit on the treatment table, feet dangling over the side. Butterflies going crazy. And she bows in namaste to me, and then she begins the secret transmission of the attunement. I close my eyes as she asked me to and listen and sense. I hear her wristlets and bracelets clacking over my head. It is very close, and my spine suddenly straightens and I begin to feel energy coming down into my body through the crown of my head. A kind of gold color washes through my mind and I can see other colors behind my eyelids. What is happening? Then my hands and feet start to get very hot. There is more to it, but I'm floating. Dr. Alison laughs, as she tells me we are complete. And it was finished. We bow to each other, hands folded at the heart.

"I'll meet you all downstairs in the teaching room in about ten minutes, Maggie, as I need to ground first after all those attunements" as she smiles, nodding at me as I then turn and exit.

Later, she did tell me that she had been delighted to see how hot my hands were getting during the attunement. That it showed I would be able to work with the energy very well when giving treatments.

And I walk out knowing I have just received some sort of empowerment. I can still see gold in the air around me. What just happened?

Taking my seat in the circle I look around and several of our group are lying on their stomachs on the rich carpet, reading their manuals. Tiya has opened the window and is standing out on the porch in the late sunshine. I know we are not supposed to talk but I feel like I need some grounding. Did anyone else feel that shift?

As one, Tiya and I turn to each other and meet eyes. Somehow, we know each has agreed to speak and I step out on the porch with her and we say in unison, "How was that for you"? She shares her experience of seeing colors and also experiencing what she thinks could be a past life. Arabella joins us. We hear the front door's bells clang. Dr. Alison must be going outside to ground.

Arabella asks, "Did any of you see lights and colors?"

We each share what we saw along with our appreciation of the mystery of these attunements. None of us expected something so powerful or shifting. Dr. Alison had warned us. I guess this is what she meant.

"Oh my god, and this was just the first one!" Tiya said.

"Yeah, we have one more tonight and two more tomorrow. How much more higher, lighter and accelerated will my progress be and after this?" I ask, with perceptible glee in my voice.

"But that is her secret plan is it not?" Tiya asked.

"What do you mean?" Arabella.

"Well, remember when she said she decided to help after she'd originally gone into politics to help protect the Earth, and instead saw that it was more functional working to evolve the world by getting people freer by working with their consciousnesses, and then this upliftment would benefit humanity and the Earth? That's why she created the Vibrational UPgrade System."

"Sure, I remember that. Someone asked her why she does what she does, and she shared that motivation and love for people and the planet . . . she wanted to bring more joy to the world—more healthy life-force. So, both humanity and the planet could shift. I think it was something like that," I said.

Tiya immediately responded without missing a beat, "I can see how if all of us could wield that kind of light she has . . . ."

I still wanted to talk more about what I'd experienced. "Whew that was intense for me. At one point I thought the top of my head would pop and then suddenly all the energy whooshed back down through my toes and I felt this total calm."

We heard the room door opening inside and scurried back in so we were not caught talking. What is it about how we treat teachers that sometimes we feel like naughty children?

Dr. Alison took a seat in the circle. Looking around she said that we were all glowing. It was true that we all were.

"So, you all, please keep in mind that these ancient sacred teachings and power mysteries were never written down in the beginning days. This was all orally transmitted. Like the symbols you'll be taught at the second level used to have to be memorized overnight and the papers burned. So, the focus here is on the attunements and a few key secrets.

"When dealing in ancient power mysteries an initiate does not just learn new ideas as a student, that 'information only' gig, but is thrown into the experience of the mysteries in real day to day living, as we have done here, within the Mastermind program overall, being on this retreat going to the sacred spots we're going to out on the land, this training and especially, these attunements. It's also why we started off with you receiving attunements without even knowing anything. This is so that *you will have more ability* to truly *master* in your lives these ancient power mysteries, and then be able to be better utilized in Service to help the lives of others."

Dr. Alison paused and looked around at each of us.

"I've added to my original level I manual, which you'll be able to see from the differences in the font. My original manual, being so close to the first person in the West to be able to share these teachings, is in 1950's typewriter font. Here, let's open up to the first page."

She walked us through some of the more esoteric points in the manual, including an explanation of what an attunement does (but *not* what's done in it, that was key, she said, for the Master's level) and asked for questions. So, the people who either were more able to follow along and wanted to ask questions for more information did. And then those who needed to clarify some of the material—well she did that too. As Dr. Alison slowly explained this stuff, we all took notes. Although, seriously, some of us were really spaced out.

We were given time for a bio break where some went and made themselves some tea to stay awake, others to the WC. Somehow for a couple of us the massive amounts of the high energy influx was making us sleepy. Actually, as we found out in the next teaching session, as the energy dislodges entrenched density into the system and it's free-floating as it makes it way up and out, feeling a bit sleepy isn't unheard of after such a strong energy experience, especially when there's more distance from how we are on a daily basis, vibrationally, to how high these attunements are.

We learned more as we continued through this first day's manual. Dr. Alison told us we'd get a new one tomorrow, but that we'd want to have today's with us again tomorrow. She suggested that we take some time in the morning—our itinerary was planned for that space—to review today's manual, "Because this information will appear a bit different for you, after a good night's sleep, where

You're integrating these attunements." That way, we'd be ready to ask whatever other questions we had, tomorrow.

Then it was time for the second attunement. Same deal; we wait for the humming of the singing bowl. Again, the sound reverberates through the woodwork and ceiling of the house. I decide I am going to be a bit braver this time and I tell my group of initiates that I would like to go third. "Cool, thumbs up, OK no problem, and go for it" are a few responses. I feel supported and safe with these women (and a man).

OK my turn again. Will it be the same I wonder? What happens in a second attunement? Each one is meant to be equal in power, although Dr. Alison told us her opinion from what she's observed over the years, is that there are certain ones we're likely to feel more. So, yeah, each attunement is equal to about eight full ones on one energy medicine session. And with the power that Dr. Alison has I am appreciating that is life-changing in such a short period of time. As I mount the stairs, I think back to walking the land and how juiced my body felt after that. What is this next blast going to accomplish?

And I decide to relax and trust the process. Not my usual jam but it feels safe here. Seeing Dr. Alison in this very loving and magical setting is reminding me of being a kid, being safe and on an adventure. It reminds me of love and stuffed animals and being cared for. Weird, I think to myself. All that from energy. Well, it's likely it's also due to the person transmitting it, I think.

I sit down on the table again. And I close my eyes. I pay a bit closer attention this time. I was both wanting to relax and trust yet also I was finding my attention field strangely heightened. Again Dr. Alison looks like she is covered in golden light. Is it the bulbs in this room? It didn't look like this when I first walked in. Oh well.

Closing my eyes again I see in my mind a great jeweled temple. I seem to hear a sistrum and some kind of bell. I smell copal incense, or cloves and frankincense—how do I know those smells? There hadn't been anything burning when I came in the room. I hear the blessing in that special breath she seems to be doing again—reminding me of a dragon's fire—then my lower body begins to tingle and my knees go cold. My heart suddenly feels light and then I see blue lights inside my eyes up around my forehead level. Wild. And it is done.

When I open my eyes and see Dr. Alison smiling at me, I am filled with some sort of gratitude. Like finding something you thought you had lost and then getting to take it home. "You had a beautiful heart opening there. Good receiving." We mutually bow and I go out and down the stairs in a sort of embodied trance. My body feels at once more my own and at the same time completely different than when I came up here today. Nobody had prepared me for energy medicine to be this powerful. I am excited to learn more.

Female Teacher—Authentic Presence

Student: Powerful Authentic Presence is a hallmark of the female spiritual teacher. The purification of years of study, practice, and personal cultivation must result in an alteration of vibration such that it is usually palpably obvious at which level the teacher is operating.

I see you embodying and honoring this self, while it is modeled by you, Dr. Alison and also cherished in all of us, by you, our teacher.

One meaning and outcome I've gotten out of your training and clearings is to get us to be in constant contact with the Observer, so at all times we're now being able to choose awareness, joy, or another desired experience.

AJK: Yes, that's the very design behind Vibrational UPgrade System!

Student: Judy Garland said it's better to be a first-rate version of yourself, not a second-rate version of someone else.

What is your definition of authenticity—and presence? And why is it important? If it is?

AJK: I remember when I came back from Asia and I started to see the trends here in the United States about people talking about authenticity. I have no ability to be other than authentic. So, I didn't understand it at first. Where I have gone in understanding what people mean by that, when they have said it to me in order for me to be able to serve them, and I've leaned into the energy of what they're asking for, what I understand is that if you even have to talk about authenticity you come from a world of lying to and hiding from yourself.

I remember a really strong awareness I had that's related here. It's also what leads to, in part, where I said in my second book, I had been seeing so much that the throat chakra is becoming the one to focus on. In part, as the one directly north of the heart, and remember, I've come to call this 'the creators channel?' 4th to 5th?

Yes, because of the 5th chakra containing the aspects of courage to choose, and choices being made from the throat chakra, this includes also seeing possibilities that you have loads of choice rather than limitations mostly, where your neck ends up stiff from feeling limited in choices? These are the higher levels to the throat chakra. I feel like the throat chakra has come on board now, in such a way that has me calling it the second power center now. Where it always traditionally has been the solar plexus as the sole power center.

I've noticed that I used to tend to diminish the communication aspects and the communication blocks that people come in with on the throat chakra, that first level to it, because I've been focusing on that higher level of the throat chakra, since around 2015. Yet that communication element of it affects the higher aspects of courage, choice, and possibilities perceived and chosen, becoming more accessible. Like all the communication aspects need to be more activated, to support the higher level—where the choices come in—of the 5th.

It was funny because I was working with a Dutch married couple weekly, each of them. They were also regular students of my weekly yoga and meditation class too; that's how I'd met them. I said this to them, "Does it strike you that people in America say, 'Yeah, let's have dinner sometime or yeah, let's get together' a lot but they don't mean it?" Again, tuning in to this whole authenticity trend and why people were speaking so much to it and what was actually behind it. Now this is a Dutch couple who has lived in America for decades. They both came over as adults in their 30s or early 40s. "Yeah so Americans tend to not tell the truth as much," was their response. I was flabbergasted!

I remember saying my version of that about the Chinese culture. I had never heard that said about Americans. Especially considering my experience when Americans had been contrasted to the Chinese culture, while living and working in Taiwan. Americans, there, are in contrast and by the Chinese, considered direct and honest. I was given this perception over and over again, from my experience as an expat living over there and my conversations as a result of interacting with expats from around the world, and the local Chinese.

However, where I've gotten to with this is that I do find that people feel obligated to say something nice. As if to close an interaction, yet with something that may not be true. There is this level of "polite society", and I know America is not the only one with it. We are operating in circles of polite society where you are required, or You're obligated. All of that is throat chakra related by the way. To interact in a certain way whether it's true or not so that you can maintain an appearance of being a certain way. That was eye opening for me.

On another note, when we talk about the hiding aspect that's the opposite of authenticity, relating back to the conversation we had about wholeness. If I'm not hiding or a trauma is not tucked in my root chakra so it's the right glute, or butt cheek, that has its chronic pain or the sciatica is starting to hurt, or lower back sacral area . . . I don't have a trauma stuffed down there so my body isn't tight and it's disease free. Or I don't have a whole level of "I'm not OK with this" stuffed down while I proceed to do the think I'm not OK with.

Once a person moves beyond that all, and comes into clarity and alignment within themselves, that cohesiveness then creates the emanation of coherence where there's no space for authenticity to even be a question. It just is. I believe what people are asking for with "becoming more authentic" was how do I become *that*? That level of alignment within myself, so that my field is coherent.

Student: Yeah, that's really important. That's sovereignty to me. Sovereignty is that aspect of continuing to maintain connection to the neutral observer and the presence of reality of choice in a situation. It is also allowing or being present to the fact that that is an entitlement to every being. The description of the world, I think Joseph Campbell, talks about something about it. The shared agreements between people in cultures and all that.

AJK: Yes. I think so, in his *Power of Myth*. And Carl Jung spoke about that too. It's a part of his collective unconscious theory.

Student: The description of the world it really is like what you were talking about when you were talking about the A-frame framework and renovating it, downsizing, or rightsizing or dismantling it a little bit and coming in with a new way—because of these times it's causing us to. It would be really useful because a lot of people are globbing on to the whole ascension this and that. Instead of having a lofty tactical conversation about something that can actually be done.

AJK: Yes. For me, it's not about the channeled information only, and how cool that is to be able to gain that information—if it can even be trusted. Always, always it's about the application of the information to improve your life, for genuine behavioral change.

Like after assessing intuitive information for its ring of truth, or alignment, *always* it's then the *application* of it within your life to make the requisite changes so that your life evolves and you live up to more of your potential within the vast possibilities that are opening up for us now as we shift from the old paradigm to the new.

Student: So, OK, let's talk about that practical information. I know that when I've worked with other spiritual teachers, it turns out that all of a sudden there is a four-hour conversation every time we meet about how things are on Lyra or Sirius. Indeed, that's the same as like if I'm talking to a scientist and he or she doesn't want to figure out how to solve world hunger, but they want to figure out how to get to the moon and live there. There is something about being grounded. To me that's spiritual maturity.

AJK: I don't think that's spiritual maturity. Nor would I call that a spiritual teacher.

Student: No? Then what is it?

AJK: It's a necessity. It is an absolute necessity. While I hear you framing it from your perspective of being spiritual maturity, I'm going to be so bold as to say, I'm one of the few on the spiritual path as a spiritual teacher talking about what I talk about, and I don't use the word, "accession." I don't even talk about Atlantis much. I don't talk about galaxies or star gates as much as I say "this is the influence of the planets on us on earth" in order to thrive in our bodies on planet Earth. I'm by no means faulting those who do, I've attended some of their events, when I feel as if the person has some element of their channeling that resonates within me in such a way that my consciousness flags it intuitively as something that can first be *trusted as clear perception free of projection*, then be applied to help people better understand how to live their best life ever, here, now, while also serving others by being lighter.

I find with the old school spiritual people who will meditate or connect in with their archangels it's to feel that unconditional love that they haven't experienced in their life while in their bodies or they don't feel now, so they leave to connect in with something that feels like more towards home like, hearth and home types of feelings, like the unconditional love. Then there is also just the fascination with the intellect when it's not properly reined in that I've seen people have applied to the metaphysical world when they start learning about Lyra and Sirius and Orion and ancient Egypt.

All of these fascinating topics that you chew over as if its raw meat, but if you don't let it impact your life and improve it in any way, what's the point? It's just as if it's intellectually fodder and it remains "out there." That's a comfort zone for people because they're like *visiting* with the higher vibrations, but then they don't have to face themselves and they don't have to go within and do the work. When it's used in this way, I find it's used as an excuse. You get it, by now, yes?

Student: What I love about some of the stuff you talk about a lot it's exactly what you just said. It's allowing people to thrive as human beings on planet Earth.

AJK: With the connection to the divine. In their sovereignty throne, as a bridge between heaven on Earth, but *on* Earth. Bringing the higher vibrations *down*, to benefit earth and the rest of humanity. That's THE key!

CHAPTER 8

Initiations in Life

SUNDAY NIGHT

Early Sunday night, after our first round of attunements, and training is complete, Dr. Alison asks us if we want to go for fish and chips together. "The best fish and chips in town. In fact, voted in the top 10 of fish and chips shops in the UK most years. And going at this for over a hundred years. Who's in?"

We all totally want to go and seem to have a ton of energy all of a sudden.

So, some walk that short distance, while others wait while Dr. Alison closes up and then drives the rest of us. We all get there at the same time.

We stand in the queue reading up on the menu board. Dr. Alison points to the fish filets already in the hot window and says, "The servings here are huge. I know many of you are likely ravaged. Please let yourselves eat what your body wants. It's likely your food cravings will be different for the rest of this retreat. Your body may require more carbs, so if that's not your norm, please do honor your bodies. You're processing a whole lot of energy, and that requires energy. So, no worries, please, OK? Let this, instead of being a cheat meal as it is for me 'cuz of the fried breading and chips (fries), be a cheat week, if you need, OK?"

We all seem to be both relieved and yet a bit concerned by that update.

"No worries, you all. Just be present, and if your body tomorrow afternoon wants something You're not used to eating, just let yourself. I don't mean as a vegetarian suddenly eat a cow, but you know what I mean, right?"

"Sure. All good," Sam places his hand on Dr. Alison's arm reassuringly.

"And, well, I am surprised, but I do want a hunk of protein right now," Arabella said, coming up on the other side of Dr. Alison.

"Yep. That's along the lines of what I mean."

"Hey what's a 'faggot'?" Sam asks, looking up at the menu board.

Dr. Alison laughs, saying, "I had the same reaction when I first came in here. I had to ask—it's offal, like the intestines etc. It's an old Black Country dish from up in northern England."

"Oh, OK."

We all line up and give our orders. Then Dr. Alison suggests we go into the room where the big tables are by the fireplace. We all agree and follow. It's pretty natural, how we all just flow together. There was no weirdness about who sits where on the long table, we all just sat down.

"Hey if you have to go to the bathroom, they're up those cool stairs," Dr. Alison says, pointing to a really tiny, tightly fitted stone staircase.

"This place just had its 110th anniversary I think last year. And yes, it's an old building. Cool, huh? There's an outdoor garden or patio area if you all wanna walk around a bit.

So, some of us get up and do that, while others stay seated.

Jan moves closer to Dr. Alison. She begins talking with Dr. Alison in a rather low voice. Dr. Alison listens, responds briefly and then excuses herself. She walks towards the front of the restaurant, it seems.

We begin to chit chat about what we're noticing on the walls, and the cool knick knacks over the fireplace. Dr. Alison returns with a ginger beer and the server is right behind her with some of our food.

"I'll go get the girls out on the patio," I volunteer.

So, I do. When I get out there, they're all in what looks like an intense conversation. "Hey you guys, food's here."

They all turn to look at me, "Thanks, Maggie," and make a bee line for the door.

"Gawd I'm starving!" Molly says as she whips by me.

I laugh and follow Molly, while the rest come in after me.

"Hey, you guys will you pass me the malt vinegar please? It's the only reason why I eat the chips with the fish, is for the malt vinegar," Dr. Alison laughs.

Sheila asks, as she passes it down, "Is that really good? I've never had it before?"

"There's no purpose in eating fish and chips if you don't have malt vinegar, in my opinion. It's like a tradition for a reason—one of the good ones. You know?" Dr. Alison responds.

"Holy shit that fish is huge!" Sue blurts out as the server returns with the remaining meals.

Dr. Alison looks up and laughs, nodding with a wide grin, as she looks like she's emptying the entire contents of the malt vinegar bottle onto her fish and chips.

"Hey, you guys may need to reach to that table next to us and grab that bottle of malt vinegar, this one is almost out," Dr. Alison says.

Jan reaches over and grabs it and begins to do much the same as what Dr. Alison just finished doing.

So, we all begin to happily dig in, talking at times with our mouths full, while making sure to cover our mouths when laughing. And there was a lot of that.

Suddenly, we are all slowing down, realizing the near empty plates in front of each of us.

Dr. Alison gets up and returns with what looks like five more ginger beers. They're in really small brown bottles.

"I love this stuff! It's one of my favorite drinks I get access to whenever here. They're nonalcoholic even though the word 'beer' is attached to 'ginger.' Does anyone want one?" Dr. Alison offers out her right hand holding three.

Sure! Myself, Sue, and Heather all reach for one. Dr. Alison then puts down her ginger beer and reaches in the pockets of her big warm wool sweater and pull out two more.

"Anyone else?" Sam and Jan both say yes.

"Anyone else?" No one else, no.

The others were having either warm teas or ciders.

Jan clears her throat and asks, "Dr. Alison, do you have any suggestions on how to manage the need for attention?"

Dr. Alison looks up and some look crosses over her face I can't quite read. She shifts in her posture, takes a drink of her ginger beer, and says, "Jan, why don't we go outside to the garden patio area?"

"Ok."

"Anyone else who wants to be in on this conversation is welcome to ʼr. Alison says as she gets up.

ʼe, and Molly do. As do I.

FEMALE TEACHER—TRUST SOURCE AND PROCESS

So, once we're outside, Dr. Alison says, "So, I can go about answering this in a couple of different ways. Let's go this direction, first, it feels like it'll be the most helpful." She takes a swig of her ginger beer, looking really satisfied, pauses and then begins, "You know how I've repeatedly spoken about how from ages zero to two we feel and think what our parents do? That there's no separation between us of their emotions, feelings, thoughts with ours? How we feel what they feel and don't know them to be not ours, up until age two?"

I nod, while Jan and the rest say, "Yes," out loud.

"Well, so then at the terrible two's stage we start going. 'No, no!' And that's the beginning of the separation. Where we're beginning to form into our own separate ego-identity, and beginning our own personality development?"

"Yes," I say, along with everyone else, but Sue, who nods.

"So, this is a combination of what I learned in Western developmental psychology and then contrasted it with what I knew from meditation and the formation of our ego-minds, neurology, and then habituated thinking patterns. Then my training with the chakras also fed into this. Meaning to say, it seems well-informed," Dr. Alison laughs at herself.

"So, coming into play from ages two to eight is when we sit there, we look around and we ask, OK, how do we do this thing on planet Earth?' In a sense. So, if this is when we're trying to understand how to do life, we'll have something like—let's take it from a woman's perspective—let's say that she grew up with, um, her parents really busy working and they didn't spend a lot of time at home with her and she didn't have a nanny. You with me so far?"

Dr. Alison looks at us, "I know it's been a full-on retreat, the land and all its input, and then being here in the heart chakra of the planet, where the consciousness that needs most to rise to the surface does, and then your trainings and those attunements."

"Yeah, I'm following," Jan says and the rest of us nod.

"OK, cool. So, in this example, this girl comes home after school and gets her own snacks, does her own homework, very disciplined, very good girl. Yet she felt like there was something wrong with her because her parents weren't spending a lot of time at home. And so, she had that locked into her subconscious. Because it was in the formative, developmental years, and with that childlike logic of figuring out how to do life on planet Earth, her child-like conclusion *because she is a child* is: 'this is how life is on the planet. I don't get a lot of attention. People aren't around me a lot of the time.' Right?"

Dr. Alison checks in with us again and we nod.

"Jesus, that's the exact way it was for me growing up," Jan nearly whispers that.

Dr. Alison looks over at her and says, "Well you should know by now my examples aren't just pulled out of thin air, but out of you all, yes?" She has this twinkle in her eye as if teasing Jan.

Jan shifts on her feet and shakes her head and says, "Yeah."

"So, when I'm doing this clearing work later on with adults, I see so much of the time, this childlike, beautiful, sweet logic. That's not like advanced *logic,* but it is childlike logic, and you can see how 1 + 1 added up to 2, when the child was attempting to understand what it takes to live on planet Earth, and how it is within their family, school, etc. It's so sweet! And so those subconscious conclusions they're left there. Those are wired into the subconscious and then the unconscious becomes involved, because that's where the conclusions reside where we're unconscious about our beliefs that are the undercurrent to why we act the way we do, choose what we do and n't choose what we don't.

"And then add to that any traumas we experience and those are wired into—stuffed down into—the subconscious. It's buried. We can't feel them. But when the childlike logic has those unconscious conclusions and then they either came in because of trauma or there are traumas related to that on top of that, these are really much more stubborn behavioral patterns, because there's a lot more wiring to undo.

"And those two elements together—that the incoming trauma is both new and it's shocking to the ego-mind—then your ego-mind can't simply go into, 'Oh, what is this coming in? Let me find a label for it,' because it's too much traumatizing, energetic, shock that in that moment, the ego mind cannot do its function. So, we shove that perception of the trauma down into our subconscious, and the ensuing emotions and illogical but oh so limiting unconscious beliefs that result from that get deposited into the body, relevant to the chakra that that trauma is related to. So, if it's sexual abuse, for example, it's the root and typically the sacral too. In this case let's just stay with the root, because the underlying right of the root chakra is that "I have the right to be here." And thus, the feeling safe in one's body corresponds to this innate right, or belief, to the root chakra, and due to the trauma, one does not feel safe to be here, so all sorts of blockages at the physical, emotional, mental, and spiritual level that correspond to the root chakra's aspects have some blockage. Some of the other aspects to the root chakra are around not fitting in, abandonment, and fear of rejection.

"So, we'd have a propensity based on all that I just mentioned—and more—that with at least 85 percent, of our daily choices being made from the unconscious and subconscious, to perpetuate this existence, based on that childhood trauma and those childlike conclusions, in the formative years, from what they experienced. Not that we hear those subconscious and unconscious thoughts like we can of the conscious mind. Rather, at that level it's robotic and unconscious—'un' meaning *not* consciously heard—and subconscious—'sub' meaning *under* the conscious mind, so not consciously heard. So, it's like driving. Once you master any skill, you don't say, put the car in reverse, take foot off brake, put foot on gas. No. You don't do it anymore. It's relegated back to the subconscious.

"Yet our daily choices in life are made also that robotically, or unconsciously or subconsciously 85 percent of the time, at least. That's the cause for energy medicine clearings and activations. To get at those, to *break* the mind-body connection so that automation stops—so the triggers cease—and then the consciousness gets freed up, that's when new behavior genuinely begins to become available. We can then have access to that fresh vital life force energy and become more conscious. Right? You're still with me?"

Jan says, "Yep. I think so."

The rest of us also say yes out loud.

"Excellent. And by now, I would expect this to all be repetition, frankly. So, if we're working on our conscious mind with that form of applied mindfulness I teach to come in after the clearings and activations, after we're able to have that scissors that comes in and cuts that automatic trigger, and we've made the progress to understanding our capacities to work with our conscious mind, so we know we're *not* our thoughts and embody that in action, that is the first level of liberation.

"And then we move into the second level of liberation: 'Oh my God, I not only am not my thoughts, I can *question* my thoughts! I don't have to believe every thought my ego-mind pumps out, just because it has a thought!' Even there is a propensity for the thoughts you're fielding with mindfulness. You're now observing the habitual storylines from all of the buried unconscious and subconscious, now made conscious. And so that's when the energy medicine comes in *again*. To create even more detachment at that point from the old storylines. That's why I have developed Vibrational UPgrade System as a coupling of energy, medicine, *and* mindfulness, but *this specific form of mindfulness*. Not just being present as you eat an apple, and call that mindfulness, and think you've got it.

"So, if we only do the clearings and the activations, meaning we only do the energy medicine, we don't have the integrated behavioral change. You need, on a daily basis in your daily lives, this mindfulness because the mindfulness is where the person takes over ownership—where you take over ownership, and soon where *You're* going to be guiding *your* clients to take over ownership—recognizing the pattern that's been released by the energy medicine, making sure that automatic mind-body connection is cut, so then the training wheels can eventually come completely off, with this level of mindfulness.

"Meaning so you've had the clearings and activations of the positive around why at a young age you concluded that you don't get a lot of attention. And then as a result, as we unravel that ball of yarn of what I call the family of entangled beliefs within a core, or foundational behavioral pattern, you also have cleared those behavioral compensatory patterns that you've engaged in to get attention, like passive aggressive manipulation, where, for example, you've learned to get upset so that people will pay attention to you, where you've learned to create drama so people will pay attention to you. So, the entire A-frame that frames that family of entangled beliefs, like a ball of yarn, can finally come tumbling down, and you are trigger less, eventually, within a group dynamic where you don't have all these odd coping behaviors in order to ensure you get attention. Or where you no longer just have yourself fade into the background, when in group dynamics, which is another direction that child could've taken her conclusions from that environment in her formative years.

ke sense?"

..ᵒ silent for a moment. I say, "Yes," as do the others.

"Where, ultimately, I'm working to get each of you to, is so that you can do this and then escort your clients to be able to do this. Where you, or they, can see they're not triggered, within a context where they once typically were. And yet, they can also see the thought coming into the ego-mind where it's just habitual momentum, say within a group dynamic, that "OK, this is where I go weird." Yet, they have more choice now how to not just react, but *respond*, understanding that they have that choice to make new and different choices about how to not be weird in that dynamic. And that they haven't failed, just because the ego-mind still had the thought. The trigger is gone; it's no longer automatic.

"Choice now resides, where you've become conscious. The energy medicine hasn't failed just because that thought came in after you've received a clearing on it. That 'this will never change,' or 'I'm stuck with this habit' or 'the pattern isn't accurate', just because the ego-mind is pumping out the thought still. It's winding down its momentum! But You're able to see it now, and as a result, have a choice of how to respond.

"Without that combination, the grounded, rooted, structural behavioral changes that affect your daily life just don't anchor and don't happen. And then also a person can just end up in the head, with their storylines, able to identify and see their storylines, but yet not have radical change. Nor will they have, uh, a body resplendently emanating joy. They have to also have the clearings around *that* repeated thought, replaced with the activation *for the positive behavior,* so they have access not only to a *different* choice, *but to the preferred or optimal one.*

"And this is where You're able to choose what you want, keeping you going in the direction you actually desire. So, much of the time choices are made out of these triggers, these habitual patterns due to having the blocks we've spoken about, that cause you to use your own free will to choose against something. Like making sure you're protecting yourself from something bad happening. In this example, it would actually be protecting yourself against fitting in or being weird within the group dynamic, because it goes against your unconscious beliefs about how life is for you. Out of old wounds, beliefs, karma, conditioning, imprints, ensuing storylines, etc. And that choosing against something is what keeps your life stale and stagnant, not new and exciting.

"We're talking about that kind of automatic choosing machine of the ego-mind when it's not worked with at all. And if you think about it, also, that's why the word 'ego' is put in front of the mind, because it's who your parents have pointed to you and said that she's like this, or who your sisters and brothers and friends have labeled you as. And that locks you down even further into seemingly automatic choosing done as if *for* you, even though it's being done *by* you.

"Yeah. So, it's that choosing mechanism, but it's also the rationalization behind the choices, which you need—rationalization—if You're busy automatically choosing, and it's *against* what *you* really desire—as automatic choosing is, typically.

"So, then you go into rationalizing why, i.e., if in case you need backup, you can say, well, I didn't choose that because in my family, we never do that or whatever. And you're taught that. So, the ego-mind feels as if it has a pass, and has avoided another possible new choice, which it construes as a challenge.

"Or when you're sitting there opening emails from some coach or mentor whose list You're on, and you're reading, seeing what else is possible by seeing testimonials of somebody else who has gotten the kinds of change, like in their business, where they're now doing wnat they love and they're making money—and *you've wanted that*, but you don't take the action to get yourself on the track that person went on who now has that, *when the way is shown right there in front of you*. Because your ego-mind, is pumping out the old storylines, 'Oh, hold on. Um, people around me just aren't that free. I'm supposed to have some kind of restriction or contraction,' Now You're not going to actually hear those words, most likely, right? You just won't choose it.

"So, you choose against that freedom, and against that increased money flow, and against that fulfillment, like your ego-mind talks you out of it, so *you choose against what lights you up*. There, that's a bit more conscious, as you can see, You're wrestling through a decision, or as I say a choice, but when it shows up in that wrestling way, it's feels more like a decision than a choice. But it's still choosing against yourself, abasing yourself and your genuine desires, so that your choosing still is in some form of automatic choosing, because it is locked down into limited possibilities, limited choices, as your storylines tell you, that's the way it is for you.

"And what it feels like, as we step more into becoming co-creators of our lives and recognizing that responsibility coupled with the absolute freedom it is, is what we're meant to be living up to, within this new era—Possibilities and Potential, baby, it's all about that now, breaking out of the old. Because after all, you contain the divine spark within you, You're a child of this universe, and You're meant to live up to that potential within you. And in doing so, you reflect your gratitude to the Source of all life, *for this life*.

"The loving undercurrent to all of life wants only the best for you. Which, interestingly, is a magnetic energy for abundance. *This* is the era of construction, our new paradigm that's coming in now, where we can be—and I would say *need* to be—aligning with the divine within you, and all around you, and that pull of vital life force energy to create a vital life! One that recognizes the loving force in all of life, behind it all. That's my two cents. Now I'm going to go in, say goodnight, and head home. I feel like my bed is calling me and my system wants some rest. Yes? But if you all want, you can stay here and hang."

"I kinda want some space on my own," Jan says.

We all walk back inside. The group who remained at the table looks happily engaged in conversation. Dr. Alison asks who's ready to go, and most everyone gets up. Heather, Sam, Sue, and Arabella choose to stay. So, the rest of us walk out with Dr. Alison, and once outside say goodnight to her. Then a group of us—Jan included—hang out in my room, chatting and goofing off with our new toys we'd bought so far in town—drums, crystals, oracle decks, books, runes—until we're all totally aware we need to go to sleep.

CHAPTER 9
Choosing Joy

Monday day

ANOTHER DAY UP and going in the new normal of this retreat. Get up, upgrade energy, get out on sacred land or to sacred sites, receive blessings, have transformative conversations, laugh. "Oh, my goddess", I heard someone say the other day. Love that.

So, we meet in front of the B & B and mill about chatting while waiting for the driver and Dr. Alison. One is brushing her hair, one is going through his bag looking for something, one is putting on lipstick, one is texting her husband. I feel a bit guilty because I haven't reached out to my husband in the last twenty-four hours. I am just not sure how I feel. As this retreat progresses, I find my needs for companionship being met by those I'm on retreat with. Then I wonder, do I still have a good connection with my spouse?

We don't laugh very much, and everything is a task-based conversation. Up till now I have blamed either him or work or the news . . . anything except taking responsibility for myself perhaps changing into something unrelatable to him. Until working with Dr. Alison and especially now on this retreat, seeing as how this work has all been exponentialized in new and different ways, I didn't know how pretty much physically dead I had felt. Ugh. Now what do I do?

So, anyway. I luck out and end up sitting up front in the car that Dr. Alison is driving. And I am not intending to talk with Dr. Alison about any of my concerns so she can have her space. I don't want to be a hog or one of "those" types of needy students. Dr. Alison points out a hill off to the left that she tells us a story about. Then we continue to drive along, enjoying the sights and chatting about what we're seeing while Dr. Alison tells more stories about the local folklore. It's really mystical stuff that has gone on around here. So, we talk about this cool stuff, going into the mystical more and we're all able to ask questions it feels like we've always wanted to. Even Dr. Alison. Like we can't get enough of it. Wow. I can't remember the last time I felt this, I don't know, in the right place with the right people, feeling the most like me, just being me. Just no *trying*, nothing forced, no way "I had to be."

Suddenly it seems we have arrived at our destination. It had been so fun, all this chit chat about stuff I may have thought about before, but never have had people to talk about with.

I know we are almost there because we have just passed a grove of oaks on the right and I see standing stones near the trees, and all around the rotary (or roundabout as they call it here). There is that energy again. The stone energy seems to snap me back into consciousness again of where I am.

"We're almost there," she says, then turning to me, "and so are you. You are circling in on your decision," as she glances off the road to smile at me. What? I didn't even ask her anything about that! Geez, she's good. Wow.

So, I relax a little bit just to try that out as Dr. Alison doesn't ever seem to worry or flip back and forth between what to decide. And plus, it feels good to be so relaxed, *for god's sake*! Out the window there is a small tavern with some really huge trees around it. Modern homeowners would have cut those down as a risk but these trees and this small wattle and daub plaster and thatch building have obviously stayed side by side quite comfortably for many centuries. Like a married couple, grandparents.

We turn right into a drive and follow it around to a gravel parking lot. There is a big new barn which seems to house a cafe and some restrooms for visitors. There is also a shop, with very magical stained-glass dragons in the window and we lose half the party to that as soon as the doors open.

I look at a beautiful pond surrounded by trees as people start to move back towards the entrance. I see a dragonfly and a frog. I enjoy a quiet moment of natural beauty as I feel the energy of the place. This whole trip has been an eye opener. The place where I bought some milk this morning is older than any of the historic buildings in my neighborhood in Manhattan. And none of the locals seem to understand how quaint it is. For them it is merely normal.

So, I see Dr. Alison coming from across the parking lot. It looks like she went the opposite way from the rest of us. She lets us know she has already done some clearing and preparation for us to be introduced and more accepted on and connected to the land. Oh!

We all stand in a group, quietly centering ourselves, taking our cue both from what Dr. Alison had just said and what she'd taught us to do that first day, while some folks walk by on a tour. Perhaps they are paying attention to where they are walking yet the energy in our intimate group is much different than theirs.

"As you walk down the avenue," she says, "here take these," And she hands each of us one of these cool copper dowsing rods. After we have received them, Dr. Alison tells us they're handmade and that she had them especially made for us to use for our first time here, preparing us more for what we'll eventually be doing if and when we get to the Dragon Master level. She proceeds to explain their history and then shows us with hers how to use them.

"So, this'll help you further learn to embody your intuition. Have your dowsing rods handy so you can use them. See if you can perceive the energy lines and currents now on your own. Then, without the dowsing rods, see if you can feel the purpose of some of the stones and formations we pass by now that your consciousness has been attuned to be able to. At the end of the avenue we'll stop for a bit and form a circle. There are some special things that want to happen while we are here that'll delight you with joy. You'll see."

So, we walk, stepping mindfully. Dr. Alison cautions us about the big piles of cow dung. "I know they look like mud pies and everything looks so much more alive and magical on this land. So, your first instinct is you may want to play with it, but I'm not helping any of you clean up afterwards should you choose to play in shit," she winks, teasing us. "And I know You're paying more attention to speaking with your dowsing rods and the land, but just beware there are piles of cow pies to avoid too."

So, then we all proceed towards the avenue. I let my feeling sense move out a bit past my body, as I learn to work with my dowsing rod, and so I can more easily feel what she's guiding us to sense. I hold my dowsing rod and do as she'd shown us to. That's so cool! Whenever she comes near me, the rods turn away from wherever I'm asking them to take me and show me, and swing towards her. She gets a real kick out of that, like a little girl's mirth. "I guess it's 'cuz I'm voltage, too?"

We cross a small road and walk through a gate. And then she asks us to stop. She takes off her shoes and pulls out some sage and a lighter. "Let's do a clearing of your fields while out here, on the land, in this way with the sage. Your fields are already higher, from all the other sites and the attunements, but let's clear out any excess noise and help the land have that kind of relief, too. That way, you can notice more of what is happening, while also contributing to this sacred, loving land." And she does this for each in turn. And then someone does the sage clearing for her.

I look down "the avenue" and it is a line of massive standing stones. It seems to stretch into the distance, but we are on a slight hill, so I am not sure where exactly it ends. Looking left there seem to be sheep, and also the remains of a stone circle. Somehow, I am not attracted to this one as I was to the one where we went the other day. I keep walking along, and I touch a couple of the stones as I go by.

"This one is warm," says Molly, who is a bit further ahead. She aligns her spine with the rock and seems to not want to move.

Next to her Jan is doing the same. "This is my favorite," Jan says. "This is my stone."

"This one is mine," says Laura, who is doing the same three stones down. "My mind is shut down when I am near this stone. Ah peace. Yes, I'll take it."

Dr. Alison walks by saying, "You all take your time. Feel as many stones as you want so you can discern how they're different. Feel free to spend as much time with the ones that speak the most to you."

I continue to walk through the medium-tall grass. I don't feel I am going to claim any of the stones for myself.

A bit later on, after I'd spent quite a nice amount of time laying down on the grass by a pair of stones, I especially liked how I felt around, Dr. Alison calls us over to the right side of the avenue, next to an especially huge stone. She asks us to form a circle and join hands.

"Ohmmmmm," she begins and by halfway through she ends up with this odd reverberation coming out of her throat. When she'd done, "Would you all do three Ohm's with me please, so we can bring in even more of the sacred, and possibly bless this land?" So, we all do this together. And by the last one, it felt like there were reverberations off of the stones. As we stand the light changes as the sun slants a bit. And a light breeze comes up, rearranging my hair. Am I hearing some sort of singing? Or a buzzing? I sway a little bit.

Dr. Alison says we can drop hands and asks us all to touch the soles of our feet with our hands if we are feeling lightheaded. Or if our shoes aren't easy to take off, she reminds anyone of us who are feeling a sense of spinning, that we can plunk our tailbones down on the ground and touch the copper rods she gave us for dowsing rods to our knees and shins and ankles, to help us stay balanced with the energies.

Then, after a bit, she asks us each to gather back together in a circle and hold hands again, and to say a word that sums up what is our vision or intention for the collective that we'd like to see more of— to speak it into the circle we now were in. Love. Prosperity. Healthy children and healthy body. New job and happy home life. Peace on Earth. One by one people speak theirs. Joy, I say. And we remain in this circle, pretty impressed by the vibes that are coming to us from this exercise. A few people walk by, including the folks who passed us in the parking lot. And a couple people wearing sandals and rainbow knitted sweaters decided to stop and watch us. They looked unsurprised to see a ceremony happening along the way. I feel like someone is playing a drum somewhere a bit far off.

After a minute more, Dr. Alison asks us, "Does anyone want to attempt to describe what You're observing you are feeling in your bodies?"

People report energy surges in their feet and spines. Sheila reports, "I feel I may have been a priestess here in some other life."

"OK," says Dr. Alison.

Tiya speaks up, saying, "Yes, I felt like I could see some sort of a procession, of some sort."

"OK, good," says Dr. Alison.

I reported, once again I have a loud ringing in my ears.

"OK, that's typical, Maggie."

After those who wanted to speak did, we then kept walking down the avenue. I can see now why they call it that. It seems like every time we stop and Dr. Alison asks us to focus in on our experience, that I become more effortlessly aware of things happening around me.

Like now I can fully see into the distance, how the line of stones goes for hundreds of yards. I can see the small grove of oaks that we drove past before reaching the parking lot. And I feel an opening of my mind and my perspective becomes naturally more positive. The energies of this place are for sure doing some sort of work on me.

We reach the very bottom of the avenue, and there is a large stone, sort of shaped like the state of New Jersey. And it is surrounded by cows. I love cows. I respect animals in their own habitats, so I don't go up to them, but I sit down on the grass for a few minutes and watch them munch grass. I see one of our party going up to one of the cows with a handful of grass. She offers it on the flat of her palm, but the cow doesn't take it. There is so much juicy grass all around that I am not surprised.

All of a sudden, I notice that there is laughter. I look over and Dr. Alison is with Sue, Arabella, Laura, and Sam. They're opposite the big New Jersey shaped stone at one just as big and they're all looking at a cow and the cow is looking at Sheila. I don't know what they're laughing at.

A few others are lying down in the grass on their backs, looking up at the sky.

I get up and walk toward the New Jersey stone, and put my back to it. I love this stone. This is my stone, I say to nobody in particular. And I start laughing too. I have never taken any drugs, b·

ɜy is making me high. We are all so light and joyful.
.s singing songs to the cows.

. know that other people are not having this experience because
I can see various other parties or individual visitors and they are all
just walking along. What is happening here?

I ask Dr. Alison about this and she says that there is a way to walk
on the land. There is an etiquette, and a way of politely approaching. And when one does, the land responds back. And that there
are certain stones with certain internal constituents that along with
where they're placed according to the Earth's currents, really give off
beneficial energies. And that these two big stones we're now around
are known, have been measured, for their electromagnetic field and
that the field they each emit lowers people who stand by them down
into the brain wave state—I think she said alpha—and Hz—I think
she said 7.8—that creates feelings of well-being.

And she describes some of the work she has been doing with elementals, and the energy currents and Ley lines on the planet daily,
for years. And even with other planetary-minded individuals around
the globe. Like she has done daily clearing work for years as a leader
with other leaders in some global community on the global money
supply, clearing money itself of the masses' projections humanity
have placed on it, to clean it up and free up the flow. She is always
doing what she can to help the awakening and joy of the planet and
its inhabitants. And she says this in a very light way. Very matter of
fact. And I think to myself, who does this stuff? Who thinks about
clearing the land and the money supply?

Yeah, she has opened some sort of portal, I am convinced. Why are
ₓ so much more fun, and getting so juiced up? Yes, she has
ething for sure. I like it.

ₑ while we start back, and she advises us to walk on the
ₓ when we came down the avenue so we can feel what

the energy is like on the other side. As we walk people remark they feel masculine or feminine energy, luck or heat. One says she feels a kind of sexual charge on one of the stones and, laughing, most of us walk over and touch that one.

Before exiting the gate we are advised to thank the land. Somehow this feels sacred to me. I feel like this is the right thing to do. I thank her as well. We all do.

We all pile into the car so we can make it back for the evening attunements. As I eat an apple I had packed for myself, I mull over all that is happening on this retreat. Although it has been a couple days, I feel like I have been in the bath of this energy for about a month. When I mention this to Dr. Alison, she says that actually I *have* been, because she begins creating the energetic for the retreats as soon as she announces them. So, yes, I say, that makes sense. And tonight, we have two more attunements. I am going to be fried at the end of this.

And I find myself thinking back to the first time we spoke, on an "Open the Drawbridge call". She'd said, "At a certain point joy becomes a technical issue." Throughout my time of working with her, I've heard her repeat, "Choose Joy no matter what it takes." —

FEMALE TEACHER—CHOOSING FORWARD

Student: I had this client the other day, an old client who I'm working on completing my work for him after this current project ends. Meaning I am firing him. He just came at me again yesterday, with anger. He's just too angry.

AJK: There's your power, _____ (student's name). This is me, dancing a little jig at a party, celebrating you stepping into this empowerment, that you are standing your ground instead of being intimidated, by saying if he continues. . .threatening him back, using his "language" so he gets it. Well done and woo-hoo!

It's a balance it seems, as bullies purge *their* density too—remember, this is happening for all of humanity and our Earth—and these bullies aren't likely dealing with it nor understanding why they're being pulled mostly unconsciously, in the ways that they have been.

Part of my glee is that you've really taken in that distinction my work with you all is, between the "old-school" "lightworkers" rise above/be compassionate/forgive and what I teach which is, no not that *all the time* anymore, *not* in these new times. Where everything is rebalancing.

Instead, You're here, with this choice, exhibiting more sternness, so that you are saying back to them, that *this is theirs and not yours to process.*

The material is rebalancing with the spiritual, right? That means on both sides of the spectrum. Spiritual people becoming more phys-icalized and OK with material possessions, like abundant money flows. While the materialistic folks who've not connected in with whatever they want to call that which keeps our Earth suspended in the galaxy and our bodies breathing, i.e., the divine balancing that with their orientation towards the material.

And so, this becomes less about the inevitable question I get asked all the time, about "protection." And "how to deal with that nega-tive energy."

My response, is yes, raise your vibration, which'll help deflect lower vibing people and situations in the first place. Raise your vibra-tion, also, so you can make different choices, like to become more embodied, stand your ground and allow yourself to have what you actually desire. Like show up for yourself, right?

And that corresponds to what I was saying, around 2013 and 14, that "Christ is coming off the cross," right? It seems why I was shown that (it took me months to understand that one!) Is that it's no longer about the burden and the responsibility of our own "stuff" or density, ("sins") being carried by someone else, first. And second, that it's no longer about burdens and heaviness, as much as it's about learning the essence of the Christ consciousness: love, purity, unity, and connection with the lightness of that Christ consciousness, that golden light.

Ultimately, learning how to live more honoring the gift of life! Learning how to exist as if there's nothing wrong, (My first book's title, what is it? Oh yeah, *What if There's Nothing Wrong?*) in the divine juice of possibilities that being alive gives us, while in a body.

Living more from the freedom through choice—and what you just described. That makes me think of that scientific measurement I frequently quote, that have come about to say it's at least 85 percent of all of our daily choices are made from the subconscious and the unconscious. Meaning so much of our lives, when unconscious, is in robotics mode, just a repeat, or a stamp or imprint, of the past. Wash, rinse, repeat. When, in fact, in our daily flow of activity implied *is* our human gift of free-will: *choice*. And as your story just showed. So, we are always making choices, even not making a choice that we know we need to make is still a choice.

So, you reminded me too, of the idea of going back to the beginning of what we were talking about of being tethered to anything outside of yourself, where I have had student after student after student ask me, mostly females this particular question "Um, when my spouse, isn't seeing what I'm seeing and isn't raising his vibration, so to speak, how can I get him to change?" It is much like that, although we've been talking about a client of yours who you work for so it's your "boss," and not a spouse.

But what I bring them back to is, OK, it's not about you getting him to change. Raise your vibration. Your emanation will help him shift. And maybe he shifts into a healing crisis and he chooses even worse and worse and worse, then you separate, or he raises and goes along for the ride and does his own inner shifting. And I want to say inner work, but it's not just work, right? Because you get free. So, using the word "work" seems like a bit of an oxymoron, because there really is such total play with learning how to best develop and actually use your capacity to choose.

But the way through that frustration with the non-changing spouse? Or boss? So, the non-changing "other" that makes the individual student, not you, feel stuck because they perceive they're—or define they're tethered to that "other" as in, "I need him, he pays my mortgage," for example. So, what you did, instead, is recognizing the choice here, as you let the long-standing frustration become anger. Because a lot of the times it does show up as anger.

Due to having done this work, you then saw with more clarity. And you see your implied choice and see where you actually have more choice. But that anger allows us to use that fire to draw boundaries. It only comes up, true genuine bodily anger, not head created anger, when we need the fire to draw boundaries because someone has over-stepped.

So, that anger is eventually able to be fuel. But you have to turn it outward because you, as a non-bully don't tend to do that; don't turn the anger inward, right? And so then, after the use of the anger, then dropping into the heart is always the instruction I give.

Yet before the anger is that seeming quagmire of "I'm a victim to my spouse's crappy choices," and thus they conclude they're stuck, and the situation has difficulty shifting.

But after doing this vibrational upgrading, You're also able to get to compassion for the spouse because of being able to see more from their own personal experience or path or journey or process. You've purified your consciousness, you've done the clearings, you've done what it takes to get to more clear seeing. Which is also meant to lead to clearly seeing where there have been choices you've been making on autopilot, not recognizing where you have been making choices.

So, there is a gradual shift that is occurring. It's not just about "protection" as so many people ask me, "What do I do when the people around me are a lower vibration and they bring me down?"

But now we're able to drop into compassion, the anger dissipates as a by-product into compassion, because you've seen what it's taken to shift your inner world to reframe it. And to reclaim your power. And then so the anger when properly worked with, turns into compassion—both for yourself and the "other." It's a beautiful and very consistent process within my response to "How do I come out of this perception that I am stuck because of what my spouse—or boss or someone I'm close to—is choosing?"

And ultimately, it comes down to choosing joy, no matter what. And then after that, there really is another stage. One of my Grand Dragon Masters has now reached it, after two years of saying to her, within the context of all the energy medicine and mindfulness coaching, "Choose joy no matter what." That next stage? The "no matter what" can be dropped. And the natural inclination becomes, increasingly, just living from just the first two words: "Choose Joy."

CHAPTER 10
Initiations in Energy

MONDAY PM

AFTER WALKING ON the land as a group, and also spending time walking around by myself, I was looking forward to receiving my second series of attunements. Certainly, I had experienced the power of Dr. Alison's command over energy these past months, both on the group calls and zoom meetings, and also during my own daily life as she performed the energy sends in the Mastermind program. The whole thing coming together here in the retreat though, the experience on the land today, in combination with everything else, was kind of blowing my mind.

So, we waited out front as a group, looking forward to seeing the beautiful temple house once again. We were all quite quiet, comparatively. Not subdued exactly, but relaxed and contained. We were a cohesive group by this time, and so we didn't really need to be social. Plus, it seemed like we were all anticipating these next two attunements and their power.

We'd all walked the five minutes to the training tonight after our break once we'd returned from our time out on the land. After being greeted at the impressive entryway by Dr. Alison, it was the same as the night before, where she did the sage clearing, but before even entering the house tonight. There was some laughter because she made a few curlicues in the air around some people's heads or hearts. This persistent lightheartedness is such a relief after the super serious way that most of us go through our lives. Seriously!

Once again, we sat in the circle, but this time we were in the crimson red room. And tonight, we were receiving the attunements downstairs, in the basement. I didn't even think that there would be rooms down there. I had been downstairs to get tea on the previous visit and had seen only that kitchen and a dark hallway down there.

"That's an interesting choice, to have such elevating attunements done in the basement tonight," Jan said. Huh? I'd not even considered that.

I again decided to go third. And nobody objected. I sat reading the new manual that we'd just been given, for the next section of this level's training. Someone opened the long window and sat outside on the deck. Finally, it was my turn and I was told to turn right, immediately *before* the kitchen. Oh! So, I wasn't going down the dark hallway I thought. And off I went, down the skinny, small, old staircase.

Walking into this new room I was struck by its cocoon qualities. There were leaves and roots painted on the walls, and there was what looked like a stone druid seat at one end. And Dr. Alison was standing behind it. "Welcome to the earth goddess's room. Take your throne," she said. And so, I sat.

The butterflies were back in my stomach. Why does that keep happening? I closed my eyes and followed the instructions given in a quiet and transporting voice. I could feel the energy presence and yet also felt like the whole room opened up into a forest or something. I lost track of time during the attunement. And only when I heard the bracelets above my head did I come back to my awareness of the room. What is it with the lighting around here I thought, why do they use gold lightbulbs?

It was weird, when I opened my eyes and saw Dr. Alison, it was like looking in two dimensions or something. She was for sure standing there and yet also I could sense some distant view, like seeing a landscape behind her. I knew it wasn't the decor because the landscape was of an ocean front. OK you are all set, she said. And I waivered a bit upon rising. My hands were so hot I thought they might catch fire.

I left the room and turned right, bumping into the dark end of the hall, and Dr. Alison called out, "It's the opposite direction, Maggie. Turn around," as she laughed. So, I then turned around. At this point I was able to see the kitchen and as I walked by the room I'd just been in with Dr. Alison she laughed again, and said, "Yup, it's like that for you right now," and then I proceeded to go upstairs to get the next person.

"Did you see any colors?" I asked Laura, who was sitting next to me. She'd already received this third attunement.

"Yah, like a rainbow when Dr. Alison was doing stuff at my hands, and then it turned to gold. Why? What about you?"

"Gold. Like are the lightbulbs gold or what? What is up with the lights in this place?" Laura laughed.

"I know," she said, "But for me, I keep seeing blue everywhere."

"Not gold?" I asked? "I keep seeing gold." It was really mystifying me because it was so vibrant and real.

"Hmmm. No, I am seeing mostly blue, but then also some purple."

"Does it mean anything to see a specific color?" Sheila, who was sitting on the other side of me, asked.

"I don't know. But that is cool that we are all seeing something different."

"I thought the attunements where just authorizing us to do the energy medicine on ourselves and eventually on others. Are they supposed to be a light show?" Sam too, done with his third attunement, joined in on the conversation.

"I don't know. But my hands got really hot," I said.

"Yeah, mine too. There is definitely something up with this energy stuff she's working with and these attunements," Sue, who'd just sat down from her attunement, said, while turning over her hands and looking at them.

"For sure. But don't call it, 'energy stuff.' Remember what Dr. Alison said in the pre-retreat call?" Laura said.

"What part?" Jan asked.

"When she said that it is really almost ignorant to dismiss or discount energy these days. And that further, we're no longer to refer to it as 'energy work' because that's what folks who are just playing around with energy without understanding that it's a science by now, subtle energy is, while yes, it's based on ancient wisdom. She's suggested to us to re-read *What if There's Nothing Wrong?* and has apparently even been considering making it a required reading for these trainings. And to now use 'energy medicine' as we step into professionalizing it, like her, as we step out as Vibrational UPgrade Practitioners. Really, if you think about it, too, when we see all the proof of its efficacy in the program within our own changes, you know? And all the work she has done to provide the proof where it exists and the methods behind and why 'this energy stuff' really works." This last bit Laura said using air quotes.

"Yes, she went a little into mama bear mode when she was saying it. Like fierce. And I guess she is breaking through all the layers of conditioning and sludge for all of us to wake up to what is around us all the time. And what else is really possible for us and for the world," Molly murmured.

"OK thanks, I know we are not supposed to talk so let's read our manuals," I said, wanting to get into this more and out of my own head. I was here to learn, and there clearly was something going on that I didn't understand. So, well, perhaps if I read the manual I was given, I would? Duh. Really, that woman teaching us has a point about how we so easily overlook the obvious, while leaping to the complicated. Silly, obnoxious ego-mind.

While much of the manual contains secret stuff and things that need to be given via transmission, here are some things I learned that I can tell to anyone. Energy is the Grandparent of Matter, Energy, or the light, has an intelligence all its own. There is a systematic way to be more able to call to, and work with, and bring down, and direct the light, or energy. The attunements create "antennae" as if we are establishing cell towers atop our heads, calling to it. We can trust the purity of the energy in this program, as we'd already clearly experienced ourselves.

And that within Dr. Alison's own Usui Reiki lineage, her first of the five different energy medicine modalities she'd been trained in prior to creating Vibrational UPgrade™ System, she's only six removed from the founder of it, back in the late 1800s. And while it's not only Usui Reiki we're learning and getting attuned to, this is part of it. At the very start, anyways . . . (Dragon Master comes later.) And so, this makes us only seven removed from the founder of Reiki. So, the lineage is really, really pure. I even have the person's signature who Dr. Mikao Usui passed on the lineage to, both the person he passed it down to while still in Japan, and then the 3rd person, who ultimately brought it to the West. Wow. Super pure!

Dr. Alison J Kay has created her own blend of transforming subtle energies with her exclusive new Vibrational UPgrade System of

Energy Medicine and Mindfulness Coaching, using her 10 years spent in Asia studying subtle energies and her 25+ years in the holistic health and wellness field. She has a PhD as a Holistic Life Coach, as well as 26 years teaching meditation that in part are what combine to be the mindfulness coaching part of the Vibrational UPgrade System that I'm getting certified in. Oooh. I had no idea, honestly, what has gone into all of this. I just knew to say yes to working with her and to coming on this retreat. Wow, this is more than I'd even thought, there's just so much more there. Of course. That makes sense.

It's unique, in depth, and clear instruction. And I am now acquiring an in-depth understanding of how subtle energy and chakras work and how energy flows work within the human mind-body-spirit system—which is from her being trained and certified in Asia, both in Chi Gong and Yoga. Plus, I'm learning about how energy flows on the land, once I'm at the Dragon Master level, with much the same in-depth knowledge of how it flows within the human mind-body-spirit system. Plus, the hands-on individual vibrational attunements (which *are* upgrades. Huh.) received directly from Dr. Kay's "super hands".

She's been doing hands on sessions with tens of thousands of people from around the world now for 24 years. That's where so much of this knowledge comes from; the practical experience of actually being with people, running energy medicine into their systems. She then realized when continuing to do so part time while in Asia, alongside her classroom teaching career, how much coaching she'd been doing within the energy medicine sessions. So, she—always the logical one!—got her PhD as a Holistic Life Coach while in her last two years living and working in Asia. Her first book is actually built upon her dissertation.

So, I know I'm in good hands, both figuratively and literally. Ha! I look up from my manuals, at the painting on the wall of the goddess with her arms raised wide in the air, forming a "Y."

Besides all that expertise, I know one of the main things I really appreciate about Dr. Alison and it makes me trust her more is that she's widely known to "walk her talk," and "be a living example of her work." The vibrational entrainment she's talked about, well it leaves us all immersed in a feeling of well-being and safety due to the authenticity to these teachings and the natural elegance to the process that she is clearly cultivating for us. I can see how connected she is, to be able to do so. I can tell there's more at work here—like magical stuff.

This last point, I guess, is why so many of us travel from around the country and world to work with Dr. Alison . . . they know her teachings are genuine, her vibration is authentic to her teachings, and the power of this gets translated to each student and client. I hear that expressed too, all the time, when new folks just coming in after using a product of hers or hearing her speak on an interview, on the monthly free Vibrational UPgrade call.

Wow, I seem to be having a moment of pride over my mentor and teacher. She did say to us all about the retreat that we will NOT be able to leave as the same person we each arrived as. Clearly that is happening.

Female Teacher—Receiving and Allowing

Student: Then the thing on initiations was, there's a sense of you explaining how people function within the initiations as you explain in Magic, Manifestation and Money Flow, like when they feel things have gone still or slow or not changing as fast as when they first got in, how that's the spiraling around a foundational issue, or pattern, going deeper, and as they rear up for another, bigger release, that's how it shows up, and hence staying with the listening of all the clearings and activations on the mp3's you provide, continuing with the work within the weekly modules and attending the live calls, so that they continue to deepen this process, where it's actually sped up, while working within the natural pacing and way that this stuff clears out and we then expand, again. And that as they go upwards, spiraling, or circling around to clear out more density—you always mention how the spiral is such a repeated shape within nature and give examples—bumping against things as they clear out more, then winding around the corner as the upgrade becomes clearer, and they're again more uplifted and shifting perspectives, you know, the way people get initiations within Vibrational UPgrade is, um, is more, is more a bias towards ease rather than a bias towards wrestling and fighting and vanquishing.

AJK: (Laughing) That's a great bunch of receiving and allowing you've done there, to perceive that with such clarity. You're reminding me, with that reflection, of how I've had as my mantra for decades now, "Universe, help me increase my tolerance for bliss." So, thank you for that perspective; I'm grateful.

Yeah, you know I've hesitated using the word, "initiations" because of the negative connotation to testing or difficulty.

But really, if I reflect back, now with having worked out what is meant by initiations on the path to empowerment within these ancient power mysteries, the way that I have designed each retreat is just that—an initiation. Now I've not ever said this before, but what I'm seeing it as is the whole thing, what I'm doing and what I have *us* doing on the retreat—and inclusive of the attunements—all culminates into a massive unleveling, which is the essence of an initiation. Right?

So, if you think back, there are certain themes in each season I have us going there. Whether it's Beltane, the season of thriving and new beginnings, in the awakening of the land. Or it's the season of Samhain—Halloween—the worshiping of our ancestors and, um, going within, getting ready to go within for the dark winter and looking at the shadow. We're also celebrating harvesting. So, they're opposite ends of the Celtic wheel *and* the two most sacred times of year for the Celts. But I did not plan that rhythm; I didn't even realize it when scheduling the first year of retreats, you know. How great is that?

Student: Completely great, yes! That's that natural elegance or grace to this all, where we can perceive how connected you are, that breeds extra magic around all that we're up to. It's simply grace. And it makes us trust more in the process, you know?

AJK: Excellent!

So, I remember your—and this overall is very much why I include the goddess work, to help with increased embodiment for all—trauma that you had gone through and the disconnection with your body. And the almost distaste—while I don't want to say distaste, because you did not have body image issues the way other women do, while you're beautifully tall. Like I view your stature as just eloquence.

So, Um, you still were really shattered in your ability to ground your presence or your being into your body. That's the distaste I mean. Like it was almost like there was no choice. You had, you just had an automatic lever that whenever you would consider grounding your beautiful being, spirit, soul essence down into your body, rather than hovering above in the spiritual world and in the intellectual world, it was almost like there was a lever that you just couldn't push. You just wouldn't consider it, actually dropping down into your body. And so, I remember in particular, this was a Samhain timed retreat. And I had us go through a certain process, all of us, including myself. And in that process, it was a ceremony I chose for us to do because of what had been going on for all of you leading up to the retreat, where the whole retreat actually was themed on getting you guys into your body.

And again, this is part of my intention in bringing in the goddess work, particularly within the retreats.

And in that ceremony, there were other people ending up in tears. There were other people having first time breakthroughs with feeling the sacral chakra. And they've never been the same since. I'm thinking of two women in particular. I mean, that was a breakthrough where instead of rejecting the body, I'm focusing on it, particularly solar plexus down. It was revelatory for most of you, if not all. Like, Oh my God, my body contains some of that intuitive stuff too! I'm used to having to meditate, or listening to angel meditations, or going up above my head to connect with you! You mean I can connect with myself and my intuition down here, too?

Student: Mmm, yeah, I remember that one.

AJK: And I'm like asking throughout the entire retreat in so many different ways, Hey sister, how about coming down and feeling that beautiful body of yours? Um, and so the shift out of "I gain wisdom from only up here, around my head," gig, I had already done a fair amount of work around this with you guys within the calls and clearings done for months leading up to the retreat. So, you'd already had much more than just an introduction to how the heart is the place where the spirit resides and that intuition is there too. So, you guys already knew that there was intuition coming in from the heart as well as up here at the head, but your orientations were all still very much up here at your heads. Strong intellects, and some quite heady folks, all of you for different reasons. Yet You're all successful women . . .

Um, and so there was discomfort. There was somebody who even left the room and as I was told later was outside crying and then there was somebody else who had no idea how to tune in down there, and was really uncomfortable doing so, and had to have a lot of extra time spent on assisting her to feel safe to tune in and feel what her body was really feeling, what she, in her feeling life, had been really feeling.

So, dropping you all down below the heart, to the actual bodily emotions of the inner GPS. I don't mean to say emotions. I mean to say feelings, and it's hard to distinguish this because we've overlapped these two terms in English for so long. I don't mean emotional reactivity. I don't mean a blocked second chakra, which makes you be *overly emotional* and not sorted with your emotions. I mean, the feelings of bodily wisdom, you guys were just beginning to understand that you have that in your lower body and that you could tune in. And there was some lever that finally got pulled, that I saw happen for the majority of you, but you, I don't want to say, but you, in particular, it was everybody, there was just some proverbial lever that was pulled so that allowed everybody to begin a whole new embodiment, a whole new level of connection with their body that they had never experienced. For some it was their first time—like you—being in their body so that their center wasn't nasally in here, (she points to her forehead's center) their center was recognized to be in the sacral.

Student: Yeah. Yeah, yeah. But you know I had no idea that's what you were up to at the time. It was only afterwards, when I recognized how differently I felt, did I start to understand. Like once I was home and I reported on that next Mastermind call that I could feel my feet? And that prior to that, they'd been more of a concept than a physical actuality.

AJK: (Laughing) Yep, I totally remember that. I *so* celebrated that! You were in such wonder and awe. Totally cute; like a little girl who'd just been given what was to be her favorite gift, ever! It was fabulous to watch and witness as you reported this new phenomenon.

And what you've been able to do since then, like you all had had enough clearings around feeling safe prior to going over there and taken out on the sacred lands and being given the attunements and the trainings in that context of the heart chakra of the planet with the sacred sites and the sacred place that it is, Glastonbury, Goddess bless it. You all had had enough work done around feeling safe to be in your body. Enough clearing work had been done on past lives when you may have been killed. You guys, by that retreat, had had enough work previously done, where all of those past life causes and the traumas that cause people to hover above their head and check out and feel safer up here rather than like viewing their body as their vessel, their temple, that houses the spirit while we're here . . . So, that you guys could do that, drop down finally, because it's, it's really, it's fascinating to me, how much work has to be done, on people before they'll allow themselves to become truly embodied.

And to allow themselves to actually *be* present, and drop down into the lower body, the masses of people. This is another tangent. It's not just you guys, but specifically because we're working with ancient power mysteries and living from this empowerment increasingly, being in your body is a must.

Nonetheless, it seems to me the masses of people live up here in the head. And then it's whether they're intellectual because that's been the conditioning. Like if you work the intellectual track, that's how you're going to get the material gains and success in the eyes of the culture. Or it's the people who have recognition of their spirituality. And they've had past life trauma when they've spoken truth to power and they've been hung or they've been viewed as witches and they've, or they're being guilty to speaking truth to power or whatever the causes were. But I also see that the massive catalyst that even when somebody is on the line with me, going from Magic, Manifestation and Money Flow and being invited into Mastermind, there is an element of this typically involved.

So, that's a main reason why people don't want to drop down in their body because they have the unconscious conclusion "there's been trauma or suffering occurs whenever I'm in this thing, whenever I'm in a version of this thing." Plus, it seems there's—and I came to this after at least a decade of working with people—like this inherent trauma of disconnection from our Source, and so everyone is like, looking for that. It's huge, yet it's really overlooked. And from what I've learned through the years, our faces don't change much from lifetime to lifetime. And I don't know that our body length, the typical dimensions, I don't know about the body, but from even just indications of pictures, like when somebody has been put into past life regression or hypnotized, and they've been taken back in order to heal a medical issue with doctors trained in hypnosis, for example, um, the person comes up with their name in Ireland at that lifetime and like the name of the pub their family owned, and the family's name. Then the staff of the doctor traces that information back and they find a picture of that person's face in that life time—name of family and pub in Irish town all check out, too—and there's a similarity.

There have been studies done on that. Meaning going back to the previous lifetime described with factual data if it can be traced—it is fascinating to me, how much is needed to be cleared in order for people to feel safe to ground down, and genuinely occupy their body. Because, even like personal trainers, even at the gym, there are people; you can see the difference who will lift a weight and they're doing it robotically because they're doing it from the head. How many times do I do it? I just had a student who I gave some yoga poses to. She's like, "Oh, how long do I say, do I count to five?" And I'm like, no, you actually inhale. And on the exhale where there's tension *because You're tuning into your body to perceive this*, while you're in the pose, you direct your exhale to that area of the body.

And when you feel like there has been a palpable element of release, however slight because this is gradual opening and lengthening in yoga, in accordance with where You're at with the tightness (i.e., chronic, injury, pain thresholds etc.), then you can move out of that pose. Right? So, I mean, you can see the headiness of people, even who are physically active, um, and even the headiness that newbies will approach physical activity with. So, I don't mean to say that if there's an athlete, they're totally in their body. No. I mean, in fact, they're probably being pushed to an extreme, so that it's much more heady.

Um, so the, the amount of time it takes, this is a real gradual, um, one of the most, if not the most gradual process to get somebody fully in their body here, allowing themselves to feel what they feel after having been able to feel safe enough to ground in the body, allowing themselves to feel their groin, their hips, to feel their pelvis, to feel their tailbone, to feel their knees.

And when You're grounding in your body, you can receive a whole lot more light. Once You're receiving more light, that means You're able to have more light in and around your body, in your field. And when that's happening it becomes easier to manifest, because the Universe has an easier time finding you and well for other reasons too that we don't need to go into here, now.

And this is also what the Earth needs from us, to be lighter on her, not just with our physical waste and use. Being a bridge between heaven and Earth is what is needed by each of us. So, you have to be in your body first, for this to happen.

Student: Now I feel I'm used to feeling my feet down there. Nowadays, my feet are warm.

AJK: I know it was so wild watching you go through that.

Student: And my feet were like, so frozen all the time. Like people would tell me that my feet are cold. And I would walk into things.

AJK: Right. The, the clumsiness, the tripping, the dropping things frequently—all of those are signs of not being in the body. OK.

Student: Yeah. I mean, today, I started just because it was, I don't know, there's some sort of big surfacing going on. I could feel it was a big surfacing of some kind. And I was, I was sort of, it took me like, I don't know, maybe an hour and 15 minutes to realize that I had for the third time over poured the liquid while I'm watching it. But for some reason my, my brain is not matching up to, it was like, I, wasn't *not* paying attention. I wasn't talking to someone. I was literally watching it pour and I kept pouring it over the side of the glass. I'm like, what's going on in your finally? I said, Oh, I think I'm out of sync somehow. So, I went and sat down on mother earth.

AJK: Perfect mindfulness and knowing the tools to remedy it. So, let me come back. There are two things here from the out of sync thing. There's the part that's the rocking of all of us and how it feels to be on planet earth—so different!—that's happened since December 21st, 2012. Um, and the increase of, uh, the frequencies we're living in now to go spiritual. You can see it society-wide, you know, more interest in yoga, more into some type of meditation, more interest in crystals, and more interest in spirituality. Um, but it's because we're meant to be balancing the physical with the metaphysical. And so, it seems like I'm helping somebody learn how to deal with this increased awakened presence. And if they'll let me, like you, then that becomes learning how to use these times to not just deal, but thrive, as they're meant to be doing.

A lot of people go even heavier when they don't know why they feel the way they do. They blame themselves rather than work it through and ultimately lighten, which is what is meant to happen.

The ego-mind is so self-absorbed, so when it's helpful to take in the bigger picture, and someone is not, then there's more suffering, where they're blaming themselves rather than understanding the bigger perspective—like others too, around them, are feeling wonky due to these times, and so that calls for more boundaries and more self-care.

Student: Yeah. I had the headache and it was like, I hadn't had, like I said, what, do I not have copper pennies in my shoes? What's going on here? Why am I having a headache? You know?

AJK: Great there too, you had the tool of the copper pennies in your shoes. OK. So, the ability to then bring, let's just say, you're already grounded. You've, you've gone through that initiation described. To then continue to allow the expansiveness of your metaphysical presence to bring in the metaphysical frequencies is what comes next. That's the other part of this. Instead of getting jammed up at the head by the throat chakra—by not recognizing your power to choose new possibilities, nor even that opening to your power to choose—typically then, your energy isn't able to flow all the way down to your lower body.

Having the ability to continually allow for that to increase is what will create more, uh, magic, more richness, more capacity to manifest, because if you're floating above your head, and you're just thinking about what you want to manifest, then that has no power compared to when you're down in the heart. And that coherence is doing the organizing for you. And when you're in your tailbone, because then the universe has a target of where to bring what you're asking for.

I feel like sometimes people are so used to just taking notes, to taking in information online or at teachings, and that the tendency is just to take notes and to have it be cerebral. And while they'll leave an event from me feeling lighter, if it's all just been about information with another event they've attended, it doesn't get past the throat chakra. It's not just information with me. It's energy, it's the application of these concepts. The energy has to, or wants to, go past the throat.

Student: Yeah. So, we expanded all the way down.

AJK: Yeah. And that's definitely an element of initiation. I've had people, so many, come into Magic, Manifestation and Money Flow and they lose weight without dieting or even trying; like I'm not actively working with them from a position of a personal trainer with fitness nutritional certification working specifically on weight-loss.

No, it's from the energy clearing and their vibration raising, as it's designed to within this Vibrational UPgrade System. Their taste buds automatically change; their desire for cleaner food automatically shifts. And that's pretty consistent if you're raising your vibration and getting a cleaner consciousness, you're going to be geared towards cleaner, higher vibratory food, for sure. It's across the board with anybody, this work, but there's an element of embodiment that is, it's so much a part of my me and my mission.

Like I've always been in my body. I, you know, I mean I'm lucky to be in a body on planet Earth. Let me jump out of a plane. Let me climb this mountain. And what else? Let me, let me learn how much good fun I can have, like great sex, or what new food I can taste in that new country, or yoga, or running barefoot on a beach, or sticking my toes in mud in the jungle on my way to a Mayan ruin, or whatever other experiences I can have within a body on planet Earth. What that feels like. Let me dance all the time. Let me hula hoop. Let me see how much I can weight-train, let me see how I can shape my body. You know, I mean, all of it is about enjoying being in the body, the sensual, and that doesn't mean it's all about sex.

It's *sensuality*. And that's the sacral chakra. Like even eating a peach, like when I lived in Israel on that rishpon and I was picking peaches for a season when I was backpacking across the planet once done with that campaign season, with my first career in politics. On that Rishpon in Israel, I'd get up at five in the morning, I was living with this French woman, crazy wild French woman, um, in her fifties and I'm in my early twenties. And then this younger German girl, like 19, and then this other, I think American, I don't totally remember that fourth person. And we would get taken out to the fields for the peach trees, by the farmer, in the wooden truck bed where we'd put the full buckets of peaches. On the way down in the morning, we'd sit there with the stack of empty buckets and he'd take us out for like a five-minute tractor ride down to his fields because the Rishpon— not a kibbutz—was where the farmers bought communal land. And if they pooled their money together, they got more land. So, it was different than a kibbutz because it wasn't centrally owned, um, and organized. It was each farmer had their own land, but they were just able to buy more land 'cause they pooled their money.

So, we go down on the tractor at 5:30 in the morning, everything's starting to wake up and we'd be taken to the peach orchard. So, I'd be just really waking up, taking a ladder from tree to tree, climbing up the ladder to where the fresh peaches were to be picked with my bucket in one hand. And I would eat the peaches for my breakfast in the other until I was full. And I would have juice dripping down my chin and I, my fingers would be sticky, and I'd be getting the juice like all over me. And I had to wash my clothes every single night, by hand. You know, it was just phenomenal.

The sensuality of eating a peach, you know, awesome. They are so great. So, like that texture peach skin is. And then at night, I was dating a British bloke, and he was working for the potato farmer (no joke) and there was a plum tree grove by the green houses where I'd go pick fresh mint for my tea. So, we'd scurry under the plum tree branches into the open part of the patch and make out. Then we'd meet everyone in the old bomb shelter that had been turned into a bit of a pub for the expats working the fields and have beers. All of that was so natural, so engaged with the Earth, my body, bodies, the sensual, textures . . . Like I loved playing with my skin, like using the dry brush and then using like really beautiful royal jelly moisturizer or the Shea butter I get direct from Africa. And it just, the feeling of that, like the Shea butter, once it gets warm in your hands and then how it distributes in your skin, as it soaks it up. And then the feeling of soft skin, like yes, sensual engagement. With all of that, it's physical.

CHAPTER 11
Service Orientation

TUESDAY DAY

WAS I READY for more, out on the land? Part of me wanted to sleep in for a day. Apparently, this is not uncommon as we sometimes need more sleep to integrate when there is so much acceleration in our subtle energy system in such a short space of time. Our bodies need to catch up. Our minds and levels of consciousness need to integrate it all. But one of the girls had said I should drink extra water, so I did and that helped. Then I remembered Dr. Alison had suggested electrolytes, so I went out to the corner store and bought some and that helped even more. Phew! Feeling a bit more like I'm ready for more.

So, some of us met out front to walk over the Abbey together and visit the weekly marketing on the way. We were going to have a guided tour with Dr. Alison.

We saw a couple of others from our group walking back to the B & B with bags and parcels. Hard to pass up a really good quality market. We passed stalls selling breads, jams, and vegies. But also, beautiful spirit rings, talismans, mead, wall hangings, musical instruments, crystal, and carpets. Not to mention handmade witches and wizard's cloaks, Viking swords, pomades and face potions, art, t-shirts, handmade shoes, and so much more.

I didn't buy anything because I didn't want to walk around with it all day. And it was getting close to the time for the tour. So, we all walked across the street, right by the town hall Dr. Alison has spoken at what seemed like weeks ago but only a few nights ago, and through the big medieval wooden gates of The Abbey. We were right on time and Dr. Alison was there to meet us. A couple of the women walked up to flank her. A bit like high school I suppose, wanting to be with the cool kid. All good.

"How are you lovelies doing today? Looking bright I must say." She stood there smiling, her green tea in hand.

"We're going to have a lovely day of integrating all that you've received, to ground it all in, with the loving, soft energy of the land here, that the Abbey is on. You'll see."

The rest of us followed up through the ticket line. Dr. Alison had already secured our admission and we went smoothly through the big wooden turnstile. Into the grounds.

Dr. Alison took us into a 12th century chapel that had Archangel Michael in the stained-glass windows, and on the opposite wall, a mural of Mary Magdalene and another one next to her of Goddess—Saint, in here—Brigit. Dr. Alison told us some stuff, and then we went outside to catch up with the local tour guide for the Abbey. I caught Dr. Alison going back inside, putting coins in the box and lighting a red candle, while seeming to say a prayer, then placing her lit candle with the others there.

We were met by a tour guide dressed in brown robes as a monk. Is it the Franciscans who have the brown robes and bald top of their head? Or the Benedictine? He introduced himself as brother something. I was struggling to hear as that ringing was back in my ears. And my eyes were full of the beauty of the grounds.

He showed us the old kitchen, called the Abbot's Kitchen. Dr. Alison said that it was one of her favorite parts to the Abbey. Then we went back out of the Abbot's Kitchen, and around the grounds. We saw foundations of stone ruins of the many monk cells, as we were guided towards the main part of the structure. Two of our group were looking at the foundations of the monk rooms and one lay down on the grass to find that monks in those days must have been quite a bit smaller than we are today. They quickly scrambled to get up and catch up with our tour group.

He took us over to the main building, open to the air. He told us the story of how The Abbey had been destroyed. And when he mentioned the passing away of one of the historical figures, I felt my knees buckle underneath me. I didn't faint but I somehow lost control of my body when I heard about the death.

Dr. Alison eyed me and came over. She just simply stood next to me. There had been some speculation in the group about maybe I had been there in another life and so hearing about that time brought something back. I was truly fine, and actually enjoyed sitting on the ground for a bit, as Dr. Alison sat down, while we just lay back and looked at the sky, the rest were standing, as we were told of the holy relics, and the death of King Arthur, and how the landscape of the area had changed through the years.

After the official tour was over, we spent a bit more time exploring the grounds, with Dr. Alison guiding us to various spots on the grounds. She pointed out the hidden healing well that none of us had noticed before on the guided tour and spoke about how that was the well that originally brought so many people on pilgrimage to the Glastonbury Abbey for healing. Although now closed, Dr. Alison reminded us of the history of pilgrimages throughout the centuries to Glastonbury for the original and still eternal she said, flowing, healing red spring of that sacred well we went to on our first day. Somehow, I keep forgetting about that very first thing we did together. I wonder why.

I was asked if I was OK, which I was. And we talked amongst ourselves in the bright sunshine, out on the grass, under a giant Yew tree that Dr. Alison had guided us over to, after talking about some of the energy currents on the land and some of their nexus points, and how they interact with Ley lines, asking us to feel them out too. Apparently, the Mary Ley line ran through here. She also showed us this cool, "Oracle Stone" that women used to sit on, like in Delphi, and deliver their oracle messages.

"If you were to use your embodied intuition—as it *has* become more embodied this week—tell me what part of this land from that wall to that one"—she motioned—"do you most get pulled towards? Walk to that and stand on the spot. I'll do the same once you all are done. When you get to that spot, do what it is I taught you to do to connect in and perceive."

Female Teacher—Non-Hierarchical

Student: Power? Not just political power. My womanly power? How do I tune into that more?

Another thing is that I am just getting to be able to do since working with you, Dr. Alison, is to have women friends because we are not competing over men. I am not blaming the men or the women for this. Although I could blame but that feels like it just makes me a victim. So, this "sister wound" of us not supporting each other, how can that get fixed?

AJK: All that we are up to is to bring forth your "womanly" power. Or your power overall, whether man or woman.

You know how when you all first saw me when we met at the front of the Abbey, and some of you ran up next to me, while others held back?

Stop doing that. Both the squandering of attention and the withdrawal from even going for it. Just be. Clear, without the old playground dynamics that the ego-mind perpetuates.

There is so much to female power when women join together. It is so much more than when either competing—which drains energy—or going at it alone. You know the circles we form at times on the land? How powerful does that feel? And notice please, Sam is the kind of divine masculine consciousness who sees this aspect of women, and is not challenged by it, nor wants to conquer it, but wants, instead, to be a part of it, to support and nurture it. Well, we've got to do the same.

Competition reduces power, when done in an aggressive way, making it about "the other." Or said in the language of Vibrational UPgrade, when approached from the ego-mind. The competition I have found to be the only form that is really functional is within myself, competing against the old versions of myself, to become stronger, better, freer. And when I'm doing that within myself, it's only natural that I'll work symbiotically, when part of a team, say a professional sports team in an actual competition.

Like that oracle stone we saw outside the Abbot's Kitchen. Oracles were all female back in Ancient Greece. That was women using their voice, not shrinking back, nor manipulating in back-stabbing ways to squelch another woman's voice.

There is more abundance when there is more harvested, yes?

Student: Yes, of course.

AJK: And there's more harvested when each plant grows to its most robust fullness, right?

Student: Yes.

AJK: Well, check-in with how you feel now. And how you've felt most, if not all, of the time when on retreats. As you all are more in the vibe of being a cohesive unit, all going for your greatest flourishing. Which feels better, the competition or the cohesion?

Student 2: The cohesion.

Student 3: The togetherness.

Student 4: The acceptance.

Student 5: The support.

Students: The cohesion, yes.

AJK: So, be like the plants. Work around obstacles that other plants may present without harming. Go for your greatest flourishing, your grandest harvest. Follow nature's way.

CHAPTER 12
Leadership

AFTER THE ABBEY we go to the house of one of Dr. Alison's local friends, a couple, who have invited Dr. Alison for tea. And she also invites all of us to come along.

There's a lot of back and forth while we all gather in their lovely conservatory. The sun is splashing in, the big wooden table we're sitting around is comfy. It seems easier to relax now.

After a lot of laughter, storytelling, and chit chat about the nature of living in or visiting Glastonbury, Tiya asks, "Dr. Alison, what is your view of being a spiritual teacher in this spiritual marketplace nowadays?"

Dr. Alison had been somewhat quieter, although laughing a lot, during this exchange. She shifted her position in her chair, putting her legs down and feet on the floor and her tea cup on the table.

Smiling, she said in quite a soft but clear voice I wasn't used to hearing—meaning not her teacher, tour guide, fierce mama bear, clearing/activation voices, "Why don't we let one of our two hosts, who see so many spiritual teachers or speakers on spiritual subjects come through this Mecca, respond to that. Would you like to, either of you?"

The female of the couple, Samantha, who I really enjoy—she's so caring, said, "I feel like part of spiritual teaching is showing the students what to adopt and what to abandon. When working with the level of transformational power that comes with highly skilled use of energy, one must take into account the level of conditioning the student is working with at any given time.

"Teaching people how to use positive destructive power, which is necessary for any kind of healing or even growth, is a key part of the work of a female spiritual teacher. In order to become empowered, whereby the student can achieve mastery and independence from the instructor's constant presence," She finishes and looks over at her husband, smiling, "David, what do you think?"

David clears his throat and says, through smiling eyes, "I've seen through my practice of martial arts, how training students to tap into their own higher cognizance and connection to higher vibratory energies functions to give a way to allow for the highest possible choice. And that when it's truly embodied, it can be made in a moment, right there on the mats. So, there's this sense of gaining confidence in one's own ability to inherently be making the best possible choices in the moment, that eventually arises, after much development of that musculature, over and over again. And training them to release, let go of, or outright end patterns that no longer serve their evolution, as appropriate, is just as key. When trauma or other old, or stagnant energy is cleared from the body, something fresh rushes into the new space. Learning how to self-lead, to choose in accordance with the soul is key."

FEMALE TEACHER: AUTHORITY

AJK: Yes. Helping each person learn to tap into their own inner authority, aligned with their Higher Self, is key. Then the need for external authority figures, deflection of one's own responsibility, and the whole dance around resisting both forms of authority, can dissipate.

What if it doesn't have to be so complicated? What if it's meant to be easy? What would it take?

CHAPTER 13

Learning from a Female Spiritual Teacher

TUESDAY NIGHT: FULL MOON ON THE TOR

THE LAST NIGHT of the retreat found some of the women eager to stay up all night before their shared taxi at 5AM to the airport for their early flights. I didn't know if I could stay up that late, but because it was a full moon, I opted to go with the crew up to the top of The Tor again.

Laughing and giggling our party found the tavern Dr. Alison had asked us to meet her at. She said she doesn't typically drink nowadays, but will every once in a while, when it felt right. So, this pub she had us meeting at? It was directly on the way to the Tor, ironically. Like the last place before it.

The whitewashed Tudor exterior gave on to a low ceiling. It was an uninspired place inside, but when we walked through to get to the open-air beer garden in the back. Dr. Alison was there, speaking with a few locals. She waved and smiled. Once again, several women struck up conversations with nearby customers. Some of us went over to join Dr. Alison, others stayed chatting with nearby customers.

After a beer or cider each, Dr. Alison gave us a farewell, hugging us each. She then walked back to her B & B where I believe she was staying for a few more weeks. I knew at least our next mastermind call that was in two weeks, she'd still be here for, anyways. But I think after that, our next call would be when she was traveling to more sacred sites and megaliths, I think she said to Scotland, then to Ireland again. I especially loved our calls when she just has been at a bunch of power spots. Her clearings are even stronger, the activations with even more buzzing to the energy. I usually ended up with particularly interesting dreams afterwards. See you soon, Dr. Alison, I thought to her back as she walked away. Hopefully here again, for the next retreat. This was life changing. Thank you!

The rest of us walked the few minutes left to get to the Tor and carried on up the side of the magic mountain again. The approach was totally spooky under the full moon. The land felt extra intense. But maybe it was the full moon and land interacting with our systems after receiving all those attunements?

"Hey, are any of you feeling this more tonight?" I ask the rest of them with me, huffing a bit on the ascent. We'd not even gotten to the steep part yet.

"Yeah, my hands are really buzzing," Jan replied.

"Mine too," said Laura.

"My ears are like supersonic," said Heather.

One foot in front of the other, I made my way up on the heels of the others who were like mountain goats. Almost running up the hill. Passing by the gate and the tree where some of us had tied the first time we were here with Dr. Alison. I hear from the top the sound carrying of a group of people sitting at the top, playing drums. And the moon was just beginning to rise. Slowly, slowly, hands on my thighs to push myself forward I could start to also hear the laughing and singing from those at the top.

One switchback and then the next. Three glowing red dots proved to be three people smoking on a bench. And then I rounded the last turn and saw a man running down the hill and tumbling and laughing. Followed by another. They were clearly unhurt as they ran up again like children and had another go. As I walked round the base of the stone tower, I saw that the group with the drums had also carried a full-sized sofa up with them! And six of them were sitting playing and singing the music I had heard below.

Three of the women in our retreat—Sue, Heather, and Jan, were already speaking with the group with the sofa and it looked like they were all going to make some new friends, as Sheila and Laura were just approaching the group. Myself, being a bit quieter in my pleasures, I went to the other side and lay down on the grass. Not totally caring about possible gifts from the sheep . . . Oh heck. Whatever. I saw in front of me, down the hill like two rings of the labyrinth down, a sheep lying comfortably on the ground, her four legs tucked under her, eyes front like a kind of Sphinx.

Remarkably there was very little light pollution, and I could see so many stars. I would think about tomorrow in the morning. Tonight, I just wanted to be. And this was new for me, which I recognized. Wow. That's good. So, much had happened on this retreat. So, much of value to me has transpired. In a way I thought that I could pretty happily live here. At the tavern one of the other ladies had said that to me too. Some kind local said that a lot of people end up thinking of this place as their magical home. I could see that. But Dr. Alison's friends had said living there had its challenges, in part due to all the people coming there and purging their stuff and then leaving. Still. I'd had such a magical time here.

Laughter and more music coming from around the other side. The sheep and I happily relaxing on the land in the dark. Room for everyone. And now I was getting a little cold. I would brave the walk down in the dark and go back to my room and write in my journal. Such a lot to remember. So, I said bye to my Tor trek partners, and went back to our B & B. I loved how safe it was here, to walk at night, alone, as a woman.

When I got back and settled into my journaling, I wrote: Integrated spirituality and everyday living—in unity.

Open-eyed meditation of the sacred process daily life can be and life choices.

Women teach about power—love power, temporal power, ancient power mysteries, voice power, body power.

People put women in roles: mother, daughter, nag, sister, competition and so forth, each according to conditioning or background. The woman herself, is just herself. And female spiritual teachers, being women, must also skillfully navigate the thicket of judgements on their tones and clothes and appearances, what their roles are and can be and need to be, and suppositions of the people in front of them in order to even begin to *serve* the students in front of them.

In the age of commercial systems, where an exchange for teaching is handled as a sale rather than a voluntary gift, then it is also up to the individual woman to organize the exchange. Charging for services is a normal part of the matrix of benefit in a cash economy. Exchange is very necessary between teacher and student else a cycle of spiritual debt is created. When a teacher is part of an institution people seem to understand a need to make an offering. As many female teachers operate outside the usual hierarchical framework it is important to view the exchange as a means of thanking the individual and of supporting the work itself.

My definition of power is defined as energy + choice.

Power. New. Mine.

Joy. New. Mine too, it seems now. Hmmm.

Possibilities . . . .

EPILOGUE

SO, WHAT DID I finally decide? I am on my way back to London now on the train. I shared a taxi to Bristol with two of the girls in the retreat. I feel like I have made sisters for life with these people. We talked all the way through breakfast, and all the way to the station about the pros and cons of staying in my marriage or going on to a new adventure. But each of them let me know it was my choice and that they would support whichever way I decided. And I seemed to be choosing both staying in the marriage and moving on to a new adventure.

I know what Dr. Alison would say: Why not go for both, combined together? Try that out for a bit to see what else is possible. And if, after making that choice, you see it's showing up lighter, keep making that choice. And if not, make a different choice. Power= energy + choice. Seems I should add onto my equation, actually: Power=energy + conscious awareness + choice. Yep. That's *it*.

I watch the hedgerows pass by the windows, feeling the land here. So, many feelings about the land have come alive due to the experiences of the retreat. Part of me feels like just getting off at the next station and going back to Glastonbury. Instead, I take out my tablet, and set it up on the table at this 4-seat location I have chosen. I lean back, preparing to send an email to husband. The usual email, about when I will arrive, how is the dog. And all of that. The train is slowing into Bath. One day I want to go to the big bath and soak in the waters. Dr. Alison does these regular natural mineral baths all over the world and raves about them. She said the ones here were good; a bit commercialized. She'll likely do retreats to those natural mineral baths too. I heard her planning one to an Italian island she'd been to. I want to go. Her pictures from there were almost unbelievable in their beauty.

Into a reverie about natural mineral baths, Italy, England, Bath, Jane Austen, and how society has changed, I do not notice that a man is standing next to the chair behind me, putting a small bag into the overhead rack at my table.

"May I sit?" He asks.

"Of course," I say.

Very attractive in a rugged backpacker way, he looks like a 15-year younger version of my husband and I think to myself, "What are the odds?" that someone who reminds me of the better days of my marriage would present himself, here, *now?*" Memories of how my husband used to treat me, where we used to go together, how our intimate moments seemed to stretch out for hours due to our love for each other. Seeing this lookalike man reminds me of that.

But it reminds me of something else. It reminds me of how I was too, back in those times. I was simpler. Life was simpler. Feeding the dog and making the bed were not political acts back then. It didn't take one entire salary to pay for our apartment back then. Hmmm . . . has my marriage become a thing that just requires work and effort? Have I forgotten to look for the love and joy in my marriage? Have I been so unawake in my body, that it had carried over into my marriage? I saw this week what it feels to feel awake, alive, and more ready to thrive, with energy pulsing throughout my body, seeing colors really clearly and vibrantly, hearing more. Hmmm.

I have just spent the whole weekend learning about the magic of energy, my connection to the land, and about living in the joy, in the lightness, in the possibilities. Could I actually apply this to my marriage? The girls seem to think so, and we spent time speaking about it while sipping a second cup of coffee. I have decided. I will walk back into my marriage and change from the inside. I will apply what I have learned about myself, and about a new way of being a woman. And I will command that my marriage be something that nurtures both of us. Plus, the dog too, of course.

Now, one year later, we are three plus the dog. The great healing skills, and all the healing changes I have made since the retreat made my body want to become pregnant. And the close connection re-kindled between my husband and me created the sacred bond of love to call in the child. Little did I know that so much goodness and change would come from what seemed like a simple choice to travel by myself to a small patch of land and spend time with a teacher. But she is a teacher of magic. So, manifesting this new yes became possible.

Being introduced to the magic of energy medicine, in combination with the magic and energy of an awakened, clearly perceiving consciousness, and the sacred wisdom of the land, was an incredible combination. It is very different to go out onto the land with someone who knows the etiquette of energy and ancient ways. It is very different to go out into the countryside and sacred sites with someone who can see and speak about the energy and shift the living currents of the land and open portals and doorways. It is an adventure and a sacred journey that is not to be missed.

NEXT STEPS

DUE TO THE power contained and woven into this book, you have been receiving transmissions (an ancient modality of communicating more than just words), blessings and energy to accelerate your evolution. Sometimes the awakening of new areas of our life and body can show up as changes in bodily sense, sleep patterns, appetite, as you've already seen described.

What might also occur is possibly an area of your body—many times the neck and shoulders or hips and knees—gets tight for a bit, as awakened energy, due to a chakra opening more, is now able to distribute fresh vital life force energy, where once it was blocked, so the musculature had been tight, but is now receiving this vital life force, so pain occurs at first as this once deadened area, awakens.

You may also feel yourself weepy, angry, frustrated or really, really hopeful.

That brief list is intended to give some examples of what may appear as a problem which may in actuality represent a healing reaction. Which is in fact, a good indication that what is behind this book actually contains more possibilities for you. And if you've felt nothing other than your typical experience when reading a book, no worries. All good. Everyone is where they're at.

If you feel the stirring to work with Dr. Alison as a result, here are some suggestions:

1. Check out the waters, get your big toe in the pool by sampling her monthly Activate Your Magic. membership. https://activateyourmagic.com

2. Step right into clearing your chakras, with the Chakra Attunement Audio Series. https://www.alisonjkay.com/chakra-healing-audio-series/

3. Step right in and UP by checking out her signature program, Magic, Manifestation and Money Flow. https://www.alisonjkay.com/work-with-me/programs/magic-manifestation-money-flow/

4. Find out about working with Dr. Alison privately, which she still does, on a limited basis. https://www.alisonjkay.com/work-with-me/work-1-1-privately/

But whatever you do, make a choice for your joy!

CPSIA information can be obtained
at www.ICGtesting.com
Printed in the USA
LVHW021450260121
677516LV00004B/323